British Battles of the
War of Austrian Succession
& Seven Years' War

British Battles of the War of Austrian Succession & Seven Years' War

Twenty-Seven Battles & Campaigns of the
First Global Conflict, 1743-1767

ILLUSTRATED WITH MAPS & PICTURES

James Grant

LEONAUR

British Battles of the War of Austrian Succession & Seven Years' War
Twenty-Seven Battles & Campaigns of the First Global Conflict, 1743-1767
by James Grant

ILLUSTRATED WITH MAPS & PICTURES

First published under the title
(Extracted from) British Battles of Land & Sea

Leonaur is an imprint of Oakpast Ltd
Copyright in this form © 2018 Oakpast Ltd

ISBN: 978-1-78282-714-6 (hardcover)
ISBN: 978-1-78282-715-3 (softcover)

http://www.leonaur.com

Publisher's Notes

The views expressed in this book are not necessarily
those of the publisher.

Contents

Dettingen 1743

This eventful battle, the last in which a crowned King of England and Scotland drew his sword, was fought during the war of the Austrian Succession.

The Elector of Bavaria was chosen Emperor of Germany at Frankfort-on-the-Maine, and was crowned as Charles VII., on the 11th of February, 1742. He was, however, a most unhappy prince; his electoral dominions were overrun by the Austrians, the French were driven out of Bohemia, and the King of Prussia, under the mediation of King George II., concluded a peace at Breslau with the Queen of Hungary.

The King of Britain resolving to take a more active part in the war, an army, under Field-Marshal John Earl of Stair, was ordered to embark for the Netherlands in the summer of 1742, for the support of Maria Theresa.

Early in the year 1743 the Earl of Stair marched this army towards the Rhine, and in May encamped near Hochst, on the Maine.

At this time the loose coats and breeches of the line were tightened, and the hats looped up on three sides; while the 7th, or South British Fusiliers, and the 21st and 23rd, or Scots and Welsh Fusiliers, figured for the first time in those peculiar conical caps which came into vogue with the Prussian tactics. Their coats had collars, their skirts were buttoned back and faced with blue, but numbers were not put upon the buttons until 1767.

About the middle of February, the roads through which the troops had to march were almost impassable on account of the snow. When at Kellenbuch and Aschaffenberg, in that beautiful district of Bavaria, where the slopes are covered with vines, and the timber is floated down the Maine and Rhine from the dense forests of Spessart and Oldenwald, the army found itself hemmed in and all supplies cut off by the able dispositions of the French commander, Marshal Noailles, who, in the beginning of June, had crossed the Rhine with an army of 60,000 men.

In this condition His Majesty George II. found matters when he landed at Helvoetsluys, and assumed the nominal command of the army, on the 9th of June.

Lord Stair had determined not to decline a battle, and had marched up the Rhine to Aschaffenberg with that view, while the enemy kept pace with him on the opposite bank. As the Allies pursued the course of the river, and the French took the direct line, the latter gained the wood near the bridge about the same time that the Allies reached the town.

When the king, accompanied by the Duke of Cumberland arrived, he found the contending armies encamped on those fertile and beautiful plains which border on the Maine, opposite each other, under a ridge of hills covered with wood in all the full foliage of summer. The Allies lay on the north, and the enemy on the south side.

Four miles east of Aschaffenberg is Dettingen, in the circle of the Unter Maine, where that river is about sixty yards broad. For about a league the land through which it flows is low and level, after which it becomes mountainous and beautifully wooded. A mile below Aschaffenberg the small river Aschaff, brawling and foaming among vine-covered rocks, runs from the hills to mingle with the Maine. Another rivulet, called the Beck, falls into the same river just above Dettingen, between which and the Aschaff is the picturesque little Bavarian hamlet of Klein Osten. On the south of the Maine rises the spire of Hochstadt, and facing Dettingen is the village of Mainpling.

The southern bank of the river is generally much higher than the other, and the lower portion of the ground, to within a mile and a half of the edge, consisted of wild and tangled woods, with wet morasses. The position of the Allies extended about two miles from Aschaffenberg, one of the strongest forts in the Elector's dominions, to Klein Ostein, and inclined towards the wooded mountains a few hundred paces from the river.

The right wing, composed of the white-coated Austrian battalions, was at Klein Ostein; the blue masses of the Hanoverians, posted in two lines, formed the centre; and the British on the left—all posts of honour being in those days assigned to foreigners—occupied the town and vicinity of Aschaffenberg.

From the bridge of the latter the enemy readied to the river at Selingenstadt.

The Allies were suffering so greatly from the want of provisions, that Voltaire asserts it was found necessary to hamstring the horses, as they were without forage; and in fact, they were nearly surrounded, when tidings came of a sudden success of Prince Charles of Lorraine, in Bavaria, and of the speedy coming of 12,000 fresh Hanoverians and Hessians, who were within two days' march of Hanau.

It was justly apprehended, as the enemy commanded the lower part of the river, that any troops attempting to advance beyond Hanau would be intercepted. The king, however, was determined that the junction should be accomplished; and resolved to march for that town and join his countryman, the Prince of Hesse-Cassel, who was expected there, and who was acquiring great wealth by trafficking in the lives of his subjects, whom he lent to Britain to fight her battles in America and elsewhere.

On the night of the 13th of June, Marshal Noailles moved his camp farther into the woods, to frustrate the king's purpose: and on the same evening his troops set fire to great quantities of wood and straw, which at first led the Allies to suppose they were in retreat; but in reality, under cover of the confusion and obscurity caused by the smoke rolling among the woodlands, they were hard at work with pick and shovel, intrenching themselves. So wisely had Noailles taken all his measures, that it was thought that the Allies, then about 40,000 strong, would be forced to capitulate as prisoners of war, or be cut to pieces.

The king, detecting certain movements on the French left, ordered all tents to be struck at gunfire, and the troops to remain under arms till break of day, when they were to move from the right in two great columns. As he felt confident that any attempt of the French would be on his rear, he ordered the three battalions of the British Guards, and four of those of Lunenburg, with twenty-six squadrons of Hanoverian cavalry and a brigade of guns, to cover this operation.

Noailles, shrewdly suspecting the Allies would commence their march under cloud of night, gave orders that Antoine, the Marshal Duke de Grammont, should cross the Maine at Selingenstadt, to prevent this intended junction with the Prince of Hesse. He also dispatched 12,006 men towards Aschaffenberg to get possession of the bridge on its being quitted by the Allies, calculating that he would leave them no retreat on that side; and to conceal these movements, they marched in profound silence from the banks of the Maine circuitously through the woods.

9

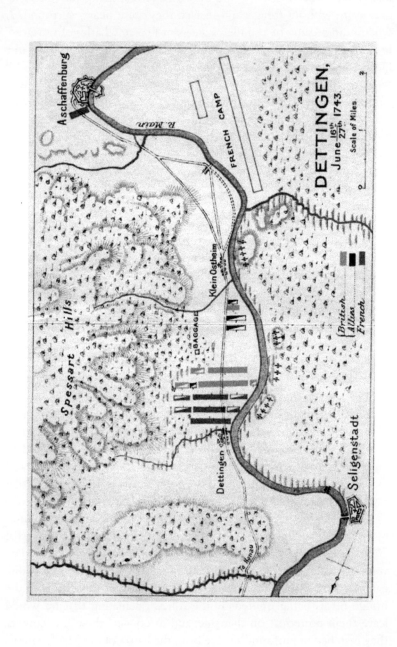

DETTINGEN,
June 16th 27th 1743.

Scale of Miles.

British
Allies
French

Aschaffenburg

R. Main

FRENCH CAMP

Klein Ostheim

BAGGAGE

Spessart Hills

Dettingen

Seligenstadt

To Hanau

So, the morning of Dettingen dawned. On this day the king appeared in the same red coat which he had worn thirty-five years before, under the Duke of Marlborough. Thackeray says:

> On public occasions he always displayed the hat and coat he wore on the famous day of Oudenarde; and the people laughed, but kindly, at the odd old garment, for bravery never goes out of fashion.

The route begun at daybreak by the troops was a dangerous one, as it lay between a mountain and the Maine, over which the French had been permitted most unaccountably to erect many bridges. Thus, it was soon discovered, states the *London Gazette*, that they had passed over bodies of troops in the night.

The king rode at the head of the seven battalions of Guards.

Sunrise saw the French Army drawn up in order of battle, in two long glittering lines, on a green plain behind a wood where the right wing of the Allies was posted. Their right was covered by the Maine, and protected by a battery on the other side of the river. The splendidly-accoutred troops of the Royal Household were in the centre, supported by infantry of the line. The left wing extended towards mountains covered by vineyards and copsewood.

In the morning the French infantry, says one relation, crossed two bridges at Selingenstadt, while their cavalry forded the river at the same place, taking possession of the village of Dettingen.

Having made all those dispositions, by which he flattered himself he would compel the Allies to attack the French under the greatest disadvantages, Marshal Noailles, with his staff, recrossed the Maine, in order the better to watch the various movements of the hostile armies.

Meanwhile, the Duke de Grammont, his nephew and lieutenant-general, who held Dettingen with 30,000 men—all select troops, among whom were the princes of the blood and a host of noblesse, all eager for battle—passed the defile behind which they were posted, and advanced into a small plain, called the Cock-field, where the Allies were in order of battle.

Noailles, when he beheld this unexpected movement, was filled with astonishment, and even with grief, at the rashness or madness of Grammont, in foregoing all the advantages of his position.

"Grammont," he exclaimed, "has ruined all my plans!"

He made all the haste he could to form a new disposition; but he arrived too late to repair the fatal mistake.

This was about twelve o'clock in the day; and on the approach of the French, who were now the attacking, and not as their general intended, the attacked force, the king ordered his first line of infantry to advance, under his second son, the Duke of Cumberland, and Lieutenant-Generals Clayton and Sommerfeldt,

Lord Carteret relates that as His Majesty rode down the line, he brandished his sword, crying—

Now, my brave boys! Now, for the glory of old England, advance boldly!

Halfway on the line of infantry halted, and gave a hearty cheer, after which they continued a rapid advance towards the enemy. During some of these movements the king was nearly taken by the enemy, and would have been so but for the valour of the 22nd Regiment, who in remembrance of this wear a sprig of oak in their caps on gala days.

From their right, the troops of the French Household advanced on the left of the Allies, or Confederates "as they were called, and commenced an irregular fire, which rapidly became general along the whole line of both armies, and then the entire field of Dettingen presented a scene of smoke, slaughter, and dreadful uproar

The Allies still continued to advance, notwithstanding a tremendous front and flank fire from the enemy, which galled them severely, and laid the dead and wounded in piles over each other.

On the left, the French cavalry, with horses spurred at full speed, fell sword in hand upon the Austrian cavalry; and many a hussar and *cuirassier* went down to rise no more. The Austrians were at once disordered:

But the British and Hanoverian infantry, animated by the presence of their sovereign, who rode between the lines with his sword drawn, stood firm as rocks, and poured forth an incessant fire, which nothing could resist. These impenetrable battalions, however, by a masterly manoeuvre, on the approach of the French cavalry, led by the nobility and princes of the blood, who rushed on in desperation, opened their lines, and afterwards closing again, made great havoc in that gallant body.

Before this took place, however, the French, in their headlong charge, drove in the King's and Ligonier's regiments of horse, which had been sent to the front by Lord Stair. They next drove in the Horse Guards, under General Honeywood; and then it was that the infantry opened their ranks, and executed the manoeuvre by which the Household Cavalry of France were totally destroyed.

Accompanied by his *aide-de-camp*, the Earl of Dumfries, the Earl of Stair then rode up to the infantry, and told them that they might yet have the entire glory of beating the French, whose third line was now seen drawn up in beautiful order.

Three hearty cheers were the response to this, and once more the grand old British line resumed its steady advance; and their attack was conducted with such impetuous gallantry that the whole French Army gave way, their confusion being increased by the Hanoverian artillery, which came galloping through a wood, and suddenly opened fire upon them.

Absolute terror is said to have seized the French, "Save himself who can!" was the cry on all sides.

In Voltaire's *Age of Louis XIV.*," he states that the Marquis de Puysegur, son of the marshal of that name, called to the soldiers of his regiment, and tried in vain to rally them; and that he even killed some that were rushing from their ranks with the cry of "*Sauve qui peut!*"

Marshal Noailles found himself compelled to retreat across the Maine, with the loss of 5,000 men; and had he been hotly pursued, the broken masses of his army must have been totally destroyed. He had many drowned in the passage of the Maine, and lost three pairs of colours.

The loss of the Allies was about 3,000 men, including Generals Murray and Clayton. The Duke of Cumberland, the Earl of Albemarle, General Huske, and many other officers of rank were wounded. Voltaire observes that the French suffered greatly, and the excellent dispositions of their generals were rendered abortive by the same precipitation, ardour, and want of steadiness which lost France the Battles of Poictiers, Cressy, and Agincourt.

After the junction was formed at Hanau, the Earl of Stair proposed that as the numbers were now equal on both sides, the French should be attacked at once: but, to the astonishment of all Europe, the king declined.

On this the earl, who was one of the first soldiers of the age, and had ever resented the king's marked preference for Hanoverian over British officers, resigned his command, and returned to Scotland. The pine woods which adorn his house of Newliston, near Edinburgh, are said to have been planted by him in the position in which he had arranged the allied troops at the Battle of Dettingen.

Though honourable to those who won it, the victory was productive of no decisive results; and both armies, after some unimportant movements, retired into winter-quarters in October.

An aged soldier, named Robert Fergusson, who died at Paisley in 1811, in his ninety-seventh year, preserved to the last, as a precious relic, the old red coat of Handyside's Foot, the 22nd Regiment, in which he had been wounded at the Battles of Dettingen and Fontenoy, just as future years may see some veteran preserving the faded, and, perhaps, bloodstained tunic which he wore when with Raglan at Alma, or with Havelock at Lucknow.

BATTLE OF DETTINGEN

Fontenoy, 1745

On the 7th of March, 1745, William Duke of Cumberland was commissioned as Captain-General of the British Army, being the third and last in succession after the Dukes of Marlborough and Ormond who has held that high rank. He was, moreover, appointed commander-in-chief of the Confederate forces, and at a Council of War held at Brussels it was agreed that these should be ready to take the field on a chosen day, if he approved; and on the 7th of April he reached the Belgian capital, and commenced his inspection of the troops.

To garrison the towns sufficiently it was computed that 18,000 men would be required; hence, from this cause and other detachments, the army did not muster more than 43,450 men.

Maurice Count Saxe, who commanded the French, had obtained great celebrity by the skilful manner in which he had managed his retreats in Germany. Not only had he shown great military talents, and coolness and intrepidity, but he also evinced the knowledge of a skilful commander. According to Voltaire, he brought into the field 35,000 more men than the Confederates; his strength being 106 battalions and 172 squadrons, while they had but 46 battalions and 90 squadrons.

The campaign opened with the investment of Tournay. The Duke of Cumberland and the Austrian general, Marshal Count Konigseck, marched for Halle, and on the 22nd of April were at Soignies.

Louis XV., accompanied by the *dauphin*, reached the camp before Tournay, when Marshal Saxe told the former that:

> He expected the Confederates were bold enough to give battle; therefore, as he was conscious that the French troops were unable to stand before the British forces fairly in the field, he was determined to depend upon stratagem rather than open strength, and accordingly made the best preparations for a brave defence against a noble attack. (*Cumberland's Memoirs*).

The disposition of his troops was most advantageous.

To block up Tournay he left 18,000 men; the defence of the bridges of the Scheldt, and to keep the communications open, he assigned to 6,000 more. The siege of Tournay had been pressed vigorously when the Duke of Cumberland advanced to its relief unwisely, as he had only 53,000 men with which to make the attempt. The Dutch, who proved worse than useless in the campaign, were led by the Prince of Waldeck, a leader possessed of as little skill and experience as the former, who though Captain-General of the British Army, and so obese and unwieldy in figure as to be scarcely able to ride his horse, was only in his twenty-fourth year.

Konigseck, who commanded our Austrian Allies, was aged, and long past the time for campaigning; and thus led, the Allies advanced to engage one of the finest armies in Europe, led by the first general and strategist of the age, Count Saxe, Marshal-General of France and Duke Elect of Courland and Semigallia, an officer so esteemed in Europe that the Marshal Duke de Noailles was content to serve under him as his first *aide-de-camp*.

His army was led by five princes of the blood, and sixty-seven general officers, all of noble families; but at this time Saxe was so ill as to be unable to sit on horseback or wear uniform; thus, he accompanied the troops in a litter.

He took up a position at Fontenoy, a small village which is situated on rising ground four miles east of Tournay, and on the left bank of the Scheldt. Along the summit of the eminence which there slopes upward from the plain, he formed his line of infantry. The village of St. Antoine, near the river, covered his right flank, and the defence of it was entrusted to the Regiments of Piedmont and Biron respectively, under the Counts De la Marche and De Lorges.

The wood of Barri covered his left; it was full of troops and guns. They had a battery at St. Antoine; another in their centre, at Fontenoy, intrenched and fortified; another at the wood; and, according to *Cumberland's Memoirs*, they had also batteries in rear of their wings:

> Which were to open at a proper time, and make way for the horrible destruction expected from them by cartridge shot. They had cannon planted, almost invisible, on their intrenchments, pointed breast-high, and loaded so as to do dreadful execution; while their own forces were almost secure from danger, by being intrenched up to their necks.

Battle of Fontenoy

There were also abattis of felled trees, fascines of baskets, and walls of turf.

The lines at Fontenoy were defended altogether by 260 heavy cannon and field-pieces. The village he committed to the Count de la Vauguyon, with the Regiment du Dauphine. On his left were the brave corps of the Irish Brigade, under the gallant Lord Clare. On their left were the French Marines, under the Count de Guerchi; and in their rear, was the Regiment of Angoumois, in the castle of Bourquembrai, on which a white banner with three *fleurs-de-lis* was flying.

It was impossible to turn the flanks of the French, and to assail in front their superior force thus posted evinced either the extremity of rashness or of ignorance. Moreover, the reconnaisance made by Cumberland was most imperfect; yet he ordered his army, consisting, as we have said, of only 46 battalions and 90 squadrons, to advance at once to the attack. He had ninety pieces of ordnance; eight of these were mortars, but many were only three-pounder falconets. The whole position of Saxe rose with a gentle ascent from a flat and fertile plain, where the young grass was sprouting in the fields; and this he could sweep by the concentrated fire of 260 pieces of ordnance.

The night of the 30th of April was chilly, dark, and moonless, and mist was enveloping the banks of the Scheldt, the wood of Barri, and the slope of Fontenoy, when, at two o'clock on the morning of the first of May, the Allies began to advance over the open plain. The atmosphere was so still that they could hear the village clocks striking, as in the dark the columns of attack were formed.

The right wing was composed of British and Hanoverians, who, under General Zastrow, formed a portion of the centre, and were formed in four lines before a village named Veson. The left wing, composed of Dutch and Austrians, reached to the wood of Peronne. In front of Veson was a redoubt mounted with cannon, and manned by 600 Frenchmen; and this point Brigadier Ingoldsby had special orders to storm at the head of four battalions, while the Prince of Waldeck was to assail Fontenoy at the head of the Dutch. And with these orders to fulfil, the troops, encumbered by their knapsacks, blankets, kettles, and great-coats, stumbled forward in the dark, over hedges, through water-cuts and the growing grain, till they formed open column of regiments at quarter-distance columns of companies, and there deployed into line three ranks deep.

With the British Army in the field there now appeared a regiment of Highlanders for the first time—the famous Black Watch, now numbered as the 42nd. They were in the division of Ingoldsby. Their dress, being so well known, requires no description, save their bonnets, which were flat and blue and bordered then, as now, by the fess-cheque of the House of Stuart, with a tuft of black feathers. Their arms were a musket, bayonet, and large basket-hilted broadsword; these were furnished by Government and such men as chose were permitted to carry a dirk, a pair of pistols, and around shield, after the fashion of their country. Their sword-belts were black.

Lieutenant-Colonel Sir Robert Munro was their leader on this day.

The Brigade of Guards was led by Sir John Ligonier, son of Colonel Francis Ligonier, a French Protestant refugee.

At a quarter to four a.m. the cannonade commenced, as the mist cleared away, and the earliest beams of day began to lighten the flat horizon, and it continued without intermission.

Sir John Ligonier was ordered to advance with the Brigade of Guards and seven guns, to check a destructive fire from the enemy's field artillery, and the moment they were silenced the whole line was to advance upon the French position.

The seven guns were grape-shotted, and the brigade advanced with bayonets fixed at a rapid pace. Several officers fell; two lieutenant-colonels, Douglas (son of Lord Morton) and Carpenter, of the Scots Guards, were unhorsed and killed at the same moment: but speedily the Guardsmen were among the French field-pieces, bayonetting and cutting down the gunners before they could limber up and retire. The *History of the War* says:

> The Guards and Highlanders, began the battle, and attacked a body of French near Veson, where the Dauphin was posted. Though the enemy were intrenched breast-high, the Guards with their bayonets, and the Highlanders with sword, pistol, and dirk, forced them out, killing a considerable number.

The Guards and Black Watch then fell back and rejoined the first line, the formation of which was complete by nine o'clock; when Sir John Ligonier sent his *aide-de-camp* to acquaint the Duke of Cumberland that as the guns were silenced, "he was ready, and only waiting for the signal of Prince Waldeck to attack Fontenoy." The troops then moved forward with astonishing intrepidity to their respective points of attack.

The "advance" was then sounded by many a trumpet and bugle,

while, amid a stunning roar of musketry, the troops rushed on; the Dutch under Waldeck against Fontenoy, Ingoldsby to assail the redoubt in front of Veson, and the first line of British and Hanoverians, led by Cumberland in person, to attack the centre.

So quick was the rush, that the duke and other officers rode their horses at a canter; but their men fell fast on every hand while passing between Barri and Fontenoy, "the fire of the cannon making whole lanes through the ranks of the Confederates particularly the English."

Under this the Dutch, who covered their left, fell into disorder, and could be rallied no more during the day. The cavalry also became disorganised. The Earl of Crawford, colonel of the Royal Scots Dragoons, remarks that:

> The conduct of the Dutch had an extremely bad effect on the mind of the troops in general, though not so much on ours, who were the first ranged, and still marched towards the enemy, the noblest sight I ever saw, and never stopped till they got through a shower of bullets and musketry.

Brigadier Ingoldsby, who had special orders to carry the redoubts at the Bois de Barri, imagined the difficulty to be greater than it was; and instead of storming the works at once, and scouring the wood with the bayonet, he returned to the duke for artillery, thus affording the enemy time to strengthen the works. For this he was afterwards tried by a court-martial, but vindicated himself by denying that he had ever received orders on this occasion, and added that those he did receive were so contradictory that he did not know which to obey.

Led by the Duke of Cumberland, attended by Lord Cathcart, K.T., the first line succeeded in passing Fontenoy and the redoubt, and got within thirty yards of the enemy's muzzles. Receiving fire therefore, at this distance, "the British doubled up in a column, and advanced between the batteries," all of which were playing upon a spot not quite half a mile in breadth. The slaughter was indescribable. Whole ranks perished, but the intervals were closed up, and after two terrible rushes with the bayonet, they broke the brigade of French Guards, and hurled them back in disorder upon their supports, the Irish regiments of Lord Clare. The French cavalry now advanced, but went about, unable to face the fire that mowed down horse and man.

At this portion of the battle there occurred two episodes worth repeating. We find one in Voltaire, and the other in the *Records of the 42nd Highlanders*, which had been withdrawn from Ingoldby's division

PLAN DE LA BATAILLE DE FONTENOY
PAR L'ARMÉE FRANÇOISE
Sur Celle des Alliez sous les
Dédié au Roy par son très humble très obéissant Serviteur et

EXPLICATIONS.

BRIGADES   BATAILLONS.
ET RENVOIS.

INFANTERIE.

1 Les deux Redoutes du Bois de Bary défendues par le Régiment d'EU - 2
2 Le Village, Eglise & Cimetière de Fontenoy, défendu par la Brigade de DAUPHIN & d'un Bataillon de BEAUVOISIS : la Brigade de DAUPHIN s'est joint pendant l'Action un Bataillon du Régiment du ROY fait en tout - 5
3 Redoutes entre Fontenoy & Anthoin, soutenues par des Détachemens de DIESBACK & de BETHENS - 0
4 Retranchemens d'ANTHOIN.
5 La Brigade de PIEMONT composée de quatre Bataillons de PIEMONT & un de ROYAL LA MARINE, gardoient les Retranchemens d'Anthoin - -
6 Bataillon de BIRON qui avoit été placé derrière la Brigade de PIEMONT, a été porté dès le commencement de l'Action en ligne entre Fontenoy & Anthoin, à la droite de CRILLON - 1
7 NORMANDIE, il n'arriva que pour les dernières charges que les Troupes du Roy ont faites ; cette Brigade eut encore assez de temps pour s'y distinguer avec honneur. - -
8 ROYAL CORSE - -
    Deux autres Bataillons étoient dans le Château d'Elmont

9 BUKLEY - - - -
10 DILLON - - - -   Brigades Irlandoises
11 BERWICK - - -
12 LALLY - - - -   de chacune un Bataillon.
13 ROOTH - - - -
14 CLARE - - - -

15 ROYAL VAISSEAUX - - 1
16 HAINAUT - - - - 1
17 ROYAL - - - - 1
18 SOISSONNOIS - - - 1
  ayant LA COURONNE pour Chef de Brigade.
19 LA COURONNE - - - 1
20 GARDES-SUISSES - - - 1
  Deux autres Bataillons étoient aux Retranchemens du Pont de Vaux.
21 GARDES-FRANÇOISES - - 1
  Deux autres Bataillons étoient aux Retranchemens du Pont de Vaux, & dès le commencement de l'Action, deux Bataillons passèrent encore aux mêmes Retranchemens.
22 COURTEN - - - - 1
23 AUBTERRE, Chef de Brigade de COURTEN - - - - 1
24 DU ROY - - - - 1
  Deux autres Bataillons indiqués sous le même N°. étoient dans les Retranchemens du Village de Fontenoy.
25 DIESBACK - - - - 1
  Deux autres Bataillons étoient, l'un au service de l'Artillerie, & l'autre dans les trois Redoutes entre Fontenoy & Anthoin.
26 BETHENS - - - - 1
  Les Bataillons de BETHENS & de DIESBACK faisoient la gauche de la Ligne formée entre Anthoin & Fontenoy.
27 CRILLON avança jusqu'à la deuxième Redoute
28 TROUPES qui se portèrent au centre pendant l'Action aux chiffres 16, 17, 18 & 19 ; ainsi l'on y verra HAINAUT, ROYAL, SOISSONNOIS & la COURONNE.
a ROYAL LA MARINE
  Aux Retranchemens d'Anthoin. - - 1

REMPORTÉE LE XI. MAY. M.DCC.XLV.
COMMANDÉE PAR LE ROY.
Ordres du Duc de Cumberland.
fidele sujet de Beaurain Géographe Ordinaire de sa Majesté.

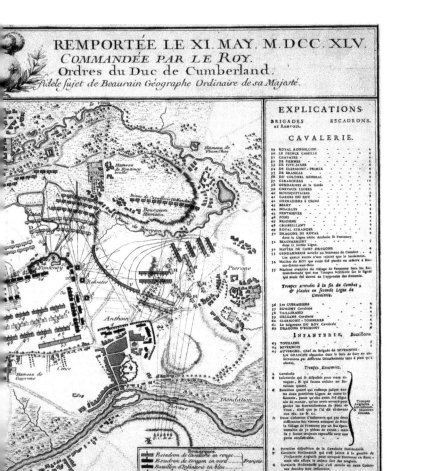

EXPLICATIONS

BRIGADES ET RENVOIS.		ESCADRONS.

CAVALERIE.

29	ROYAL ROUSSILLON.	4
30	LE PRINCE CAMILLE	4
31	CRAVATES	3
32	DE FIENNES	3
33	DE FITZ-JAMES	4
34	DE CLERMONT - PRINCE	4
35	DE BRANCAS	3
36	DU COLONEL GENERAL	4
37	CARABINIERS	10
38	GENDARMES de la Garde	4
39	CHEVAUX LEGERS	4
40	MOUSQUETAIRES	2
41	GARDES DU ROY	6
42	GRENADIERS à Cheval	1
43	BERRY	2
44	NOAILLES	3
45	PENTHIEVRE	3
46	PONS	2
47	BRIONNE	2
48	CHABRILLANT	2
49	ROYAL ETRANGER	4
50	DRAGONS DE ROYAL	4
	dans la Ligne entre Anthoin & Fontenoy.	
51	BEAUFREMONT	3
	dans la 100me Ligne.	
52	MESTRE DE CAMP DRAGONS	4
53	GENDARMERIE arrivée au moment du Combat	4
	Les quatre notes n'ont rejoint que le lendemain.	
54	Maison du ROY qui avoit été postée en réserve à Notre-Dame-aux-Bois	
55	Maison enterrée du Village de Fontenoy hors les Retranchements que nos Troupes brûlèrent sur le Signal qui avoit été donné de l'approche des Ennemis.	

Troupes arrivées à la fin du Combat, & placées en seconde Ligne de Cavalerie.

56	Les CUIRASSIERS	4
57	EGMONT Cavalerie	4
58	TAILLERAND	3
59	ORLEANS Cavalerie	3
60	CLERMONT - TONNERRE	2
61	Le régiment DU ROY Cavalerie	4
62	DRAGONS D'EGMONT	4

INFANTERIE, Bataillons.

63	TOURAINE	2
64	NIVERNOIS	2
65	AUVERGNE, Chef de Brigade de MIVERNOIS	2
	Les GRASSINS répandus dans le Bois de Bury en observations par différens Détachemens tant à pied qu'à cheval.	

Troupes Ennemies.

A — Cavalerie
B — Infanterie qui se disposoit pour nous attaquer, & qui furent enfuite en Bataillon quarré.
C — Bataillon quarré qui venant jusque dans les deux premieres Lignes se coupa en fusieurs, parce qu'elle avoit été déguarnie de monde, on nous avoit envoyé pour garder les Retranchemens du Pont de Vous, ainsi que je l'ai ci-devant aux No. 30 & 11.
D — Deux Colonnes d'Infanterie qui par deux différentes fois vinrent attaquer de front le village de Fontenoy par sa fine éventable de 30 pièces de canon ; mais ils y furent toujours repoussés avec une perte considérable.

E — Première disposition de la Cavalerie Hollandoise.
F — Cavalerie Hollandoise qui s'est jointe à la gauche de l'Infanterie Angloise pour attaquer Fontenoy en flanc ; mais elle n'a se mêsue fort peu Anglois.
G — Cavalerie Hollandoise qui s'est retirée en deux Colonnes derrière leur Infanterie.
H — Premiere disposition de l'Infanterie Hollandoise.
I — Infanterie Hollandoise en deux Colonnes qui s'étoient approchées pour attaquer le Bourg d'Anthoin ; s'étant repoussées, de même que la Cavalerie, & retirèrent l'une & l'autre dans leur derniere position pendant l'action que si passoit entre Fontenoy & le Bois de Berry.

REMARQUES.

Aux Postes d'Anthoin, Fontenoy & les Redoutes, le nombre des pièces de canon est marqué au vis des deux lignes civières, à la réserve de l'une des deux Redoutes du Bois de Bury, où quatre pièces qui y étoient n'ont point servies, lesquelles sont marquées par des lignes de quinte.
Les Canons qui ont servi à la bataille sont placés en même nombre de petits Canons vis-à-vis des Brigades de la première Ligne.

Remarques.
- Escadron de Cavalerie en rouge
- Escadron de Dragon en vert — François
- Bataillon d'Infanterie en bleu
- Escadron de Cavalerie en violet — Ennemis
- Bataillon d'Infanterie jaune
- C — Marqué avec un Chiffre qui est avant le nombre des Pièces de Canon.
- Chemin Creux

Echelle de 600. Toises ex.

Le terrain du Plan cy joint a été dessiné et levé sur les Lieux par Mr. l'Abbé aide de Camp de Mgr. le Prince de Soubise : L'ordre & la disposition de l'Armée des Alliés avec des Vües sur les explications, sont de Mr. de Beaurain.

and attached to the Guards.

Voltaire tells us that the officers of the British Guards, when in the presence of the enemy, saluted the French by taking off their hats. The Count de Chambanne and Duke de Biron, who were in advance, returned the salute, as did all the other officers of the French Guards. Lord Charles Hay (son of the Marquis of Tweedale), a captain in the English Guards, called aloud—

"Gentlemen of the French Guards, fire!"

"Gentlemen," replied the Count d'Anterroche, lieutenant of grenadiers, " we never fire first; fire yourselves."

He continues:

The British then commenced a running fire in divisions (platoons?), so that one battalion made a discharge, and afterwards another, while the first reloaded. Nineteen officers of the French Guards fell by the first discharge. Messieurs de Clisson, de Ligney, de la Peyre, and 95 soldiers were killed, and 285 were wounded; also 11 Swiss officers, and 209 of their soldiers, of whom 64 died on the spot. Colonel Courten, his lieutenant-colonel, 4 officers and 75 soldiers were killed, and 200 soldiers were dangerously wounded. The first rank being swept away, the three others, finding themselves unsupported, except by a regiment of cavalry at a distance, dispersed. The Duke de Grammont, their colonel and first lieutenant-general, who might have rallied them, was killed. Monsieur Luttaux, next in rank to De Grammont, did not reach the ground until they had abandoned it. The English advanced as if performing part of their exercise; the majors levelling the soldiers' muskets with their canes, to make their aim more sure.

In the *Records of the 42nd*, we find that this second attack was made about midday:

When the Dutch again failed, and Lieutenant-Colonel Sir Robert Munro, with the Highlanders, was ordered to sustain the British troops, who were severely engaged with superior numbers.

Sir Robert having obtained the duke's permission to let his men fight in their own fashion, they flung themselves flat on the ground when the French fired a volley, which thus swept harmlessly over them. Then, springing up, they poured in their fire, slung their muskets, and in the smoke, rushed on with target and claymore. Doddridge in his *Life of Colonel Gardiner* says:

> Sir Robert was everywhere with his regiment, notwithstanding his great corpulency, and when in the trenches he was hauled out by the legs and arms by his own men; and it was observed that when he commanded the whole regiment to clap to the ground, he alone stood upright with the colours behind, receiving the fire of the enemy.

A little work entitled, *Conduct of Officers at Fontenoy Considered*, states that the Duke of Cumberland remarked the gallant conduct of the regiment, and observed a Highlander, who had killed nine men, making a stroke at a tenth with his broadsword, when his arm was torn off by a cannonball.

> His Royal Highness applauded the Highlander's conduct, and promised him a reward of value equal to the arm.

The line of the French trenches was choked with dead and dying; while three-cornered hats, powdered wigs, weapons, and half-buried shot lay everywhere.

At this crisis the British had decidedly the advantage over the left wing. The Duke de Grammont was killed by some English artillerymen, who, perceiving that he was splendidly mounted, conceived him to be an officer of rank, and made bets among themselves as to who would bring him down. His thigh was broken by a ball, and he expired on the field. For firing this shot, a *matross* named Baker received a pension of £18 *per annum*.

On the other side. Sir James Campbell, K.B., son of Lord Loudon, and colonel of the Scots Greys, fell at their head. A cannon-shot smashed one of his legs, and he expired just as he was being borne from the field, in his eightieth year.

The standard of this regiment was borne by Sir William Erskine, then a cornet. His father, the lieutenant-colonel of the Greys, tied the standard to his son's right leg, and said:

> Go, and take care of this; let me not see you separate, for if you return alive you must produce this standard.

After the battle, the cornet rode up to his father, and displayed the standard tight and fast, as in the morning.

Unsupported by cavalry, the British infantry bore down all before

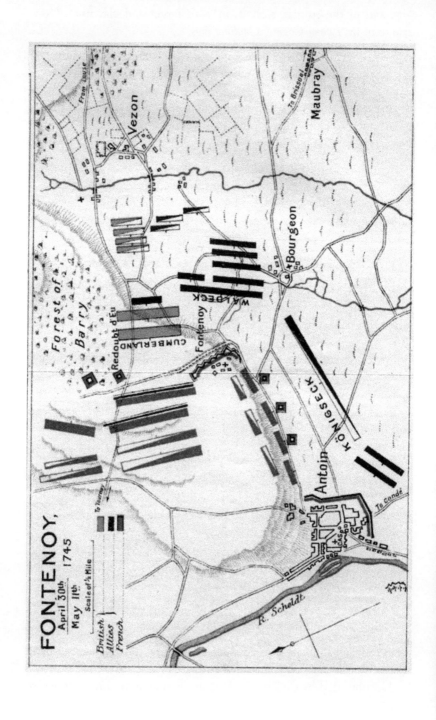

FONTENOY,
April 30th 1745
May 11th

Scale of ½ Mile

British
Allies
French

Forest of Barry

Vezon

From Tournai

Maubray

To Brussels

Bourgeon

WALDECK

Redoubt d'Eu

CUMBERLAND

Fontenoy

KÖNIGSECK

Antoin

To Tournai

To Condé

R. Scheldt

them, driving the French left 300 paces beyond Fontenoy, and making themselves masters of the field, from the ground on which they stood to their own camp. But as the left retired, the columns wheeled back, or opened and uncovered two batteries of heavy guns, which poured on the British such a storm of cartridge shot in front and flank, that it was impossible to face it. Rallying, however, they completed the disorder of the French, who were fairly beaten; and had some fresh battalions from the reserve replaced those that had suffered from the masked batteries, or had the second line advanced to enable the cavalry to get past the redoubts, the enemy could not have recovered the day.

Colonel Mackinnon says, in his *History of the Coldstream Guards*:—

According to the first plan drawn out, the French would have been taken in flank by Lord Crawford, who was to advance along the edge of the wood leading to the road of Leuse, where Prince Waldeck's regiments, with some hussars, had endeavoured to penetrate in the morning; and if the troops under Lord Crawford had been reinforced, instead of being withdrawn on the failure of the Dutch, the results of the battle would probably have been different. Lord Crawford himself gives it as his real opinion that orders were at one time issued for the retreat of the French. The left, although supported by the fire from the English artillery, did not succeed; and Fort Veson not being carried, the British were placed between a cross-fire of cannon and musketry, which obliged them to retire on the height of Fontenoy.

When the French infantry were fairly driven out of the village of St. Antoine, the Count de Saxe believed the battle was lost, and sent an officer with such tidings to the king and *dauphin*, who were seated on horseback at an eminence named "The Justice of our Lady in the Wood," where the royal standard of France was flying. The latter was immediately struck, by the order of Louis, as the officer begged that they would provide for their own safety by flight.

Guns were brought to bear on the British artillery, which in some degree slackened its fire, and gave time for the Irish Brigade to form. It was the last resource left to King Louis and Count Saxe. It was at the most critical period of that bloody day, when, after being harassed by the manoeuvres of the past night, when, after enduring a cannonade from more than 200 pieces of ordnance, after driving in the field-guns, after forcing a passage between Fontenoy and the wood of Barri, and after hurling the foe from the heights and village of St. Antoine, that the Irish Brigade, of immortal memory, came fully into action against the Confederates—the representatives of 30,000 Irishmen who had followed King James into exile—these were the veteran regiments of Clare, the Honourable Arthur Dillon, Count O'Lally, the Duke of Berwick, Rothe, and the Counts Buckley and Fitzjames; and the gallant Charles O'Brien, Lord Clare, was at their head. Fitzjames's regiment was a dragoon corps; and the regiments of Normandy and Vaisseaux were ordered to support them.

It must have been with emotions of a very mingled nature that some of the troops in that field, particularly the Highlanders, beheld the advance of the Irish exiles, who were all clad in scarlet uniform, with white breeches.

A yell rang along their ranks as the seven regiments came on, and their cry had a terrible significance. It was—

"*Cuimhnigidh ar Luimneac agus ar fheile na Sacsanach!*" which may be translated, "Remember Limerick and Saxon faith!"

Pouring in a volley, they rushed on our toil-worn infantry with the bayonet, after having successively routed the finest troops in the French service, who were now fated to be routed, and by the Irish!

Mackinnon says:

No additional corps were sent to the relief of the British, whose compact formation had hitherto enabled them to repair the repeated losses occasioned by these incessant attacks. No fresh orders were issued; no cavalry was within reach to follow up the panic which had seized upon the enemy. The Dutch did not appear in any quarter, nor was there any probability of a sortie from Tournay to aid this isolated body. . . . . . The encounter between the British and the Irish Brigade was fierce, the fire constant, the slaughter great; and the loss on the side of the British was such that they were compelled at length to retire.

The Duke of Cumberland lost all presence of mind, and his army fell back in undeniable confusion, cavalry and infantry all mingled together; and but for the steady stand made by the Earl of Crawford, with the 3rd Buffs and the Highlanders, to cover the rear, the defeated Allies had not crossed the Bruffoel so speedily, though some corps faced about to fire again at every hundred paces.

The army moved to Lessines, and encamped there near Aeth.

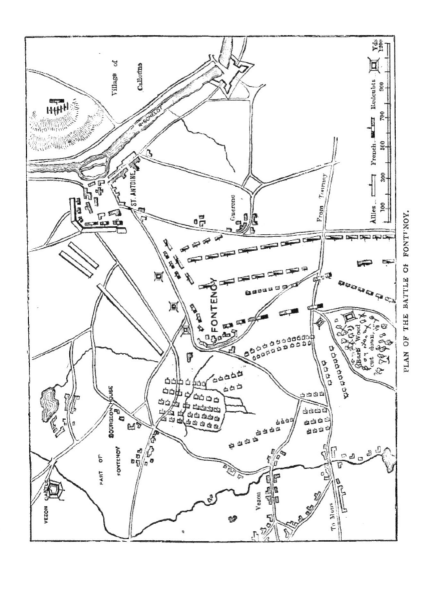

PLAN OF THE BATTLE OF FONT'NOY.

Louis is said to have ridden down to the bivouac of the Irish, and thanked them personally.

An Irish ballad, perhaps unknown in England, refers with exultation to Fontenoy:—

> *O'Brien's voice is hoarse with joy, as halting, he commands,*
> *'Fix bayonets—Charge!' Like mountain storm rush on these fiery bands;*
> *Like lions leaping at a fold, when mad with hunger's pang.*
> *Right onward to the English line the Irish exiles sprang.*
> *Bright was their steel—'tis bloody!—the muskets filled with gore;*
> *Through shattered ranks, and severed files, and trampled flags they tore.*
> *The English strove with desperate strength; they rallied, staggered, fled:*
> *The green hill-side is matted close with dying and with dead.*
> *Across the plain, and far away, passed on that hideous wreck,*
> *While cavalier and fantassin dash in upon their track.*
> *On Fontenoy, on Fontenoy, like eagles in the sun.*
> *With bloody plumes the Irish stand the field is lost and won.*

Voltaire estimates the loss of the French in this battle at 8,000 men, while the Allies had 21,000 killed or wounded. Our Household Brigade had 724 officers and men placed *hors de combat*; of these no less than 437 belonged to the Scots Foot Guards. Of the Irish Brigade there fell one-fourth of the officers, including Colonel Dillon, and one-third of the men.

The Duke of Cumberland was never able to face the enemy again, but lay timidly intrenched with his troops between Brussels and Antwerp. The following is the bulletin of Fontenoy, published at Paris on the 26th May, five days after the battle;—

> Our victory may be said to be complete; but it cannot be denied that the Allies behaved extremely well, more especially the English, who made a soldier-like retreat, which was much favoured by an adjacent wood. The British behaved well, and none could exceed them in advancing, none but our officers, when the Highland furies rushed in upon us with more violence than ever did a sea driven by a tempest. I cannot say much for the other auxiliaries; some looked as if they had no concern in the matter. We gained the victory, but may I never see such another!

From the *Diary* of the Rev. John Bisset, we learn that some of the cannon taken from the British at Fontenoy were afterwards sent over

The Salute at Fontenoy

by France to the Highland army of Prince Charles, and were landed at Stonehaven.

When George II. heard of the conduct of the Irish at Fontenoy, he uttered that memorable imprecation on the penal code—"Cursed be the laws which deprive me of such subjects!"

Such were the leading features of this memorable field; and hence the stirring words of Prince Charles Edward Stuart, when, soon after, he drew his sword before the disastrous Battle of Culloden—"Come, gentlemen, let us give Cumberland another Fontenoy!"

The last survivor of this field was the well-known amazon, Phoebe Hessel, who served there as a soldier in the 5th Regiment, and received a bayonet-wound in the arm. She died in 1821, and her monument, which is still to be seen standing in the churchyard of Chelsea, states that she was born in 1713; so that, if the record be correct, she had attained the age of 108 years.

SERGEANT OF THE 1ST FOOT GUARDS

Sea-Fight off Toulon, 1744

When the alliance between France and Spain was fully concluded at Fontainebleau, the admirals of their combined fleets which lay in the harbour of Toulon resolved to give battle to that of Britain.

While Admiral Thomas Matthews, who commanded the latter— an old, distinguished, and ultimately most ill-used officer—was at the Court of Turin on the public service, he received tidings that a French squadron, consisting of eleven sail of the line and ten frigates, had sailed from Brest, for the purpose of forming a junction with the squadron under Admiral de Court at Toulon, and thereby to favour the escape of the Spanish fleet, which had been for some time blocked up in that port.

He immediately repaired to Villafranca; and on the 3rd of January he joined the fleet under Vice-Admiral Lestock, in Hyères Bay, eleven miles eastward of Toulon. The fleet consisted at this time of sixteen sail of the line, and four fifty-gun ships; but a few days after he received a reinforcement, and ultimately his force consisted of fifty-four sail, carrying 2,680 guns, and 18,805 men. All those vessels, however, did not take a part in the subsequent action.

On the 9th the combined fleets were seen standing out of the roadstead of Toulon, and forming in order of battle as they came. At ten o'clock Admiral Matthews threw out the signal to weigh anchor, and to form the line of battle ahead. The British fleet continued plying to windward, between the mainland and the group of sterile islets named Porquerolles, Portcros, Bagneaux, and Titan, called of old the Isles d'Or; but the confederate fleets not evincing any disposition to bear down, Admiral Matthews returned to his anchorage in the Bay of Hyeres, which is overlooked by an ancient castle and steep old town of that name on the slope of a hill.

All next day the fleets manoeuvred in sight of each other, and

34

stood out to sea in a line abreast, without exchanging shots.

On the 11th. Admiral Matthews began to suspect that M. de Court had in view the decoying of the British fleet towards the mouth of the Straits, where there was a probability of his being joined by the expected squadron of Brest. The moment this suspicion crossed the mind of Matthews, he resolved to bring the French and Spaniards to close action at once.

Irrespective of frigates and fire-ships, the van, centre, and rear divisions of the enemy consisted of twenty-eight sail, carrying 1,832 guns, and 17,430 men.

The first was led by M. de Cabaret, the *chef d'escadre*; the second by De Court, in *La Terrible*, 74; the last by Don Navarro, Rear-Admiral of Spain, in the *Royal Philip*, 114 guns. His captain bore the Irish name of Geraldine.

Admiral Rowley led the British van, in the *Barfleur*, 90; Matthews the centre, with his flag flying on the *Namur*, 90; Admiral Lestock led the rear, in the *Neptune*, 90. But the latter officer kept two full leagues to windward, by which means twelve sail of the line, two frigates, and a fire-ship "were of no use except to intimidate."

At half-past eleven the signal to engage was hoisted on the *Namur*, which bore down upon the Spanish admiral, attended by the *Marlborough*, 90 guns, commanded by Captain James Cornwall, and by one o'clock the battle began. But while it continued, M. de Court, in his anxiety to reach the Brest squadron, made sail and lay-to by turns, so that the British could not engage his ships in proper order; and as they outsailed ours, Mathews feared they might escape him altogether if he waited for the division of Admiral Lestock, who purposely, as the sequel proved, lagged far astern, leaving the brunt of battle to be maintained by the van and centre.

In coming into action, the *Marlborough*, amid the smoke, drove so far ahead that Matthews was compelled to fill his sails to prevent her coming on board of him. There was but little wind, with a heavy ground swell, which rendered the gunnery practice on both sides somewhat ineffective: yet the *London Magazine* for 1744 states that early in the engagement the masts and rigging of the flag-ship were much cut up and disabled; that Admiral Matthews "hoisted his mizzen-topsail to prevent the spars and rigging tumbling about their ears;" and that this "hindered the working of the ship (though he reeved new braces three times), so that he could not give the assistance" to Captain Cornwall that was requisite. This officer had both his legs carried away by a cannon-shot, which killed him on the spot. His nephew, a first lieutenant, was also killed; another, named Frederick Cornwall, had an arm torn off by a ball, but died an admiral in 1786. She had forty-three men killed and ninety wounded.

It is also stated that the French gunners were most expert, as they had been trained for the previous three months by daily target-practice; and that the *Marlborough's* mainmast was swept away "by the board, as if it had been a twig," while Matthews' mainmast and bowsprit were shot through and through, the former "having only two shrouds left to support it."

The ships were now engaged at pistol-shot distance, but as the enemy fired chiefly at our masts and rigging, in their anxiety to escape, the admiral had only, according to one account, nine men killed and forty wounded; by another, sixty casualties in all. The flag-captain, John Russell, had an arm shot away, and afterwards died of the wound.

By four in the afternoon the towering three-decker of Don Navarro was quite disabled, and, according to the *London Magazine*, bore away out of the action, under all the sail that could be set upon her.

Smollett says:

> The fight was maintained with great vivacity by the few who engaged. The *Real* (*El Royal Philip?*) being disabled, and lying like a wreck upon the water, Matthews sent a fireship (the *Anne*, galley) to destroy her; but the expedient did not take effect. The ship ordered to cover this machine did not obey the signal, so that the captain of the fire-ship was exposed to the whole guns of the enemy. Nevertheless, he continued to advance until he found the vessel sinking, and being within a few yards of the *Real*, he set fire to the *fusées*. The ship was immediately in flames, amid which he and his lieutenant, with twelve men, perished.

He was a skilful Scottish seaman, named Mackay.

This was also the miserable fate of a Spanish launch, which had been manned by fifty seamen, to prevent the fire-ship from running on board the *Real*.

Though Admiral Lestock lingered in a manner so unaccountable, and some captains neglected orders. Admiral Matthews, in this most confused action, was nobly supported by the Marlborough, which, after the captain's and first lieutenant's fall, was fought by Lieutenant Neuceller with dauntless intrepidity; by the *Norfolk*, 80 guns. Captain

Action off Toulon

the Honourable John Forbes, son of Earl Granard; and by the *Princess Caroline*, 80 guns. Captain Osborne.

Captain (afterwards Sir Edward) Hawke, in the *Berwick*, 70 guns, observing that *El Poder*, a Spanish sixty-gun ship, commanded by Don Roderigo Euretia, maintained a heavy fire on several of our ships, which were unable to make any effectual return, gallantly bore out of the line and brought her to close action. By his first broadside he dismounted seven of *El Poder's* lower-deck guns, and killed twenty of her men; soon after he shot away all her masts close by the board, on which she struck her colours, and became the prize of the *Berwick*.

The *Norfolk* beat the *Constante*, a Spanish seventy-gun ship, commanded by Don Augustino Eturagio, completely out of the line, but was too much disabled to pursue her. The *London Magazine* says that:

> The *Cambridge*, of Lestock's division, now came up, and began to fire at five ships with which the *Rupert* and *Royal Oak* were engaged. Two ships, it is said, were brought into action by their lieutenants, against the consent of their captains, whom they confined, (an almost incredible story).

And the writer adds that Admiral Matthews, during the hottest part of the battle:

> Stood on the quarterdeck, or arms-chest, making use of his spyglass, as coolly as a *beau* in a playhouse, even while a doubleheaded shot carried away the place he leaned on.

Admiral de Court, who had been engaging Rear-Admiral Rowley, on seeing the disabled condition of Don Navarro's ship, came with his squadron to assist the Spaniards; but Rowley tacked to pursue him, and just about that time—eight in the evening—Admiral Matthews hauled down the signal for battle, and darkness put an end to the conflict. By this time his flag-ship was so shattered that he repaired on board the *Russell*, 80 guns; and *El Poder*, with her prize-crew, being unable to keep up with the fleet, was retaken in the night by the French squadron.

By daylight next morning the enemy's fleet was observed to leeward, going off with all their disabled ships in tow. Admiral Matthews threw out the signal for a general chase, and then to draw into line of battle abreast. Seeing that the British fleet was fast coming up with them, the enemy cast off *El Poder*, set her on fire, and she shortly after blew up. After five in the evening the wind died away; and as there was then no prospect of coming up with the flying enemy, the fleet brought to.

On the morning of the 13th, Admiral Matthews signalled to Admiral Lestock to give chase to twenty-one sail of the enemy that were in sight to the south-westward. The vice-admiral came fast up with them; and had not Matthews signalled to recall the chase, the enemy must either have cast off their crippled ships or risked a general engagement.

The reason assigned by Admiral Matthews for this change of plan was:

That had he continued the pursuit he might have been drawn too far down the Mediterranean, and, in that case, have left the coast of Italy unprotected, and deviated from his instructions.

The fleet kept the sea a few days longer and on its arrival at Port Mahon, Admiral Lestock was put under arrest and sent home to England.

Exclusive of those who perished so miserably amid the flames of the fire-ship, the total loss of the British in this unfortunate and indecisive action was 277. Captain Godfrey, of the Marines, was killed on board of the ship of Captain Cornwall, to whom a handsome monument was erected in Westminster Abbey.

A letter from the *Rupert*, says:

Upon the whole it was a confused running action; but sixteen English ships did engage.

And another from the *Norfolk* says, bitterly:

Thus, did fate, misconduct, and backwardness contribute to the easy escape of the enemy.

The slaughter on board the combined fleets was very great. The Spanish flag-ship had no less than 500 men killed or wounded; the *Neptune*, 200; the *Isabella*, 80 guns, Don Ignacio Dutabil, 300; and all the other ships were in the same proportion. Among the officers killed were Don Nicholas Geraldine; Don Enrique Olivarez, captain of the *Neptune*, and his first lieutenant. Two wounds were received by Admiral Navarro, who immediately on his return to port, complained so bitterly to the Spanish Ministry of the conduct of M. de Court, in not seconding him sufficiently, that the King of France superseded that officer, then in his eightieth year, in command of the fleet.

The Situation of the ENGLISH, FRENCH and SPANISH FLEETS, when they begun the Engagement in th...

The English *Commanded by* Admiral Mathews, Vice Adm.l Lestock *and* Rear Adm.l Rowle...

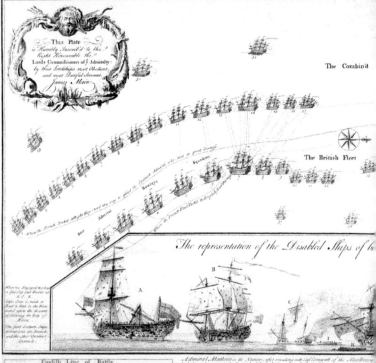

This Plate is Humbly Ascrib'd To The Right Honourable the Lords Commissioners of ye Admiralty by their Lordships most Obedient and most Dutiful Servant James Main

The Combin'd

The British Fleet

The representation of the Disabled Ships of b...

English Line of Battle

	Ships	Commanders		Ships	Commanders	
				Vice Adm.l Lestock		

DITERRANEAN, on the Eleventh of Feb.ʳ 1744, Cape Sicie bearing then N.N.E. & from the Center of the Fleet about Ten Leagues. e French by. Mons.ʳ DeCourt and Gabaret, and the Spanish by Don Juan Joseppo Navarro.

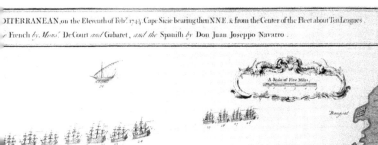

A Scale of Five Miles

Admiral Mathews

Vice Admiral Lestock's Squadron

Cape Sicie

Hieres Bay

Fleets

French & Spanish Line of Battle.

In England, Admiral Lestock became in turn the accuser of Admiral Matthews, his superior.

Smollett, their contemporary, says:

> Long before the engagement, these two officers had expressed the most virulent resentment against each other. Matthews was brave, open, and undisguised; but proud, imperious, and precipitate. Lestock had signalised his courage on many occasions, and perfectly understood the whole discipline of the navy; but he was cool, cunning, and vindictive. He had been treated superciliously by Matthews, and in revenge took advantage of his errors and precipitation. To gratify this passion, he betrayed the interest and the glory of his country; for it is not to be doubted but that he might have come up in time to engage, and in that case the fleets of France and Spain would in all likelihood have been destroyed: but he intrenched himself within the punctilios of discipline, and saw with pleasure his antagonist expose himself to the hazard of death, ruin, and disgrace. Matthews himself, in in the sequel, sacrificed his duty to his resentment, restraining Lestock from pursuing and attacking the combined squadrons on the third day after the engagement, when they appeared disabled and in manifest disorder, and must have fallen an easy prey, had they been vigorously attacked.

Many officers were examined at the bar of the House on the subject; a court-martial sat on board the London, at Chatham, where several officers were cashiered, and Vice-Admiral Lestock was honourably acquitted; while Admiral Matthews was rendered incapable of ever again serving in His Majesty's navy.

Smollett, himself once a naval officer, adds:

> All the world knew that Lestock kept aloof, and that Mathews had rushed into the hottest of the engagement; yet the former triumphed on his trial, and the latter narrowly escaped the sentence of death for cowardice and misconduct. Such decisions are not to be accounted for, except from prejudice and faction.

OFF BELLE-ISLE, 1745

In the summer subsequent to the battle off Toulon, there ensued a very obstinate engagement between a French and British ship, which chanced to encounter each other in the latitude of 47 degrees 17 minutes north.

The former was the *Elizabeth*, a sixty-eight-gun ship, commanded by Captain d'Eau, having in convoy Prince Charles Edward Stuart; the latter was the *Lion*, a sixty-gun ship, commanded by Captain Piercy Brett, the same officer who stormed Paita in Anson's expedition, Nov 12th, 1741. On the 22nd of June, the prince had embarked on board of a vessel named the *Doutelle*, 18 guns, at St. Nazaire, near the mouth of the Loire, to commence the memorable rising which ended at Culloden. He had with him a small retinue, known in Scotland now as "The Seven Men of Moidart," *viz*.: The Marquis of Tullibardine, whose younger brother, by his attainder, now enjoyed the dukedom of Athole; Sir Thomas Sheridan; Sir John Macdonald, an officer in the Spanish service; Kelly, an Episcopal clergyman; Francis Strickland; Angus Macdonald, brother of Kinloch Moidart; and a Mr. Buchanan.

At Belle-Isle they were joined by the *Elizabeth*, on board of which the young prince had placed his warlike stores, 1,500 *fusées*, 1,800 French broadswords, 20 field-pieces, and other munitions; but the two vessels had barely put to sea when the *Lion* hove in sight.

Captain D'Eau immediately went on board the *Doutelle*, and requested Walsh, an Irish refugee, who commanded her, to assist him in attacking the British ship; but Walsh, influenced by natural solicitude for the prince's safety, declined. The *Elizabeth* in consequence commenced the attack alone.

Ranging alongside of each other, these two vessels, which were very nearly equal, though the *Elizabeth* had 700 men on board, began a close, obstinate, and bloody engagement, which lasted fully five hours, by which time both ships were so disabled, and their decks so encumbered by killed and wounded men, by dismounted guns, splinters, and fallen spars, that they each crept away, one towards England, and the other towards France, where the *Elizabeth* reached Brest in a sinking state. The *History of the Present Rebellion*, by J. Marchant, London, 1747, states, that:

> She had lost her captain, 64 men killed, and 146 wounded dangerously; and that there was on board this ship; £400,000 sterling, and arms for several thousand men.

An exaggeration, like everything written by the Whig pamphleteers of the day.

Another large British ship had given chase to the *Doutelle*, which, however, escaped by her superior sailing, and reaching the Hebrides, landed the prince disguised as an Irish priest, on the island of Eriska, where the people received him with open arms as the son of their exiled king.

The disaster of the *Elizabeth* was, however, a great misfortune to him, as he thus lost all his arms and stores, with above 100 able officers who were to serve on the Scottish expedition. Had she reached the Highlands in safety, her guns would speedily have reduced Fort William, which was situated amidst the clans who were loyal to the House of Stuart; and such a conquest would have drawn to the field many who now remained irresolute and aloof.

Expedition to Morbihan, 1746

In this year the wigs of the soldiers were abolished, and all whose hair was long were ordered to "tuck it up under their hats." All officers were to mount guard in queue wigs, or with their hair tied. Brown cloth gaiters were adopted by the privates; and in the colouring for the belts, one pound of yellow ochre was mixed with four pounds of whiting.

In the September of 1746 a secret expedition was fitted out for the coast of France.

The Government had originally intended it for the French possessions in America. A body of troops, consisting of the 1st battalion of the Royal Scots, the 15th, 28th, 30th, 39th, and 42nd Highlanders, 200 of the artillery train, *matrosses* and bombardiers, was placed under the command of General the Honourable James Sinclair, son of the Master of Sinclair, who was attainted after the Battle of Sheriffmuir. He was an officer who had entered the service in the reign of Queen Anne, and had served with distinction in the Scots Foot Guards, under the Duke of Marlborough. In 1734 he was colonel of the 22nd Regiment, in which the father of Laurence Sterne was then serving as a captain; and he was a general in the year of Culloden, but served with the army in the Netherlands.

The forces embarked at Portsmouth for Cape Breton, and were twice driven back by adverse winds; hence ultimately their destination was suddenly changed for a descent on the coast of France. Accordingly, the army was reinforced by the 3rd battalion of the 1st, and 2nd battalion of the Coldstream Guards, under General Fuller, making the entire strength 8,000 men.

The *Westminster journal says:*

Early last Wednesday the two battalions of Guards, consisting of 2,000 men, met on Great Tower Hill, whence they marched to

45

the King's Stairs, on Tower Wharf, where they embarked. His Royal Highness the Duke of Cumberland was present at their going aboard, and spoke to every man as he passed with the greatest freedom.

The naval portion of the armament, under the rival and enemy of Matthews, Admiral Lestock, consisted of the *Princess*, 74, Captain John Cockburn; the *Edinburgh*, 70, Captain Thomas' Cotes, and fourteen other vessels, carrying in all 669 guns, with thirty transports.

On the 19th of September the squadron, with the troops on board, was close in on the coast of France, with special orders to destroy Port l'Orient, where the French East India Company fitted out their ships, and deposited the greater part of their stores and merchandise. Its trade was then very flourishing; its harbour was large and secure, easy of access, and sufficiently deep to float large ships.

That evening our fleet came to anchor in Quimperlé Bay, on the Isolle, twelve miles northward of L'Orient, and immediate preparations were made for landing; and though 2,000 infantry suddenly made their appearance, it was rapidly effected by the Guards and Highlanders, from whom the enemy, being probably militia, fled as the boats approached the shore.

The whole force, with the artillery, now disembarked, and in two columns advanced into the country. Some militia fired upon them from the woods. On entering the village of Pleumeur, they were fired on from the houses, which were soon set in flames. On the 22nd they were before L'Orient, when the governor sent a flag of truce, and proposed surrender on certain conditions. These were rejected on the 24th, by which time one mortar battery and two twelve-gun batteries were erected and armed. On the 28th the French troops made several sallies, Stewart of Garth says:

> In one of which they assumed the garb of Highlanders, and approached close to the batteries. On being discovered, they were saluted with a volley of grape shot, which drove them back with precipitation, followed by those whose garb they had partly assumed.

The cannonading, which had done considerable damage to the town, ceased in the evening; and General Sinclair began to perceive that he had not sufficient force to attempt its reduction by assault. Smollett states that he had neither time, artillery, nor forces sufficient for such an enterprise, though the engineers predicted that they would lay the whole place in ashes in twenty-four hours; but that all his cannon were mere field-pieces:

And he was obliged to wait for two iron guns, which the sailors dragged up from the shipping. Had he given the assault on the first night, when the town was filled with terror and confusion, and destitute of regular troops, in all probability it would have been easily taken by escalade; but the reduction of it was rendered impracticable by delay.

The ramparts had been armed with cannon taken from the ships in the harbour; new works had been raised with great industry, and the garrison had been reinforced by regular troops. Others were mustering elsewhere, so that the slender British force of 8,000 men bade fair to be surrounded and cut off in an enemy's country; and now Admiral Lestock sent repeated messages to the general to the effect "that he could no longer expose the ships on an open coast at such a season of the year."

General Sinclair consequently abandoned the siege, after holding several Councils of War, and spiking his mortars and the two heavy iron ship-guns, he retreated to the seaside in good order, and re-embarked on the 30th; but the troops had undergone considerable hardship during the few days they had been on shore.

It was at first resolved to proceed to Ireland; but during the re-embarkation of the troops, Admiral Lestock, on the 1st of October, received a letter from Captain Leke, of the *Exeter*, 60 guns (who had been sent to sound Quiberon Bay), in which he gave so favourable an account of the anchorage that the admiral, notwithstanding the adverse opinion of a Council of War, resolved to proceed with the fleet and army to that place. The town of Quiberon, in Morbihan, is situated on a long narrow peninsula of the same name, which, with some islands, forms one of the largest bays in Europe.

With the exception of some of the transports and store-ships, which, by stress of weather, had been compelled to bear away for England, on the 2nd the armament came to anchor off Quiberon; when they found that on the preceding day Captain Leke, in the *Exeter*, with the *Pool* and *Tavistock*, sloop, the one of 44 and the other of 10 guns, had engaged in the bay and in sight of the town a French sixty-four-gun ship, *L'Ardente*, and forced her on shore, where she was afterwards burned. She belonged to the Duke d'Anville's squadron, and had just returned from America in great distress.

Another landing was at once resolved upon.

Lieutenant-Colonel John Munro went on shore with 150 of the Black Watch, and took possession of the long isthmus; while General Sinclair, with the rest of the Highlanders and the 1st battalion of the Royal Scots, stormed an eighteen-gun battery, driving out the enemy sword in hand (*Records of the 1st and 42nd Regiments*). They now fortified the isthmus; more troops were landed, and all were cantoned in the villages and farm-houses, from which the scared inhabitants fled.

The next proceeding of the invading force was to assault the fort on the Isle of Houat, which lies six miles north-east of Belle isle-en-Mer, and is three miles long. Several insulated rocks secure it on the south; and on the east, where the fort stood, lie the Bay d'Enfer and Port Navalo. Here the troops landed, and speedily carried the works.

The adjacent isle of Hoedic, which was defended on the south by Fort Pengarde, and on the southwest by a tower, armed with cannon and having a broad ditch, was also reduced. The fortifications were then destroyed, the cannon spiked, the habitations of some 600 fishermen, who occupied both isles, and all the houses on the isthmus, were laid in ruins; after which the troops re-embarked and returned to England, and the fleet came to anchor in the Downs on the 24th of October.

This expedition to the Morbihan, though a somewhat puerile affair, was resented by the entire French nation as one of the greatest insults they had ever sustained; but it demonstrated the possibility of injuring France seriously, by means of an armament vigorously conducted, secretly mustered, and well timed. But nothing could be more absurd and precipitate than the duty on which the Ministry dispatched General Sinclair, to invade France with only 8,000 men, without draught-horses, tents, or a proper train of artillery, from a fleet that lay of, an open beach, exposed to tempestuous weather, in the most uncertain season of the year.

General Sinclair was subsequently employed as Ambassador to the Courts of Vienna and Turin, with Hume, the historian, as his secretary, in which capacity the latter wore a military uniform. On the death of his brother, the general became Lord Sinclair, in the peerage of Scotland, and died at Dysart, in Fifeshire, in 1762.

Cape Finisterre, 1747

The naval transactions of the year 1747 were more favourable to Great Britain, and more brilliant than any others during the war which arose out of the Pragmatic Sanction. Beyond all example was her success, but more advantageous perhaps than glorious, as she had manifestly the superior force in every engagement.

The *London Gazette* of May 16th records that the British and French fleets encountered each other in the beginning of the month off Cape Finisterre, on the Galician coast, and so called from its having been deemed before the discovery of America the western extremity of the globe.

Led by Admiral, afterwards Lord, Anson, and Sir Peter Warren, who had displayed great bravery at Louisbourg, in 1745, the British fleet consisted of seventeen sail, including one fire-ship, the whole mounted with 930 guns. Eleven of Anson's vessels were sail of the line, and his blue flag was hoisted on board the *Prince George*, 90 guns; Sir Peter Warren, as Rear-Admiral of the White, was on board the *Devonshire*, 66 guns.

The French squadron was under the Marquis de la Jonquiere and M. de St. George, and consisted of only thirty-eight sail (of these were afterwards taken six), ranging from seventy-four to forty-four guns, having in all battery to the number of 344 pieces of cannon, and manned by 2,819 seamen and marines.

There was thus a considerable disparity of force; but it should be borne in mind that in Anson's squadron the *Namur, Devonshire, Yarmouth, Defiance, Pembroke, Windsor, Centurion*, and *Bristol*, all, however, line-of-battle ships, alone engaged the enemy.

The French admirals had under their convoy thirty valuable ships, laden with stores and merchandise, bound for America and the East Indies.

Every war had conduced to add to the skill, strength, and efficiency of the British navy. In 1734, by royal proclamation, all British seamen serving foreign powers were recalled for home service; in1740 an Act was passed to prevent the press-gangs from seizing seamen who were above fifty years of age; and in January, 1746, the Parliament voted 40,000 seamen and 12,000 marines for the naval service. In the following year a uniform clothing was first appointed to be worn by admirals, captains, lieutenants, and midshipmen.

The idea of it is said to have been first suggested by George II., when accidentally meeting the Duchess of Bedford (Diana, daughter of Charles Earl of Sunderland, and grand-daughter of John Duke of Marlborough) on horseback, in a riding-habit of blue faced with white. He commanded the adoption of those colours, but the order was never gazetted, though a subsequent one, in 1757, distinctly refers to it; hence we may assume that in the battle off Cape Finisterre, on the 3rd of May, 1747, the uniform which became so identified with the naval glories of later years was for the first time worn under fire.

Frampton's Regiment, now the 30th Foot, served as marines on board the fleet on this occasion, "and received the approbation and thanks of both admirals for their general behaviour."

On the British squadron coming in sight, the war-ships of the Marquis de la Jonquiere immediately shortened sail, triced up their ports, and promptly prepared for action, forming line of battle; while the store-ships, under the protection of six frigates, bore on their course with all the sail they could carry.

The British squadron had also formed line of battle as it drew near the enemy; but Sir Peter Warren, perceiving that the latter were beginning to sheer off as soon as the convoy had attained a considerable distance, advised Admiral Anson to haul in the signal to form line, and hoist that for giving instant chase and engaging, otherwise the whole French fleet might escape them under favour of the night.

The suggestion was at once adopted. All sail was made in pursuit; and about four in the afternoon, when the sun was shining redly on the mountain peak called the Navé of Finisterre, Captain Denis, in the *Centurion*, 50 guns, brought the sternmost ships to action.

Vessel after vessel now shortened sail, and opened fire as those in chase came up; the French fought with equal conduct and valour. The efforts of the *Centurion* were nobly seconded by those of the *Namur*, *Defiance*, and *Windsor*, and they continued pouring round shot and grape into each other, with a blaze of small-arms from the tops, poops, and forecastles, till sunset began to steal over the sea; and, overpowered by the weight and force of the British, the French squadron struck their colours at seven in the evening, and were taken as prizes, but not until they had 700 of their men killed and wounded. Among the former was one captain, and the Marquis de Jonquiere, who received a musket-ball in the shoulder. He was in his seventieth year. At the moment he was wounded he had just run through the body a man who was about to strike the colours.

The British had 250 killed and wounded, according to Schomberg; 500 according to Smollett. Among the latter was Captain Thomas Grenville, of the *Defiance*, a sixty-gun ship. He was only in his twenty-eighth year, and was deemed an officer of great promise. He was the nephew of Viscount Cobham, who had been so recently serving at Culloden:

> Animated with the noblest sentiments of honour and patriotism, he rushed into the midst of the battle, where both his legs were cut off by a cannon-ball. He submitted to his fate with the most heroic resignation, and died universally lamented. (Smollett).

Lord Cobham erected an elegant column to his memory, in the gardens at Stowe. Captain Edward Boscawen, son of Viscount Falmouth, in after years a distinguished officer, was wounded by a musket-shot in the shoulder.

The admiral now detached the Monmouth, Yarmouth, and Nottingham (two sixty-fours and one sixty-gun-ship) in pursuit of the fugitive convoy, with which they came up and took nine sail, three of which were East Indiamen. The rest escaped under cloud of night.

Upwards of £300,000 were found on board the captured ships of war. The treasure was put into twenty wagons, and conveyed under military escort to London. One of the captured ships, *Le Rubis*, 52 guns, was commanded by Macarthy, an Irishman. Anson, in his dispatch to the Duke of Bedford, says:

> I have 4,000 prisoners now on board my squadron. The French compute their loss at £1,500,000 sterling; and I believe it must be considerable, for we found £300,000 in specie, and out of the *Invincible* alone took £80,000. They all behaved well, and lost their ships with honour and reputation.

It is related that M. de St. George, in allusion to the names of two of the vessels taken, his own, *L'Invincible*, 74 guns, and *La Gloire*, 44, Captain de Salesse, said, while presenting his sword to Admiral Anson—

"Monsieur, vous vaincu L'Invincible, et La Gloire vous suit."
("Sir, you defeated *The Invincible*, and *The Glory* is following you.")

Anson brought his prizes safely to Spithead; and when he appeared at Court after this victory, the king was graciously pleased to say to him—

Sir, you have done me a great service. I request you to thank in my name all the officers and private men for their bravery and good conduct, with which I am well pleased.

On the 13th of June Admiral Anson was created a peer of Great Britain, and Sir Peter Warren received the Order of the Bath. He died in 1752, and was buried in Westminster, where a monument was erected to his memory.

The 9th of August subsequent to this victory saw Admiral Sir Edward Hawke, K.B., who had shown such bravery when captain of the *Berwick*, at Toulon, cruising off Cape Finisterre, with a squadron of fourteen sail of the line and several frigates, mounting 854 guns, with 5,890 men.

As Rear-Admiral of the Red, his flag was hoisted on board the *Devonshire*, 66 guns. His special orders were to intercept a fleet of French merchant-ships which were expected to sail from the Basque Roads, under the convoy of a strong squadron of vessels of war, commanded by M. de Letendeur.

He had cruised for some time along the coast of Brittany, and at last the French expedition sailed from the Isle of Aix, at the *embouchure* of the Charente; and on the morning of the 14th of October the two squadrons came in sight of each other, as the dispatches have it:

In the latitude of seventeen degrees forty-nine minutes north, and the longitude of one degree two minutes west of Cape Finisterre.

Admiral Hawke instantly hoisted the signal to "give chase," and fired a gun; but on observing several large ships drawing out from the convoy, he changed his plan, and signalled to form line of battle.

M. de Letendeur, whose squadron carried, 556 guns and 5,416 men, at first mistook the fleet of Hawke for some of his own convoy from whom he had been separated in the night; but on nearer approach he discovered his error, and ordered the *Content* and some of the frigates to make their way seaward with all the merchantmen, while he formed the remainder of his force in order of battle.

Hawke instantly detected the design of the *chef d'escadre*, and, resolving to baffle it, made signal for a general chase. This was at eleven in the forenoon, and in half an hour after the sternmost ships of the French fleet were compelled to shorten sail, and reply to the fire of the *Lion* and *Princess Louisa*, two sixty-gun ships, under Captains Scott and Watson, who sailed right through the squadron, passing along the whole line to the van, exchanging fire with every ship in succession.

These two ships were speedily supported, as the rest soon came up, and a severe general action ensued, and was continued with great obstinacy during the whole afternoon, many vessels having every tier of guns on both sides engaged.

By four o'clock in the afternoon four of the enemy's ships had been so riddled and wrecked by shot that they had struck; and by seven two more had followed their example.

Le Tonnant, the ship of the *chef d'escadre*, and *L'Intrepide*, commanded by the Count de Vandrieul, the one an eighty, and the other a seventy-four-gun ship, to avoid sharing the fate of their companions, made all the sail they could to escape into the darkening night; but were quickly pursued by the *Nottingham, Yarmouth,* and *Eagle*, the crews of which during the chase were refitting their shattered gear, carrying the wounded below, and throwing their dead overboard.

In an hour they were overtaken, and the engagement was renewed, when there was scarcely light by which the men could train their guns; but Captain Philip Saumarez, of the *Nottingham*, a gallant officer, who had served under Lord Anson in the Pacific, being killed by a stray shot, the lieutenant, who succeeded to the command of the ship, hauled his wind, which favoured the escape of the enemy, who gradually disappeared in the offing. It is undeniable that the French maintained this conflict with the greatest bravery. Every ship that was taken was dismasted, save two, and their casualties were considerable. Of all ranks, they had 800 men placed *hors de combat*. Of these, no less than 160 were killed on board *Le Neptune*, including her captain, M. de Fromentiére, and she had 140 wounded. The British loss was 154 killed and 558 wounded.

A plain monument was erected to Captain Saumarez in Westminster Abbey.

SURRENDER OF M. ST GEORGE

When the night had fairly set in. Admiral Hawke brought to, to muster his fleet. Next morning, at a Council of War, it was agreed that the pursuit of those vessels which had escaped should, be abandoned.

The admiral then steered for England, and on the 31st of October anchored with his prizes at Spithead.

Soon after he received the Order of the Bath, as a reward for his services.

CAPE FINISTERRE.

Laffeldt, 1747

So bitterly did the King of France resent both the invasion of Brittany and the merciless treatment of the Scottish Jacobites, who had been decisively defeated at Culloden, that he ordered all natives of Britain resident in France, and unprovided with passports, to be seized; and among others who were sent to the Bastille was James Douglas, Earl of Morton, whom he only released at the request of the Dutch Ambassador.

In the furtherance of his plans for retribution, Louis proposed to make the campaign in the Netherlands at the head of 150,000 men, while 60,000 more were ordered to take the field in Provence. Marshal Count Saxe was appointed to act under His Majesty, with the title of *Marechal-General de Camp*, which empowered him not only to command all Marshals of France, but even the princes of the blood.

France was now in possession of all the Austrian Netherlands, from Dinan to Antwerp; and it was evident that she intended to penetrate into the United Provinces, which made the Confederates anxious to open the campaign before the French; so, the Duke of Cumberland landed at The Hague on the 30th of November, and took the field in February, 1747, with the British, Hanoverians, and Hessians, who were drawn out of their quarters and assembled in Dutch Brabant.

The duke fixed his headquarters at the town of Tilberg, which was then a small village on the way between Breda and Bois le Duc. The Dutch were at the former-named city, under the Prince of Waldeck; while the Austrians and Bavarians were at Venloo, under Marshal Bathyani. On paper the Confederate Army was estimated at 126,000 men, but fell short of that strength.

Marshal Saxe had collected a great train of artillery to aid the invasion of Dutch Brabant, and to carry the banners of France into the very heart of the United Provinces. He then assembled his grand army between Antwerp and Mechlin, 140,000 strong. There was also a separate force under the Count of Clermont, making a total of 158,000 men.

All being in readiness to enter Holland, Saxe instructed Count Lowendahl and the Marquis de Contades to advance from Ghent on the 16th of April, at the head of 27,000 men, while he covered Antwerp, and attended to the motions of the Confederates.

Meanwhile the Duke of Cumberland, with the force of the latter, had taken post between the two Nethes, to cover Bergen-op-Zoom, which had been besieged, and Maestricht; and Saxe resolved to blockade the latter on the arrival of the King of France at Brussels, in May. For this purpose, he advanced to Louvain; but the Confederates, perceiving his design, took post on the ground stated.

The 20th of June found them in order of battle, with their right at the town of Bilsen, and their left extending to Wirle, having in front of their left wing the village of Laffeldt, in which were posted three battalions of British infantry—the 13th, or Pulteney's, the Old Edinburgh Regiment (now the 25th), and the 37th, or Dejean's, with the Hanoverian corps of Freudman. This was the most important post of the whole position, and it was well fortified with cannon.

The confederate generals diligently reconnoitred the French, who, about nine o'clock on the morning of the 21st, were discovered by Sir John Ligonier advancing towards Laffeldt, and he instantly sent Colonel Forbes to acquaint the Duke of Cumberland that such was the case.

By ten o'clock their artillery opened a tremendous fire; and their infantry, among whom were the Irish Brigade and one or two regiments of Scottish exiles—the 108th Royal Ecossais and the 113th Regiment d'Ogilvie, Ecossais—burning to avenge Culloden, appeared coming down into the plain, in a vast, dark, and dense column, consisting of ten battalions in front and seven deep. The blaze of the morning sun upon the arms of these masses produced a magnificent effect, as they came, like a living tide, rolling onward against the small force which occupied Laffeldt, which was but a little enclosed hamlet, consisting of only five houses; and around that small spot the whole fury of the battle, which lasted five hours, was spent.

As the French advanced, the field batteries of the British opened upon them with terrible effect. The *matrosses* and bombardiers plied well their deadly work among the dense battalions of infantry, and also upon the glittering squadrons of cavalry which supported them

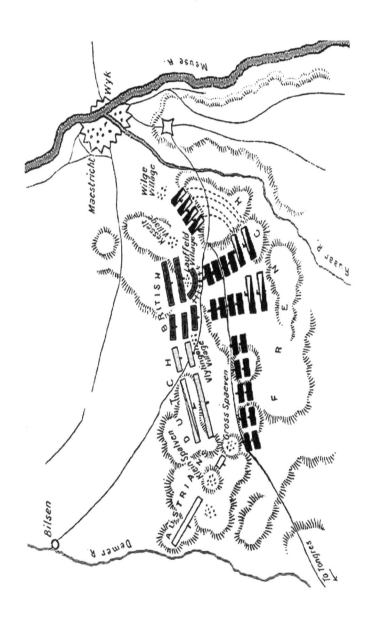

Meuse R.

Wyk

Maestricht

Wilre Village

Kesselt Village

Fuffield

BRITISH

DUTCH

Oldfield Village

Vlytingen Village

Klein-Spaeven

AUSTRIANS

FRENCH

Gross Spaeven

Bilsen

Demer R.

To Tongres

Jaaer R.

on each flank.

The second shot fired from the French batteries at ten o'clock cut in two Baron Ziggesaer, the Duke of Cumberland's German *aide-de-camp*; and a few minutes later saw the French literally swarming around the hamlet, in their efforts to storm it, but to the rest of the line all trace of the spot became hidden in the white smoke of battle.

The attack of the French was made with all their usual *élan*, and was met with equal bravery. Smollett states that:

> They suffered terribly in their approach from the cannon of the Confederates, which was served with surprising dexterity and success; and they met with such a warm reception from the British musketry as they could not withstand: but when they were broken and dispirited, fresh brigades succeeded with astonishing perseverance.

According to the *Memoirs of Cumberland*, the first French brigades which attacked the post were "dispersed with prodigious loss, as were their second, third, and fourth divisions."

Overpowered at last by the succession of fresh assailing masses, the British regiments in the hamlet were compelled to retire, leaving heaps of dead behind them; but on being reinforced by General Edward Wolfe's Regiment, the 8th, or King's, the 3rd Buffs, and the 48th, or Conway's, with the Hanoverians of Haus, they returned to the attack, and, after fresh carnage, the petty hamlet of five houses was retaken.

The French brigades, consisting of the Navarre Regiment (3rd of the line), of four battalions; the 26th, or Royal des Vaisseaux, two battalions; and the 66th, or La Marque, also of two battalions, "were entirely ruined, and the Irish Brigade suffered extremely."

Here one of the standards belonging to the latter was taken by Ensign Thomas Davenant, of the 8th, or King's, according to the *Dublin Journal*. Fresh troops were hurled in masses against Laffeldt. Again, the British were driven out, but again they retook it; so that the carnage around the place was frightful beyond all description.

In the earlier part of the assault, the Duke of Cumberland sent one of his *aides-de-camp* to inform Marshal Bathyani that:

> The left was attacked; that Marshal Saxe appeared determined to make his whole effort upon Laffeldt; and therefore His Royal Highness desired to be supported speedily and effectually.

Bathyani replied that:

He was doing his utmost for that purpose, having ordered away
five battalions belonging to the *corps de reserve*, as also part of the
squadrons that were under Count Daun, to reinforce the left.

Part of the column commanded by the count—afterwards the famous Marshal Daun, who defeated the Prussians under Marshal James
Keith at Hochkirken—arrived in time enough to enter the hamlet
and be of great service; but the five battalions came up too late, as they
were posted somewhat far to the right. The British and Hanoverians
behaved so well in line that about noon, when Laffeldt was again
cleared, Cumberland ordered an advance of the whole left wing upon
the enemy, whose infantry began to recoil so fast that Marshal Saxe
was compelled to resort to the unusual expedient of placing cavalry
in their rear and on their flanks, to drive them on with their swords.

Under the Prince of Waldeck, the centre now began to advance;
but the Austrians were somewhat slow in their motions. The French
reserves then came up, and the conflict became more close and deadly,
while the roar of musketry deepened on the plain. Five battalions
of the confederate reserve were completely overthrown by the gross
misconduct of some squadrons of Dutch cavalry which were posted
in the centre. These troopers suddenly gave way, went threes about,
and at full gallop bore down upon these five battalions, and trampled
them under foot.

One of these regiments proved to be the 23rd Welsh Fusiliers, who
resented this unforeseen catastrophe by pouring upon the Dutch two
rattling volleys that were intended for the French, whose cavalry now
penetrated to Cumberland's centre, and defeat became imminent.
Cumberland rode to the head of the Dutch cavalry, and, together
with their leader, Major-General Cannenberg, strove to rally them,
but in vain. So the infantry began to give way on all hands; and "the
hero of Culloden," defeated here, as he had been before at Fontenoy,
thought only of making good his retreat to Maestricht, about three in
the afternoon.

Even this final movement he would have been unable to accomplish, but for a charge made by the British cavalry, led by the gallant
Sir John Ligonier. The *Records of the 4th Hussars* says:

The first line of opponents was instantly broken, the brave
troopers galloped forward, and a second line was speedily overthrown. British horsemen mixing fiercely with the French cav-

alry, used their broadswords with terrible execution; but pursuing too far, they received the fire of a battalion of French infantry posted in some low ground behind a hedge. The undaunted dragoons instantly attacked and routed the infantry; but being charged by a new line of combatants, they were forced to retreat, and their commander. Sir John Ligonier, was taken prisoner. (He was captured by a carbineer).

They brought off with them several French cavalry standards; but the enemy took many men and horses. In an account of the Battle of Val, as it is sometimes named, written by an officer of the artillery, it is stated that:

The Scots Greys, Sir Robert Rich's, Rothes', and the Duke's Dragoons, with a large body of hussars, gave the French cavalry a prodigious stroke, and took several standards; but the enemy, by superior numbers, obliged them to retreat. This day's action is looked upon as most glorious on the part of the Allies who were engaged." In another account it is related that "our cavalry, led by Sir John Ligonier, charged the French cavalry with such success that they overthrew all before them.

Here, as at Minden, Waterloo, Balaclava, and many other glorious battles, the Scots Greys and the Inniskilling Dragoons rode side by side. Sir John Ligonier had his horse killed under him. In the Memoirs of Cumberland, it is stated that the French had 1,200 cavalry and 9,000 infantry killed or wounded, while the loss of the Confederates did not exceed 6,000 men. The principal officers killed in the British Army were Lieutenant-Colonels Williams and Ross; among those wounded were John, third Earl of Glasgow, and Major-General Bland. With Sir John Ligonier were taken Colonel Conway and Lord Robert Sutton, colonel of Cumberland's Dragoons, a corps no longer in existence, but which was formed from the Duke of Kingston's Horse, raised to act against Charles Edward.

In this action the Welsh Fusiliers had no less than one officer and 187 men missing.

In his retreat and in the action, Cumberland lost sixteen pieces of cannon. Smollett states that the Confederates suffered from the pride and ignorance of their generals. On the eve of the battle, when the column of Count Clermont appeared on the ridge of Herdereen, Marshal Bathyani asked Cumberland's permission to attack it before it could be reinforced. No regard was paid by the unwieldy duke to the proposal of this veteran officer; but he haughtily asked him in turn where he would be when wanted.

"I shall always be found at the head of my troops," replied the marshal, sternly, as he retired with disgust.

In an account of the Battle of Laffeldt, printed at Liege, in 1747, it is said that "the King of France's brigade marched up under the command of Marshal Saxe," and carried the village, "after the repulse of forty battalions who had successively attempted it."

A writer in the *Gentleman's Magazine* for the same year says that:

> The brigade consisted of Scots and Irish in the French service, who fought like devils; that they neither gave nor took quarter; that observing the Duke of Cumberland to be extremely active in defence of this post, they were employed on this attack at their own request; that they in a manner cut down all before them, with a full resolution, if possible, to reach His Royal Highness, which they would certainly have done had not Sir John Ligonier come up with the horse, and saved the duke at the loss of his own liberty.

A false rumour was spread in London, to the effect that the Prince Charles Edward served with these Scots and Irish exiles as a volunteer.

There were fourteen standards taken in all from the enemy, and brought to London by the Earl of Ancrum. Four of these belonged to the regiment of Belfond, and four to that of Monaco; one belonged to the Royal Cravates, another to De Beaufremont's Dragoons. There were two colour-staffs taken from Diesbatch's Swiss, and the colours without the staff of the Royal des Vaisseaux and the Irish Brigade.

Lord Ancrum was the eldest son of the Marquis of Lothian, and was many years M.P, for Richmond.

The Storming of Bergen-Op-Zoom, 1747

The reduction of this great fortress, the siege of which cost France nearly 20,000 of her finest troops, was the next great feature of the war.

The Confederates having passed the Maese, and encamped in the Duchy of Limburg, so as to cover Maestricht, the King of France remained with his army in the vicinity of Tongres; while Marshal Saxe, after amusing and perplexing the Duke of Cumberland by a series of marches and counter-marches, the object of which he could not define, suddenly detached Count Lowendahl with 36,000 men to besiege Bergen-op-Zoom.

The strongest fortress in Dutch Brabant, it had never yet been taken, and enjoyed the then common reputation of being invincible; hence on this siege the eyes of all Europe were turned.

Situated on an eminence in the middle of a morass, half a league from the eastern branch of the Scheldt, it has a communication with that river by means of a navigable canal, and is of vast strength, both by nature and art. By its advantageous situation, it not only secures an avenue between Holland and Zealand, but opened for the Dutch a way into Brabant whenever they pleased. This fortress was the favourite work of the great Cohorn. The town had a population of about 5,000. The garrison consisted of six strong battalions, supported by eighteen more in the lines, with 250 pieces of cannon. General Coustrom, Governor of Brabant, assumed the command. He was a brave and experienced officer, but so deaf that he could not hear the sound of his own guns.

To oppose the operations of Count Lowendahl, all the disposable troops in Brabant were collected, including Lord Loudon's new regiment of Highlanders, who had been last under fire at Prestonpans and Culloden. In the former battle every man and officer of them was taken prisoner.

Lowendahl carried on his approaches with great vigour. On the 14th of July his batteries opened, and they were replied to with great vivacity by the besieged, among whom were two battalions of the Scots brigade in the Dutch service (afterwards 94th Foot); and in the *Records of the Black Watch*, it is stated that "when the French attacked Bergen-op-Zoom, Colonel Lord John Murray, Captain Fraser, of Culduthel, Captain Campbell, of Craignish, and several other officers, obtained permission to serve in the defence of that fortress," as their regiment was in South Beveland.

From the 15th of July till the 17th of September, the siege was pushed on without intermission, and the loss of, life among the French in the trenches was terrible. During all that time fifty pieces of heavy cannon and twenty-four great mortars had been raining an incessant shower of iron upon the town. The bullets were frequently red-hot, hence the principal church and a great part of the streets were frequently in flames. The French made their advances with the greatest bravery; but were met by frequent sallies, which repulsed them and ruined their works.

In one of these, made on the 25th of July, it is recorded in the *Hague Gazette*, that:

> The Highlanders of Lord Loudon, who were posted in Fort Rours, which covers the lines of Bergen-op-Zoom, made a sally sword in hand, in which they were so successful as to destroy the enemy's grand battery, and to kill so many men that Count Lowendahl beat a parley in order to bury the dead. To this it was replied that had he attacked the place agreeably to the rules of war, his demand would certainly have been granted; but as he had begun the siege like an incendiary, by setting fire to the town with red-hot balls, a resolution had been formed neither to ask nor grant any suspension of arms. (So, the French dead had to lie where they had fallen).

The siege, says Smollett, was an unintermitting scene of horror and destruction; desperate sallies were made; mines were sprung with the most dreadful effect; the town was laid in ashes; the trenches were filled with carnage and pools and puddles of blood; nothing was seen but fire and smoke; nothing heard but one continued roar of bombs

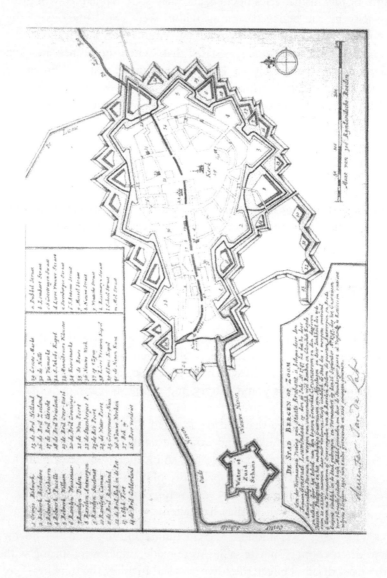

and cannon. But the damage fell chiefly on the besiegers, who were slain in vast numbers; while the garrison suffered very little in comparison.

By the 7th of September the French had, by incredible labour and loss, obtained entire possession of the lunette of Zealand, and made a lodgement in the angle of that of Utrecht. They had also ruined most of the counterscarp in front of the attack, and blown up a portion of the main gallery. This so alarmed the garrison, that General Swartzenburg, who had a considerable corps under his command at Oudenbosch, entered the town to concert measures with the governor for its defence. There were more mines sprung and more lives lost by them on this occasion than in any similar operations on record. Those of the French were thrice countermined by the garrison, and on one occasion 700 men were blown into the air in an instant!

On the morning after this terrible event, the French unmasked four batteries in front of the attack—"The first says *The Scots Magazine* for 1747, on the covered-way near the left of the Utrecht Bastion, of four guns, which fired on the right flank of the bastion of William, and two on the right face of the Pucelle; the second on the right face of the ravelin of Dedem, which played on the *orillon* of the Cohorn Bastion," where they dismounted several guns and killed many men. All that day Count Lowendahl was in the trenches, and in his presence some soldiers of the Regiment de Normandie (5th of the Line) deserted to the town.

Next day the French erected three new batteries—two on the covered way, and one on the ruins of the Zealand Bastion—but the garrison also erected a battery upon that of Holland; and so terrible was the adverse cannonade, that for hours both town and trenches were completely hidden in smoke. By the 14th several breaches were made in the works, and particularly one of great width in the ravelin of Dedem. That night the garrison made a sortie from this rough aperture, intending to spike the guns which had formed it, but without success; and on the night of the 16th, Count Lowendahl resolved to attempt the capture of the fortress by storm.

The *London Gazette* says:

The enemy began their attack on the 16th instant, about four in the morning, by springing a mine before the ravelin of Dedem, throwing an immense quantity of bombs, and firing at once from all their batteries. In the meantime, fifty companies

Bergen-op-Zoom

of grenadiers, supported by sixteen battalions, threw themselves into the fosse, and having cut off the communication between the outworks and the town, some attacked the ravelin of Dedem by the breach, while others got into it from behind, and soon made themselves masters of it.

Forcing their way at the bayonet's point through the sally-ports, some scaled the walls of the town by ladders, and mounting narrow breaches which the cannonade had formed in the bastions of Pucelle and Cohorn, they soon possessed themselves of these works, and got into position along the ramparts almost before the whole garrison could be got under arms; and many others, in the grey dawn, were seen rushing to the muster-places and getting the ranks formed while literally in their shirts.

The "account published by authority, at The Hague," three days after, states that as the troops of the garrison were got together by degrees, they were posted at the avenues of the great square towards the Steenbergen Strasse, where their fire was so sharp that they kept the enemy in check for fully an hour; but that the French ultimately forced their way into the houses of the square in which the colours of the Scots Brigade were flying, and passing quickly from house to house, as the reliefs were shot under them; thus every foot of the square and of the narrow street that led to the Steenbergen Gate was most fiercely contested. Here the Prince of Hesse-Philipsthal was severely wounded; and his lieutenant-general, Solly, of the Irish Brigade, and Major-General Thierry gave proofs of the highest valour.

The noble stand made in the great square by the two battalions of the Scots Brigade enabled the deaf old governor and his garrison to recover from their first surprise, otherwise the whole must have been killed or taken prisoners.

The Hague *Gazette* says:

The Scotch assembled in the market-place, and attacked the French with such vigour that they drove them from street to street, till fresh reinforcements pouring in compelled them to retreat in turn, disputing every inch as they retired, and fighting till two-thirds of their number fell on the spot killed or severely wounded, when the remainder brought off the old governor, and joined the troops in the lines.

Another Dutch account, quoted by General Stewart, of Garth, states that:

Two battalions of the Scotch Brigade have, as usual, done honour to their country, which is all we have to comfort us for the loss of such brave men, who, from 1,450, are now reduced to only 330, and who have valiantly brought their colours with them, the grenadiers recovering them twice from the midst of the French at the point of the bayonet. The Swiss have also suffered, while others took a more speedy way to escape.

The same account, which is also quoted in *Coxe's History of the House of Austria*, adds that these 330 surviving Scotsmen fought a passage out, and that thirty-seven of their officers fell killed or wounded. Lieutenants Francis and Allan Maclean, sons of Maclean of Torloisk, were taken, prisoners and brought before Count Lowendahl, who thus addressed them:—

Gentlemen, consider yourselves on parole. If all had conducted, themselves as you and your brave corps have done, I should not now be the master of Bergen-op-Zoom.

General Stewart tells us that Allan Maclean afterwards quitted the Dutch service for the British, in which he raised the 114th Highlanders in 1759, and the 84th Highlanders during the American War, during which he was the principal cause of the defeat of the colonists at the attack on Quebec.

The fall of this great fortress excited vehement suspicions of treachery on the part of some portion of the garrison; for after holding out with such firmness against the most vigorous assaults, it yielded at last with but little resistance save that made by the Scots Brigade. During the siege every soldier who carried away a gabion from the enemy's works was paid a crown.

Some of the Scotch soldiers gained ten crowns a day by this service. Those who performed more daring exploits, such as taking the burning fuse out of the bombs when they fell within the garrison, were rewarded with ten or twelve *ducats*.

By one account the French loss is stated to have been 20,000 men; by another more than 22,000, and that of the garrison to have been 4,000.

Mrs. Grant, in her *Superstitions of the Highlanders*, relates an anecdote connected with Bergen-op-Zoom, illustrative of the love of a foster-brother: for when a son was born to a Highland chief, there was always a contention among the tenants for the nursing of the child:

The happy man who succeeded in his suit being ever after called the foster-father, and his children the foster-brothers and sisters of the young laird.

In one of the midnight sorties, Captain Fraser, of Culduthel, who accompanied it, desired his servant, a 42nd man, to remain in the garrison. The atmosphere was pitchy dark, and as the party stumbled forward, Fraser felt his feet impeded. He put down his hand and found someone grovelling near him in a tartan plaid. He put his dirk to the throat of the crouching man, in whom he then recognised his foster-brother.

"What brought you here?" he asked.

"Love of you and care of you," was the reply.

"But why encumber yourself with a plaid?" asked the officer.

"Alas!" said the soldier, in Gaelic, "how could I ever see my master had you been killed or wounded, and I not been there to carry you to the surgeon, or give you Christian burial; and how could I have done either without my plaid?"

So, with these intents the faithful fellow had crawled out of the fortress, unseen by the sentinels, on his hands and bare knees. Mrs. Grant adds:

This faithful adherent had soon occasion to assist at the obsequies of his foster-brother, who was killed a few days' afterwards, by an accidental shot, as he was looking over the ramparts and viewing the operations of the enemy.

In the *Edinburgh Herald* for 1800 is recorded the death, at Dunse, of one of the veterans of Bergen-op-Zoom, John Nesbitt, aged 107, who had been wounded there, and discharged without a pension.

Tortuga, 1748

In the summer of the preceding year, it was ordered that all ships of war from fifty to those of a hundred guns were to carry as many marines as they mounted guns; ships of fifty guns and under were to have ten marines more than the number of their guns; and all sloops of war were to have twenty marines on board.

In the autumn of 1748, Rear-Admiral Sir Charles Knowles, an officer who had greatly distinguished himself when a captain, particularly in the attacks made on the Spanish settlements in the West Indies, was cruising off the Tortuga Bank in the hope of intercepting the Spanish Plate fleet—then the great object of ambition to our seamen—which was expected at the Havanah from La Vera Cruz.

His flag was on board the *Cornwall*, an eighty-gun ship. His squadron consisted of seven sail of the line, carrying 246 guns and 2,900 men.

On the 30th of September, he was joined by the *Lennox*, under Captain William Holmes (who was afterwards killed at the siege of Pondicherry), who reported that the day before, while having under his convoy the homeward-bound trade fleet from Jamaica, he fell in with and was chased by a Spanish squadron of seven ships of war. He added that he ordered the convoy to "shift for themselves," and proceeded to give the admiral earliest notice of the enemy being at sea, doubtless to protect the eagerly looked-for Plate fleet from La Vera Cruz.

This squadron of Spanish ships was commanded by Rear-Admiral Spinola, and carried 420 guns, with 4,150 men; consequently, his numerical force was superior to that of Admiral Knowles, who on the 1st of October discovered the enemy ranged in order of battle.

They lay near Tortuga, an island so called by the buccaneers from its fancied resemblance to a tortoise—a rocky and rugged place, covered with lofty trees, some ten miles north from the coast of Dominica.

Rear-Admiral Knowles instantly formed his line and bore down upon the enemy; and at half-past two in the afternoon the battle began. Captain Innes, in the *Warwick*, 60 guns, and Captain Edward Clarke, in the *Canterbury*, also of 60 guns, being at some distance astern, or unable to make up their leeway in time, gave the Spaniards at first the advantage.

Thus, in half-an-hour the British flag-ship had her maintopmast and foretopsail-yard shot away, and was otherwise so considerably damaged that she was obliged to quit her place in the line, with her decks encumbered by dead and dying men, and all slippery with blood.

Her place was soon supplied by other ships, whose commanders closed in, maintaining a rapid and heavy cannonade, which very soon drove the *Conquistadore*, 64 guns, commanded by Don de St. Justo, so fairly out of the line that she fell away to leeward of the *Cornwall*.

Rear-Admiral Knowles, in the latter, had by this time repaired the damage she had sustained, and shipped spare spars aloft. Then bearing down upon the *Conquistadore*, he attacked her with renewed fury. Her crew fought bravely and made a most obstinate resistance, but on the fall of St. Justo her flag was struck, and she surrendered, but not until she was dreadfully shattered by round and cross-bar shot.

Meanwhile, Captain Holmes, in the *Lennox*, had been gallantly fighting almost yard-arm and yardarm with the *Invincible*, 74, which carried the flag of Admiral Spinola, till the arrival of the *Warwick* and *Canterbury* made the action more general and furious; and the roar of so many hundred pieces of cannon, borne by the breeze and water, could be distinctly heard amid the forests and wild volcanic mountains of Dominica.

At eight in the evening the Spanish admiral slackened his fire, and ultimately "hoisting everything that would draw," bore away for Havanah, which was fully 700 miles distant from Tortuga. Along the coast of Cuba, the fugitive Spaniards were pursued by Admiral Knowles and his squadron, which fired on them whenever they came within range. However, they all got safe into Havanah, save the *Africa*, 74 guns, the ship of the vice-admiral, who had been killed, and lay dead in his cabin.

Her masts had been shot away, so her crew let her anchors go within a few leagues of the Moro Castle, where she was soon discovered by the inexorable British squadron. To prevent her being taken, the crew set her in flames, and fled in their boats; and just as they were half way between her and the shore, her shattered hull blew up with a hideous crash.

In this protracted action the Spaniards had one admiral, 3 captains, 14 other officers, and 72 men killed, and 197 of all ranks wounded. The British squadron had 180 killed and wounded.

Admiral Knowles still persevered in cruising off the mouth of the Havanah, in hope of intercepting the expected Plate fleet, till there was brought into his squadron a Spanish advice-boat, whose commander informed him that the preliminary articles for a general treaty of peace had been signed in Europe.

At home all parties had grown weary of the useless and protracted war; and the preliminaries for a complete pacification had by this time been fully made at Aix-la-Chapelle, and by the 7th of October hostilities ceased everywhere.

These tidings are said to have caused the deepest dejection on board of Knowles' squadron, whose prospect of the riches they would have shared had the Plate fleet come a day or two sooner now vanished, and he bore up for Jamaica. Some dissensions that had prevailed among the officers of the fleet were now much increased. The admiral taxed some of his captains with misconduct, and a court-martial was the result of their mutual accusations. Those who adhered to their commander, and others whom he impeached, showed against each other the most rancorous resentment.

Smollett states that the admiral himself did not escape without censure. Two of his captains were reprimanded; but Captain Holmes, who had displayed' uncommon courage, was honourably acquitted. The admiral fought a bloodless duel with Captain Paulett, of the *Tilbury*; but Captains Innes and Clarke met by appointment in Hyde Park, with a case of pistols each. The former was mortally wounded, and died next morning; the latter was tried and condemned for murder, but received His Majesty's pardon,

On the peace a general reduction of the armaments took place; thus in 1748 all cavalry regiments were disbanded to the present 14th Hussars, and all regiments of infantry to the present 49th Foot.

Beausejour and Ohio, 1755

The first year after the peace saw some experiments made in gunnery practice, which may provoke a smile when contrasted with those now made daily at Woolwich and Shoeburyness. The firing began at Windsor, in 1749, in presence of the Dukes of Cumberland, Montague, and Richmond, the Earl of Sandwich, "and other persons of quality." The pieces used were two 12-pounders, one British the other Saxon. These were discharged in succession, at 700 yards' distance, against a target twelve inches square; and after repeated trials it was found that the ball from the Saxon gun not only came nearer to the mark, but was driven deeper into the butt. In the experiment of quick firing, the British gun was twelve minutes in firing eighty-six rounds; the Saxon was fired forty-six times in five minutes. The strength of both was then tested by overcharges, on which the Saxon gun burst, while the British still remained serviceable.

The pay of a foot soldier was eightpence per day; from this, two pence was stopped for clothing. He received a new suit of uniform yearly, all save a waistcoat, which was thriftily made from the red coat of the preceding year. The cavalry were clothed anew every two years. From the year 1746 the rank of brigadier had been abolished in the promotion of general officers; and in 1751 a warrant was first issued regulating the colours and clothing of regiments, which then for the first time, received numerical titles, though such were not borne upon their appointments till some years later.

The rank of several regiments had been first established by a board of general officers assembled in the Netherlands, by order of William III., in 1694. Another was assembled by Queen Anne, in 1713, to decide on the seniority of regiments raised after 1694; and a third by George I., in 1715. All these boards decided that English regiments raised in England should rank from the date of their formation; and that English, Scots, and Irish regiments raised for the service of foreign powers should date from their being first placed upon the British establishment. Hence the 1st Royal Scots, having come from France to serve King Charles II. for eight years, took rank from 1661, and having been raised during the reign of James VI., in Scotland, and representing the Scottish Archer Guard of France, it was to take the right of the whole, and does so still.

Eight years of peace only followed the Treaty of Aix-la-Chapelle, till the undetermined limits of the British and French territories in North America occasioned a war between the two kingdoms.

Our settlers, particularly in the province of Nova Scotia, having been repeatedly disturbed by the encroachments and insults of the French, it became necessary at last for the British Government to send out a force sufficient to keep them in check and protect our frontier. For this purpose, in the beginning of 1755, the Assembly of Massachusetts Bay, in New England, passed an Act prohibiting all intercourse with the French at Louisbourg; and early in spring they raised a body of troops, which was transported to Nova Scotia, to assist Lieutenant-Governor Lawrence in driving the encroachers back.

In May the governor sent a body of troops, under the command of Lieutenant-Colonel the Honourable Robert Monkton (who was colonel of the 17th Regiment in 1759), upon this service; while three frigates and a sloop of war were dispatched up the Bay of Fundy, which opens between the islands of Penobscot Bay and Cape Sable, to give assistance by sea. This part of the expedition was under the command of Captain John Rous, who in 1745 had been promoted to the rank of post-captain in the Royal Navy, for his gallantry in American waters, while commanding a humble privateer.

Foreseeing what was to come, the enemy were prepared to offer a stout resistance, but eventually without effect.

Upon his arrival at the River Massaguash, Colonel Monkton found its passage about to be disputed by a large number of the regular troops of France, rebel neutrals, or Acadians, and by savage Indians, 450 of whom occupied a loopholed block-house, with cannon mounted on their side of the stream. The rest were posted within a strong palisade, thrown up by way of breastwork to the blockhouse.

With hatchet and hammer, one body of the British Provincials assailed this stronghold, while others opened a steady fire across the stream. The breastwork was soon beaten down and stormed, the bayonet and clubbed firelock being freely used. On seeing this the native

VIEW of BEAUSEJOUR from y S.E.

REFERENCES.

1 Officers quarters
2 Soldiers barracks
3 Gate way
4 Bastion in which y Sardine
5 Don. d. y near y Orchard

6 The Hospital
7 The Wet Ditch
8 Road to Tatamar
9 The River Beaugendie

indians in the block-house deserted it instantly, the Europeans fell back, and the passage of the river was left free.

Colonel Monkton now advanced against the French fort of Beausejour, which he invested, as well at least as the small number of his troops would permit; and on the 12th of June, after a four days' bombardment with mortars, he compelled the garrison to surrender, though he had not yet placed a single cannon on his batteries, and the French had no less than twenty-six on the ramparts and a vast quantity of ammunition in store.

The garrison he sent to Louisbourg, on their parole of honour that they were not to serve in arms for six months; and the Acadians who had joined them he pardoned, as they pleaded that they had been forced into the service of King Louis. After putting a garrison into the fort, and, under a salute of guns, changing its name to Fort Cumberland, in honour of the "hero of Culloden;" Monkton next attacked another French fortress upon the Gaspareau, a small river of New Brunswick, which empties itself into the Bay of Verte.

This fort he speedily captured by storm, and found in it a vast quantity of provisions and warlike stores of all kinds, as it had been the chief magazine for supplying the French Indians and Acadians with arms, ammunition, and other necessaries. He disarmed the latter to the number of 15,000 men. In the meantime, Captain Rous had sailed with his little squadron to the mouth of the great river St. John, in New Brunswick, to attack a new fort which the encroaching French had built there. But the garrison saved him all trouble, for as soon as his ships came in sight and the Union Jack was seen, they overloaded all their cannon and burst them, blew up the magazine, and destroyed, so far as they had time, all the works they had been executing.

In all this expedition, which completely secured the tranquillity of Nova Scotia, so active and careful was Colonel Monkton, that he had only twenty men killed and the same number wounded.

While the New Englanders were thus employed in reducing the French in Nova Scotia, preparations were made in Virginia for attacking them upon the Ohio. The colonies on the coast had extended themselves on every side, while the Indian trade had been alluring many wandering dealers into the inland country, where they found well-watered plains and green savannahs, luxuriant woods, a delightful climate, and a fruitful soil

These advantages appearing to compensate for the distance from the sea, a company of merchants and planters obtained a charter for a tract of land beyond the Alleghany Mountains, and near the stately Ohio commenced the establishment of a colony. To this part of America, the French laid instant claim, and driving away the new settlers, built a strong fort, called Duquesne, to command the entrance into the country on the Ohio and Mississippi; and from its situation it bade fair to become the most important military work in North America, as it stood 250 miles west by north of Philadelphia.

A post called Fort Cumberland was now also built at Wills's Creek; and on the 14th of January, Major-General Edward Braddock sailed from Cork, in Ireland, with the regiments of Sir Peter Halkett, Bart., and Thomas Dunbar, the 44th and 48th respectively, and with these battalions he landed safely in Virginia before the end of February.

Braddock was an officer of the Coldstream Guards, a battalion of which he had command in the Netherlands and at the siege of Bergen-op-Zoom.

Lord Mahon, in his *History of England from the Peace of Utrecht*, says thus of this officer:—

> Braddock was a man cast in the same mould as General Hawley, of a brave but brutal temper, and, like Hawley also, a personal favourite of the Duke of Cumberland. His rigorous ideas of discipline made him hateful to his soldiers; and from the same cause he held in great contempt the American militia, seeing that they could not go through their exercises with the same dexterity which he had so often admired and enforced in Hyde Park. As to the Indians, the allies of France, he treated with disdain all the warnings he received against an ambush or surprise from them; and the Indians of his own party who would have been his surest guards against this particular peril, were so disgusted by the haughtiness of his demeanour, that most of them forsook their banners.

He was destitute of the caution, stratagem, and secrecy necessary in a leader of troops.

His second in command, Sir Peter Halkett, of Pitfirrane, in Fifeshire, was a brave and honourable officer. At the late Battle of Prestonpans, he with all the officers of his regiment (the 44th) had been taken prisoners by the prince, but the whole were released on parole. He was one who, with five others, *viz.*, the Honourable Mr. Ross, Captain Lucy Scott, and Lieutenants Farquharson and Gumming, refused to rejoin their regiments at the Duke of Cumberland's command and

PLAN of the CITY and FORTRESS of LOUISBOURG, with the Attacks.

1. Barrack Sheds for 4 Companys
2. The First Wing of A New Barrack
3. Infirmary for the New Barrack
4. Powder Magazine
5. Hospital Barracks
6. Victualling Store-house
7. New House for Stock at the Governors
8. Victualling Store house
9. Rough Shed for Wet Provisions
10. New Ordnance Store-houses
11. The Sharleys & Pepperels Infantry
12. The Kings Bastion or Citadel
13. Prince of Oranges Bastion
14. Powder Magazine & Prison
15. Prince of House Bastion
16. Advanced Cannon & Mortar Battery
Of 4 Guns
17. Powder Magazine
18. Trenches

Black Cape

Morr of Gabanes

Little Pond

The Key Wall

Brazir that

Rochefort Point

Pond

threat of forfeiting their commissions. Their reply was:

His Highness is master of these, but not of our honour.

With this expedition of Braddock there was a naval force, consisting of two fifty-gun ships, under the Honourable Captain Keppel; and its departure was no sooner known at the Court of France than it began to assume a hostile disposition.

From the date of his landing, General Braddock should have been able to have entered upon action, collaterally with Colonel Monkton, early in the spring; but unfortunately, he was delayed by the Virginian contractors for the army. When the latter was ready to march, these men had failed to provide a sufficient supply of provisions for the troops and a competent number of wagons for transport. Smollett says:

This accident was foreseen, by almost every person who knew anything of our plantations upon the continent of America: for the people of Virginia, who think of no produce but their tobacco, and do not raise corn enough for their own subsistence, being by the nature of their country well provided with the conveniency of water conveyance, have but few wheel-carriages or beasts of burden; whereas Pennsylvania, which abounds in corn and most other sorts of provision, has but little water-carriage, especially in its western settlements, where its inhabitants have great numbers of carts, wagons, and horses.

General Braddock should therefore have landed in Pennsylvania; and if his first camp had been formed at Franks Town, he would not have had more than 80 miles to march to reach Fort Duquesne, instead of 130, which the troops had to traverse from their camp at Wills's Creek. By great efforts he ultimately procured 15 wagons and 100 draught-horses, instead of 150 wagons and 300 horses, which the Virginian contractors had promised him; while the provisions they furnished were so bad as to be unfit for use.

Under these adverse circumstances, he began his march through woods, deserts, and morasses; scenes very different to those where his past experience had been—the fertile plains of the Low Countries and the stately parks of London. Before he left the latter, he had received, in the handwriting of Colonel Napier, a set of instructions from the Duke of Cumberland, indicating that he was to attack Niagara, to leave the reduction of Crown Point to the Provincial forces; but, above all, both verbally and in writing, he had been cautioned by

CANADIAN INDIAN.

Cumberland to beware of ambush and surprise.

Full of his own conceit, he utterly disdained to ask the opinion of any officer under his command; and proceeded at the head of 2,200 bayonets, on the 10th of June, for the Little Meadows, the scene of Washington's reverse in the preceding year. There he found it necessary to leave part of his slender force, under Colonel Dunbar, and all his heavy baggage; and advanced with only 1,200 men and ten pieces of artillery, although he was informed the French commander in Fort Duquesne expected a fresh reinforcement of 500 regular troops. He marched on with so much expedition that he seldom took any time to reconnoitre the woods or thickets he had to pass through, as if the nearer he approached the enemy the safer he would be from danger.

On the 8th of July he encamped within ten miles of Fort Duquesne. Colonel Dunbar was now forty miles in his rear; and his officers, but more especially Sir Peter Halkett, entreated him to proceed with caution, and employ the friendly Indians who were with them as an advanced guard, in case of ambuscades. In spite of this he resumed his march next day, without sending a single scout into the dense woods which now surrounded his slender force.

About noon the troops entered a hollow vale, on each side of which there grew a dense primeval forest and thick brushwood. Suddenly the echoes of the solitude were wakened by a fatal and appalling whoop, the war-cry of the native Indians; and in a moment, there was opened upon the front and all along the left flank of Braddock's force a deadly and disastrous fire, from an enemy so skilfully and artfully disposed that not a man of them could be seen, the flashing of their muskets alone indicating where they lay. These assailants were the native Indians, assisted by a few French troops from the fort.

The advanced guard instantly fell back on the main body; the panic and confusion became general, and most of the troops fled with precipitation; and, notwithstanding that all their officers behaved with the most brilliant gallantry, it was impossible to stop their career. And now General Braddock, instead of opening a fire of grape from the ten pieces of cannon he had with him, and so scouring the place whence this fusillade was coming, or dispatching any of his Indians to take the ambush in flank, obstinately remained upon the spot where he was, and gave orders for the few brave men who remained with him to advance.

Thickly fell the dead and dying around him, and all the officers were singled out in succession and shot down, as the marksmen could

BRADDOCK'S FORCE ATTACKED

distinguish them by their dress, their gorgets, and sashes, which were now worn in the German fashion, round the waist. At last Braddock, whose obstinacy, pride, and courage seemed to increase with the peril around, after having no less than five horses killed under him, received a musket-shot through the right arm and lungs, of which he died in a few hours, after being carried off the field by his *aide-de-camp*, the Honourable Colonel Gage, and some soldiers, whom, according to Lord Mahon, that officer had to bribe by offering them a guinea and a bottle of rum each. Gage, son of the viscount of that name, died a lieutenant-general, in 1788.

When Braddock fell, the confusion of the few who remained became complete; a most disorderly flight ensued across a river which they had just passed. They were not followed, as the artillery, ammunition, and baggage of the army were all left behind; and these, together with the savage use of the tomahawk and scalping-knife on the 700 dead and wounded who lay in the little valley, afforded ample occupation for the exulting Indians. Braddock's cabinet was taken, with all his letters and instructions, of which the Court of France made great use in their printed memorials and manifestoes.

Among those who perished by the first fire were Sir Peter Halkett and his son James, a lieutenant in the 44th Regiment, and the son of Governor Shirley; among those wounded were two *aides-de-camp*. Captains Orm and Morris, and Sir John Sinclair, the quartermaster-general. What number of men the enemy had in this ambuscade, or what loss they sustained at the hands of the few who resisted, was never ascertained, for the survivors never halted until they reached Fort Cumberland, named, as we have already stated previously, Fort Beausejour.

FRENCH AND INDIAN WAR

MAP OF THE SCENE OF OPERATIONS.

The American Campaign of 1755

Had the shattered remains of Braddock's force continued at Fort Cumberland, and strengthened themselves there, as they might easily have done during the rest of the summer, they would have proved an efficient check upon the French and their ferocious allies, the scalping Indians; and might have prevented those ravages which during the ensuing winter were perpetrated on the western frontiers of Virginia and Pennsylvania. But their commander left only his sick and wounded in that isolated fort, under the protection of two companies of Provincial militia, and marched the rest, on the 2nd of August, towards Philadelphia, where they could be of no immediate service.

In one of his works, Cooper, the novelist, remarks with truth that it was a feature peculiar to the wars of North America that the toils and dangers of the wilderness were always to be encountered before the adverse armies could meet in the shock of battle. A wide and apparently impervious boundary of primeval forests severed the possessions of Britain and France. The hardy colonist, and the trained European soldier who fought by his side, frequently had to expend months in struggling against the rapids of unknown rivers, or in penetrating into the passes of mountains as yet unnamed, the abode of cunning, and hostile savages.

From Philadelphia the remains of the 44th and 48th Regiments were ordered to Albany, in the State of New York (then a small town on the western bank of the Hudson), by General William Shirley, who, in the preceding year, had been appointed colonel of one of the two regiments which were raised in America, and officered exclusively from the half-pay list.

By this arrangement, Maryland, Virginia, and Pennsylvania were left entirely to take care of themselves, which they might have done effectually had they been undivided in council; but the latter, which was the most influential of the three, was rendered incapable of defence by local jealousies and internal disputes, though £50,000 were voted for the erection of forts.

To the north of Pennsylvania our colonies were more active in their preparations for war.

New York, like New England, prohibited the export of provisions to any French settlement, and raised £45,000 for the defence of the province, which was peculiarly exposed to an invasion of the French from Crown Point; and on being succoured by a small force of regular troops, under Colonel Dunbar, they boldly resolved upon offensive measures, which, when practicable, are always wisest, and two expeditions, one against the enemy's fort at Crown Point, and another against the fort at Niagara, between Lakes Erie and Ontario, were projected at the same time, as both these strongholds were alleged to be built on British territory.

The first of these was to be conducted by a Provincial officer, named General William Johnson, a native of Ireland, who had long resided upon the Mohawk River, where he had acquired a considerable estate, and was famous as a negotiator with the Indian tribes, whose language he had learned, and by whom he was greatly beloved. The other expedition was to be led in person by General Shirley, on whom the command of our forces in America had devolved after the death of General Braddock.

The rendezvous of the troops for both places was appointed to be at Albany by the end of June; but the artillery, *batteaux*, provisions, and other stores necessary for the attack upon Crown Point did not arrive till the 8th of August, when General Johnson began his march with them from Albany, for the carrying-place from the Hudson to Lake George. There the first portion of the troops had already arrived, under Major-General layman. The whole now consisted of about 6,000 men, besides well-armed Indians, raised by the governments of New Hampshire, New York, Rhode Island, and Connecticut.

Towards the end of August, General Johnson marched forward fourteen miles, and encamped in a strong situation, flanked on each side by a densely-wooded swamp, having Lake George in his rear, and a breastwork or palisade of felled trees in his front. There he resolved to await the arrival of the *batteaux*, and afterwards to proceed to Ticonderoga, at the other end of the lake, whence it was but fifteen miles to the south end of Champlain, where stood the stronghold called Fort Frederick by the French, and by the British Crown Point.

The village near this old fort, so famous in the French and Revolutionary wars, consisted then of only fifteen log-huts, amid the mountainous wilderness which is now named the county of Essex.

While he was, thus encamped, some of his Indian scouts, of whom he took care to send out great numbers on every side, brought him intelligence that a considerable force of the enemy, in the white uniforms then worn by the royal infantry of France, had been seen on their march, by the way of the south bay, towards the fortified encampment since called Fort Edward, which General Lyman had built at the carrying-place, and in which 500 of the men of New York and New Hampshire had been left as a garrison.

Immediately on learning this, he sent expresses to Colonel Blanchard, commanding there, with orders to call in all foragers and stragglers, and to keep every man within the works. About twelve at night those who had gone with the second express returned with an account of having seen the enemy within four miles of the camp at the carrying-place, which they could scarcely doubt would be speedily attacked.

Important as the strength of that post was for the defence, and perhaps for the retreat, of the whole army, it does not appear that General Johnson summoned any Council of War, or resolved upon any plan to succour Colonel Blanchard; but next morning he detached 1,000 men, with a number of Indians, to intercept, or, as he oddly phrased it, "to catch the enemy in their retreat," whether victorious or defeated. This expedient he resolved on, though no one knew the number of the enemy, or could obtain any clear information on that subject from the Indian scouts, as they were without words or signs expressive of any great number, save by pointing to the hair of the head, the leaves of the trees, or the stars of the firmament.

About nine in the morning, the 1,000 infantry and 200 Indian warriors, under the command of Colonel Williams, began their march; but these had barely been gone two hours when those in the fortified camp heard the din of close musketry, as they supposed about four miles distant, ringing through the vast dingles of the echoing forest. As it approached nearer and nearer, they came to the conclusion that the force under Colonel Williams had been overpowered and was retreating.

The appearance of some fugitives, and soon after whole companies, in flight towards the camp, confirmed this, and then the French infantry came in sight—2,000 strong—marching in regular order to-

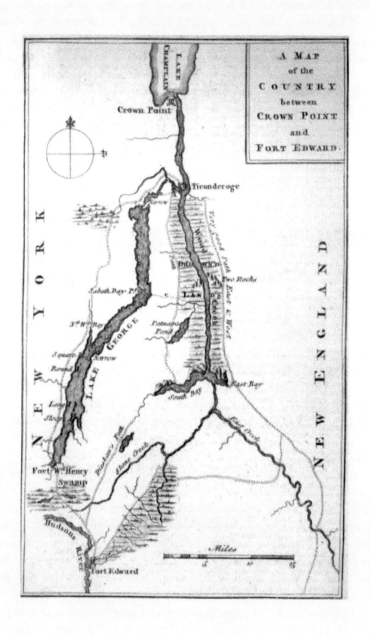

A MAP
of the
COUNTRY
between
CROWN POINT
and
FORT EDWARD.

wards the centre of General Johnson's camp, where the confusion was so great that had it been instantly attacked it must have been easily reduced; but, fortunately for the British, the enemy halted at the distance of 150 yards, and began the assault of the breastwork by the most unusual method of platoon firing.

To this Johnson responded by his artillery; on which the Canadians and Indians in the French service fled into the swampy forest on each side of the camp, and squatted among the bushes or behind the trees, whence they took occasional shots when opportunities occurred, but they never had the courage to emerge into the open ground.

Meanwhile, the Baron Dieskau, who, though a *marechal-de-camp* of that year, 1755, was an old and experienced officer, and commander-in-chief of all the French forces in Canada, being thus left with only the regulars in front of this strongly-entrenched camp, and finding that he could attack it neither in front nor on the flanks, continued his platoon and bush-firing till four in the afternoon, during which time his troops suffered greatly from the fire of the British, and were at last thrown into confusion. This was no sooner perceived by the troops of General Johnson than, without waiting for orders, with loud hurrahs, they leaped over the breastwork, forced a passage through the abattis of felled trees, and falling upon the French with the bayonet, killed a vast number, took thirty prisoners, and utterly routed the rest.

About 800 French were killed, and among those taken was the old Baron Dieskau, a soldier of fortune, who was found in the forest mortally wounded, and supporting himself against the stump of a tree. The loss of the British was about 200 men, chiefly belonging to the repulsed detachment of Colonel Williams; for few were killed or wounded in the attack on the camp, though among the former was Colonel Titcomb, and among the latter were General Johnson and Major Nichols. Among the slain of the detachment, which would have been entirely cut off had not Lieutenant-Colonel Cole sallied out to its support, at the head of 300 bayonets, were Colonel Williams, Major Ashley, six captains, and many subalterns; while among many Indian warriors who fell, none was more mourned by his tribe than the brave old Hendrick, the *sachem* and chief of the Mohawks.

It was now deemed too late in the season to attack Crown Point, as it would have been necessary to build a strong fort in the place where the camp then was, to secure communication with Albany, whence alone the troops could be reinforced or supplied. They therefore began to retire after this encounter, after erecting a little stockaded fort at the farther end of the beautiful sheet of water named Lake George, where a small garrison was left, to become, as might have been foreseen, a prey to the enemy. Great rejoicings were made in London over the repulse and death of Baron Dieskau; and General Johnson was created a baronet on the 27th of November, with a donation of £5,000 from Parliament.

For General Shirley's expedition against Niagara, the preparations were alike slow and deficient, although it was well known that all his chances of success depended on his commencing operations early in the season, Smollett says:

> As will appear to any person who considers the situation of our fort at Oswego, this being the only way by which he could proceed to Niagara.

The fort, over which a town has now sprung up, stands on an eminence eastward of the river Oswego, which has its source near that of the Mohawk, south-eastward of Ontario, and nearly 300 miles from Albany. The way to it then, in those pre-railway times, was long and tedious by land; but there was a water carriage by means of *batteaux*, which were light flat-bottomed boats, broad in the beam, pointed at the stem and stern, of great burden, and managed by only two *batteau* men, with paddles and steering-poles. Shirley was no sooner ready to march than tidings came of the defeat and death of General Braddock. The influence of that intelligence on his troops was astonishing. Their enthusiasm was damped, a panic pervaded all ranks, and many, soldiers deserted; thus, when General Shirley arrived at Oswego, he had scarcely troops sufficient to secure the British settlements in those parts, so far from having enough to assault the strong fortress at Niagara.

The attempt was abandoned; he returned ingloriously to Albany, and thus ended the puerile campaign of 1755 in America.

Minorca, 1756

This year brings us to the now-forgotten defence of Minorca, which was held by four British regiments of the Line against an army of more than 20,000 men.

But all their bravery was rendered futile in the end, by the parsimony and incapacity of the Government; so true is it, as General Sir William Napier wrote:

> In the beginning of each war England has to seek in blood the knowledge necessary to ensure success, and like the fiend's progress towards Eden, her conquering course is through chaos followed by death.

Minorca, the second or smaller of the Balearic Isles, as its name imports, was ceded to Britain by the same Treaty of Utrecht that confirmed her in possession of Gibraltar. In 1708 the Government, desirous of possessing a naval station farther up the Mediterranean than that fortress, had Minorca captured by General Stanhope, at the head of 2,600 men. The garrison made but a poor defence, and, with the loss of fifty killed and wounded, Stanhope made himself master of the place, together with 100 pieces of cannon, 3,000 casks of powder, and, other munition of war. During the forty-eight years Minorca had been under British rule, its inhabitants had prospered, and carried on a tolerably active shipping trade, by which many had grown wealthy; but, as Catholics, they had always in secret resented the rule of a Protestant king.

The troops in Minorca at this crisis consisted only of the 4th, or King's Own, the 23rd Welsh Fusiliers, and the 24th and 34th Regiments, which together mustered not more than 2,460 men fit for duty. The Government having received intelligence of extensive preparations at the port of Toulon, the object of which was generally believed to be the reduction of Minorca, dispatched early in April a fleet under the unfortunate Admiral Byng for the defence of the island.

The armament of Toulon, consisting of the fleet, under Lieutenant-General de Galissoniere, mounting 1,766 guns, with 17,700 seamen and marines, and the troops to the number of 20,000 men, under the Marshal Duke de Richelieu, arrived on the 18th of April off the port of Ciudadella, on that part of the island which lies opposite to Mahon, or St. Philip's, and immediately the disembarkation began.

Two days before they reached the island. General Blakeney, an aged officer, whose last military service had been the defence of Stirling Castle against the Highlanders, had by a packet-boat received certain intelligence of their departure from Toulon, and began to make preparations for the defence of the castle of St. Philip. As for defending the isle with a force so small as that under his orders, he never conceived it possible, as Minorca has an area of 260 square miles. Its surface, is very uneven, and its abrupt hills and knolls have been by some writers compared to the waves of the sea in a storm. It has only one mountain, Tore, which rises in its centre. The climate is damp.

The north wind checks the growth of much timber; yet the vegetation is generally luxuriant; but the grapes and the crops of wheat and barley had all been gathered by the time the French troops spread themselves over the isle

The castle of St. Philip was very extensive; numerous redoubts, ravelins, and other outworks surrounded it, and it had numerous subterranean galleries, mines, and traverses, cut with incredible labour out of the solid rock. It was then deemed one of the best-fortified places in Europe. It was well-supplied with provisions, ammunition, and artillery, which, from the rocky eminence it crowns, commanded alike the noble anchorage of the port, and the narrow, tortuous, steep, and ill-paved streets of the picturesque little town, the houses of which are flat-roofed, and perched on ledges of rock that in many instances overhang the sea.

Had St. Philip been properly garrisoned, beyond all doubt its siege might have proved one of the most desperate and protracted in history. The nature and extent of the fortifications required more than double the number of men then in the place. As war had not yet been formally declared, at least forty officers were absent on leave; the chief engineer was rendered unfit for duty by gout, and General William Blakeney was nearly equally so by old age and infirmity. He had been a brigadier of January, 1743. The natives of the island might have been serviceable as pioneers, says Smollett, but from their hatred of the Protestant religion, "they were averse to the English Government, although they had lived happily and grown wealthy under its influence." Such zealous Catholics are they, that they still are wont to bury their dead in the habit of a religious order.

General Blakeney ordered his drums to beat up for volunteers in the town of St. Philip's; but few or none would enlist, and he had no power to compel their services. He drew in all his detachments, particularly a company which was posted at the seaport of Fornella, six miles from the Toro mountain, and five others from Ciudadella, the episcopal capital of the isle, as soon as the enemy began to disembark.

Major Cunningham, an active Scottish officer, was sent with a working party to blow up or break down the bridges, and trench all the roads between Ciudadella and St. Philp's; but the task of destroying the roads proved no easy one to the major, in consequence of the hard rock which runs along the surface throughout the whole of Minorca, and, is seldom at any depth below the soil; but the street, served the foe for trenches, which otherwise could not have been dug through the living rock.

The French deliberately entered the town of Mahon, and made a lodgement close to the outworks of St. Philip's; there they found convenient quarters of refreshment, masks for their batteries, and an effectual cover for their mortar-beds and bombardiers. General Blakeney was censured for not having destroyed the town; but, says the historian already quoted:

> If we consider his uncertainty concerning the destination of the French armament, the odious nature of such a precaution, which could not possibly fail to exasperate the inhabitants, and the impossibility of executing such a scheme after the first appearance of the enemy, he will be held excusable, if not altogether blameless."

He demolished certain houses and windmills, to gain a clear range for his guns. All the wine in the cellars of St. Philip's was destroyed, and the casks were taken into the castle to serve as gabions, or as fascines, when filled with earth at the traverses. Five-and-twenty Minorcan bakers were brought into the fort to make bread for the garrison; a quantity of cattle were also seized and brought in; the gates were walled up, posts assigned, and additional guards and sentinels appointed.

GRENADIER OF THE FOOT GUARDS, WITH GRENADE AND MATCH ALIGHT (1745).

Commodore Edgecumbe, who was then at anchor in the harbour, sailed thence with his little squadron, consisting of the *Chesterfield, Louisa, Portland,* and *Dolphin,* after having left all his marines, the whole crew of the *Porcupine* sloop, and half of the *Dolphin's,* as a little reinforcement to the castle, under the command, of Captain Carr Scroope, of the *Dolphin,* who was distinguished for his bravery during the siege that ensued.

M. de Galissoniere might easily have prevented the escape of the commodore; but it is supposed he did not do so lest on any emergency or assault the crews and officers of the squadron might have reinforced the garrison.

The Duke de Richelieu was perfectly acquainted with the great extent of the works in St. Philip's, and also with the weakness of its garrison; and from these circumstances, he was quite sanguine that the place would be taken without the risk and labour of a regular siege. After the departure of the commodore for Gibraltar, a sloop was sunk, by General Blakeney's order, in the channel that leads to the harbour; and a French squadron, after menacing the town and castle, fell away to the leeward of Fort Mola, and returned no more in a hostile manner.

On the 22nd of April, General Blakeney dispatched a drummer to the Duke de Richelieu, requesting to be informed of his reasons for invading the island. To this an answer was returned by the duke, declaring that he had:

> . . . . . come with the intention of reducing it under the dominion His Most Christian Majesty, by way of retaliation for the conduct of his master, who had seized and detained certain ships belonging to the King of France and his subjects.

The duke must have been but indifferently provided with engineers, for instead of first entering the town, as he ultimately did, he erected his batteries at Cape Mola, on the other side of the harbour, where the distance rendered their fire ineffectual; while that from St. Philip, where the guns were heavier, proved so severe that the enemy were compelled to change their mode of attack, and on the 12th of May they pushed their way into the town, and at nine that night opened two bomb-batteries near the place where the windmills had been destroyed. From that hour an incessant fire from mortars and cannon was maintained day and night, on both sides; and the French continued with great expedition to raise fresh batteries in every position whence they could annoy the besieged.

In consequence of these operations, war was formally declared against France on the 18th of May, 1756.

The little garrison continued to resist with great valour till the 19th of June, when, to their joy, the fleet of Admiral Byng (son of the celebrated naval officer of that name, who, in 1718, destroyed the Spanish fleet near Messina) appeared in sight, like a white cloud at the horizon, as he had with him ten great ships of the line, two of forty-eight guns, and three frigates. The four regiments shut up in St. Philip's now redoubled their exertions, on finding succour near, and worked their guns with courage and vigour. On his approach the British admiral expressed his satisfaction to see the Union Jack still flying on the castle of St. Philip; but, notwithstanding that animating circumstance, his attempts for its relief were alike feeble and ineffectual. He would seem to have been utterly discouraged when he heard of the greater armament commanded by the Marquis de Galissoniere, and to have given up Minorca as lost.

His subsequent conduct, and a letter addressed by him to the Secretary of the Admiralty before he reached Port Mahon, seem to confirm this. After regretting that he could not reach Minorca prior to the landing of the French, he wrote thus:—

I am firmly of opinion that throwing men into the castle will only enable it to hold out a little longer, and add to the numbers that must fall into the enemy's hands; for the garrison in time will be obliged to surrender, unless a sufficient number of men could be landed to raise the siege. I am determined, however, to sail up to Minorca, with the squadron, when I will be a better judge of the situation of affairs, and will give General Blakeney all the assistance he shall require. But I am afraid all communication will be cut off between us; for if the enemy have erected batteries on the two shores near the entrance to the harbour, an advantage scarce to be supposed they have neglected, it will render it impossible for our boats to have a passage to the sally-port of the castle.

A single circumstance occurred which confuted the admiral's idea that it was impracticable to open a communication with the garrison.

Mr. Boyd, a commissariat officer, ventured to embark in a small six-oared boat, which passed from St. Stephen's Cove, a creek on the west side of the castle, through a shower of cannon and musketry, that tore the water into foam around him, and he actually gained the open sea, in hope to reach the fleet, which he saw stretching far away to the southward; but on finding himself pursued by two of the enemy's light vessels, he returned by the way he came, and regained the garrison untouched.

Next day the hopes of the besieged, which had prognosticated a brilliant naval victory to the British squadron, and consequent relief to themselves, were greatly damped by the reappearance of the French fleet, returning quietly to their station off the harbour of Mahon.

That same evening, they were informed by a deserter that the British fleet had been defeated by the Marquis de Galissoniere, tidings which a *feu de joie* in the French camp seemed to confirm. However little the French fleet had to boast of, the retreat of the British, by leaving them in possession of the sea, was equivalent to a victory; for had the admiral maintained our old superiority there, the French troops which had been disembarked would in all probability have been compelled to capitulate as prisoners of war.

The case was now entirely different. The French fleet, while Byng returned to Gibraltar, cruised about the island without molestation; and their troops daily received, by means of transports, reinforcements of men, and supplies of fresh provisions and ammunition.

Though astonished and mortified to find themselves thus totally abandoned by the fleet, the British troops in St. Philip's resolved to acquit themselves with their native gallantry; and many were not without hope that when reinforced, the admiral would again return to their relief.

The brave fellows in St. Philip's never lost heart. They remounted cannon, the carriages of which had been disabled by the enemy's shot; and they received and returned the fire of the French with a resolution that never flinched. They dragged their guns occasionally to places where they would do the greatest execution; they repaired breaches, restored merlons, and laboured with unceasing vigilance, when quite environed by hostile batteries; when their embrasures were destroyed, their parapets demolished, and they were then left exposed to a united fire of cannon, mortars, and musketry The latter was poured upon them without ceasing from the windows of the sheets, which were fully in possession of the enemy.

By this time, they were enclosed by more than 20,000 men. The fleet blockaded the entire island by sea, and they were plied incessantly with missiles from sixty-two battery-guns, twenty-one mortars, and four howitzers, besides the small-arms; yet the loss of men in the castle

St. Stephen's Cove

Part of St. Philip's Town

ENTRANCE OF THE HARBOUR

SANDY BAY

A Scale of Feet

A
PLAN
OF THE
Underground Works of St. PHILIP'S CASTLE.

REFERENCES.

A. Castle
B. No. 1
C. E.
D. St. } Bastion
E. W.
F. N.
G. E. } Counterguard
H. P.
I. W.
K. N.W. } inward
L. S.W.
M.S.E. } Ravelin
N. N.E.
O. N.W. } outward
P. S.W.
Q. S. } Lunette
R.S.W.
S. Curtain
T. High Lunette
V. Ravin
W. Queens Redoubt
X. Aroyal
Y. Aquaductor
Z. Royal Battery

a. Charles Fort
b. Marlborough
c. Hospital
d. Hardcastle } Battery
e. Reef
f. Bread
g. Wine
h. Corn } Magazine
i. Oyl & Aquavilent
k. Powder
m. Ordnance Store
n. Ordnance Shops
o. Laboratory
p. Hospital
q. Serjeant Apartments
r. Ovens s. Kitchens
t. Mills
u. Galleries for the Troops
v. Casemates for Officers & Defence
    of the Gallery
w. Stepherspller
x. Counter Mines
y. Bason for Boats
z. Bason for the Pontoon
&. Lodgement for the Pontoon.

J. Mynde sc.

was comparatively small, the most of the garrison being secure in the casemates, galleries, and other subterranean works, where neither shot nor shell could penetrate.

Incessant duty and watching so exhausted the soldiers that they frequently fell asleep under a heavy cannonade, yet they persevered with admirable resolution. (*Records of the 34th Regiment*).

By the 27th of June the batteries of the French had made a practicable breach in one of the ravelins, and so damaged the other outworks that the Duke de Richelieu deemed that now had come the favourable moment for a general assault. Accordingly, at ten in the night, the *Records of the Welsh Fusiliers* states:

The enemy issued from their works, to the different attacks, which were made simultaneously on so many different points that the garrison, worn out with seventy days' incessant duty, were unable to repel them all.

But so great was the enthusiasm, that even the sick and wounded officers and men who were in hospital seized their arms, and came rushing out to defend the breach. At the same time, the Marquis de Galissoniere sent a strong detachment in armed boats to force the harbour and penetrate into St. Stephen's Cove, to storm Fort Charles, and second the attack on Fort Marlborough, the most detached of all the outworks.

The air was literally alive with shells and rockets, and the blaze of the incessant musketry, above and below, seemed at times to shed a red light over all the walls of St. Philip.

Led by the duke in person, the French advanced with great intrepidity; but the assault was attended by the most dreadful slaughter, for as the columns drew near, stumbling in the dark over fallen masonry, dead and dying men, trenches, and gabions, the grape shot and musketry mowed them down on every hand. Several mines were sprung beneath their feet with terrible effect, so that the whole glacis was thickly covered with killed and wounded.

Resolutely the French poured on, and ultimately succeeded in effecting a lodgement in the Queen's Redoubt, and in the Anstruther and Argyle Batteries. A secret mine sent the latter work into the air, and with it three entire companies of French grenadiers.

The capture of the Queen's Redoubt was effected in the dark, owing to the weakness of the garrison, and before the circumstance was known to our officers; for Lieutenant-Colonel Jeffries, the second in command, an officer of great skill and courage, in going on his tour of duty to visit the post, found himself suddenly captured by a file of French grenadiers. Major Cunningham, who accompanied him, though he escaped captivity, was run through the arm by a bayonet, and the piece being discharged at the same time, his bones were shattered in such a manner that he was maimed for life. In this shocking condition, adds Smollett, he retired behind a traverse, and was taken to his quarters. Thus, General Blakeney lost two of his most able officers; one being disabled and the other taken prisoner.

The Duke de Richelieu, after the firing had continued without intermission from ten o'clock at night until four next morning, beat a parley, for permission to carry off the wounded and bury the dead; a request which General Blakeney granted with more humanity than discretion, as the enemy most treacherously and dishonourably took this opportunity for throwing strong reinforcements in the Queen's Redoubt and Anstruther Battery, whence they penetrated into the gallery of the mines which communicated with all the other outworks.

General Blakeney, during this short cessation of hostilities, summoned a Council of War, to deliberate upon the state of the fortress and garrison; and, believing that they had done enough for honour, the majority of the officers declared for a capitulation. The works were ruined, the body of the castle was shattered, many guns were dismounted, the parapets demolished, the palisades destroyed, the garrison totally exhausted, and the enemy already in possession of the outworks and the subterranean galleries between them. These considerations, together with despair of having any relief from Britain, all led to a surrender.

The *chamade* was beaten on the ruined walls; and at a conference which ensued most honourable terms were accorded to the conquered garrison, which was to march out with all the honours of war, under a salute from the whole French Army.

The Duke de Richelieu wrote:

The noble and vigorous defence which the British have made, in reply to the second article proposed by Blakeney, having deserved all marks of esteem and veneration that every military person ought to show to such actions, and Marshal Richelieu being desirous also to show to General Blakeney the regard due to the brave defence he has made, grants to the garrison all the honours of war that they can enjoy under the circumstances of their going out for embarkation, to wit, firelocks on their shoulders, drums beating, colours flying, twenty cartridges for each man, and also lighted matches.

The total casualties of the siege were only 89 killed, 367 wounded, and 1 missing; 23 men died of their wounds, and 10 of disease. On the other side, the French losses were not less than 5,000 men.

The French were put in possession of one gate, as well as Fort Charles and the Marlborough Redoubt; but the British troops remained in the other works till the 7th of July, when they marched out and embarked in French ships for Gibraltar. In the meantime, many reciprocal. civilities passed between the officers and soldiers of both countries. Their fighting over, all seemed comrades while in the castle of St. Philip.

Beatson, in his *Naval and Military Memoirs* says:

Thus, did four regiments and one company of artillery maintain the fort against such numbers of the enemy by sea and land, for such a length of time, as can, perhaps, scarcely be paralleled in history. The terms on which the fort was at last surrendered by a handful of men, so distressed, so shattered, and neglected, remain a lasting monument to their honour.

News of this conquest was brought by Count Egmont to Versailles, and the exultation of the French knew no bounds. The whole kingdom was filled with triumphs and processions; a thousand poems and orations lavished praises on the victors of Minorca, while the English were vilified in ballads, farces, and *pasquinades*.

In Britain the sense of disgust and disgrace was strong. The returning troops were everywhere hailed with acclamation, and General Blakeney was created a peer of Ireland. The people clamoured for a victim; and, to appease the growing storm, the unfortunate Admiral Byng, for failing to succour Minorca, was tried by a court-martial and found guilty of an error in judgment, for which, in the following year, he was barbarously shot on the quarter-deck of the *Monarch*, in Portsmouth Harbour.

Admiral Forbes (a Lord of the Admiralty) alone refused to endorse the death-warrant of Byng; and Admiral West, who was lying at Spithead in command of a squadron under sailing orders, when he heard of the sentence passed on his unfortunate brother officer, wrote a public letter to the Admiralty Board, begging leave to resign his command, and a private one to Earl Temple, the First Lord, expressive of his reasons for so doing.

Plassey, 1757

The Battle of Plassey, where 3,000 men encountered 70,000, is, perhaps, one of the most remarkable in history.

The conquest of Bengal was one of the greatest achievements of Clive, "The Avenger," as he was named—Clive, the daring in war; "he who," says Horace Walpole, "was styled by policy a heaven-born hero."

The British authorities in Bengal had from the beginning been opposed by the native viceroys of that province, until the reign of Aliverdi Khan, a wise and valiant prince, who had with success protected his dominions from the inroads of the Mahrattas. He was a friend to the British and their trade; but when he died, in 1756, he was succeeded in the office of *nabob* or governor by his grand-nephew, Surajah Dowlah, a narrow-minded tyrant, who disliked all Europeans, and soon found a pretext for commencing hostilities.

When he suddenly appeared before Calcutta, with a force that made resistance seem hopeless, all the women and children were put on board a vessel; and so great was the alarm that all the other ships sailed at daybreak with the English governor and others who were selfish enough to secure their own retreat; and after a three days' resistance, the slender garrison in Fort William surrendered.

The *nabob* entered soon after, accompanied by his *vizier*, Meer Jaffier, and though he had promised solemnly that no violence should be offered to the garrison, amounting to only 146 officers and men, he thrust them all into a dark room—the terrible Black Hole— scarcely eighteen feet square, where, during a night of the most horrible suffering, 123 of them died of thirst or suffocation, and the few who survived were found in a state of delirium or stupefaction. One of the Hindoo guards set to watch the prison on that night of horror was willing to represent to the tyrant, on being offered a large bribe, the fearful situation of the sufferers, and pray that they might be trans-

CLIVE AT PLASSEY.

ferred to a larger prison; but the *nabob* was asleep, and the soldier dared not disturb him, so while he slept the work of death went on.

Calcutta was speedily retaken by Colonel Clive, the rich city of Hooghly, twenty-five miles higher up the river, was captured and plundered, and the rage of Suraja Dowlah on hearing of these successes was unbounded, but he was compelled to make peace; and ere long Clive was induced to enter into the secret views of the *vizier*, Meer Jaffier, who aspired to the sovereignty of Bengal, which he hoped to obtain by the deposition of his odious and tyrannical master.

The measures taken by Clive to accomplish this desirable revolution did equal honour to his address and sagacity. While conducting an intricate and perilous negotiation with Meer Jaffier, he counterfeited friendship so artfully as not only to lull the suspicions of the *nabob*, but to induce him to dismiss his army which had been assembled at Plassey, a strong camp to the south of his capital, before the capture of Chandernagore, in consequence of a report that Colonel Clive meant to attack Muxadavad.

The colonel asked:

Why do you keep your forces in the field after so many marks of friendship and confidence? They distress all the merchants, and hinder our trade. The British cannot stay in Bengal without freedom of commerce. Do not reduce us to the necessity of suspecting that you intend to destroy us as soon as you have an opportunity.

So, the Surajah Dowlah recalled his army from the front, but not without great anxiety and suspicion.

"If," said he, with great emotion, "this colonel should be deceiving me!"

The secret departure of Clive's agents from Muxadavad soon convinced him that he was deluded; and, filled with fury, he reassembled his army, and ordered it to occupy its former camp at Plassey, after having made Meer Jaffier, of whom he had suspicions, renew solemnly upon the *Koran* his obligations of allegiance and fidelity.

Clive, who had hoped to possess himself of that important post, was somewhat disconcerted by this movement. The *nabob* had reached Plassey twelve hours before him, at the head of 50,000 infantry, 20,000 horse, and 50 pieces of cannon, directed chiefly by forty French officers and deserters.

Clive had but 1,000 Europeans, 2,000 *sepoys*, and 8 field-pieces.

VIEW IN CALCUTTA.

Among the former were the King's 39th Regiment, and the 1st Bengal Fusiliers and 1st Bombay Fusiliers, now, (1892), numbered respectively as the 101st and 103rd Regiments of the Line; the three corps being about 300 men each; he had also 150 artillerymen and sailors, and the 1st Bengal Infantry, raised in the same year, 1757, and styled *"Ghillis-ka-Pultan."*

On the 16th of June this slender force had reached Pattee, a fortified port on the Cossimbasar River. This they promptly reduced, as well as Cutwah, a town with a castle; but the rains setting in with unusual violence, Clive was fain to strike his tents and quarter his men in the huts and houses. Six days he halted there, waiting with intense anxiety for communications which he expected from Meer Jaffier; but the few letters that reached him told only of a complete reconciliation between the *nabob* and his *vizier*, and promised nothing of that defection in the army of the former which he had been led to hope for, when being lured so far into the enemy's country.

His position now became as perilous as the general of so small an army ever occupied, and he was too clear-sighted not to perceive that it was so. He summoned a Council of War, to determine whether the troops should cross the Cossimbasar at once, and put their existence to the doubtful issue of a battle against fearful odds, or halt where they were during the rainy season, and call in the *nabob's* enemies, the Mahrattas, to their aid.

Instead of requiring, in the usual manner, the opinions of the junior members of the Council, Clive took the initiative by giving his own, and gave it in favour of a suspension of hostilities. Majors Kilpatrick, and Grant, the next in point of seniority, followed the same course; while Coote, afterwards so distinguished in the wars of the Carnatic, protested against such policy as most unwise. He urged that nothing could be won by delay; that the confidence of their men would evaporate; that the junction of M. Bussey's French corps, an event by no means improbable, would give the *nabob* a superiority of force that would be irresistible.

Clive saw the force of these arguments; and after spending some hours in solitary thought, amid the recesses of a neighbouring grove, he issued orders for the troops to march before break of day on the following morning.

Just as the sun was rising on the 22nd of June, the troops began to pass the river; and by four in the afternoon the whole were on the hostile side, where a messenger from Meer Jaffier met them with

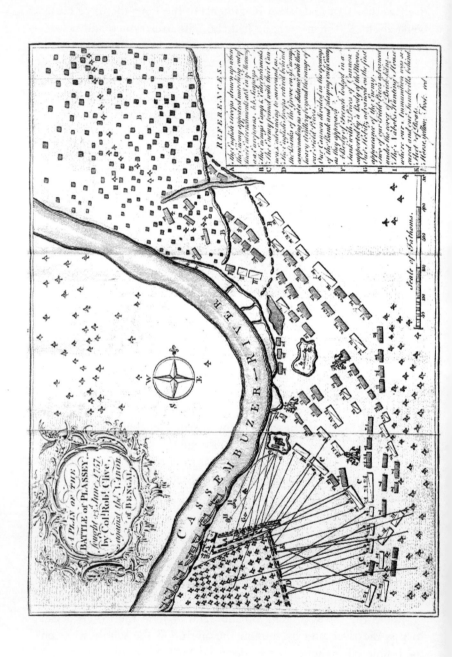

A PLAN OF THE BATTLE OF PLASSEY, fought 23d June 1757, by Col. Robt. Clive, against the Nabob of BENGAL.

CASSEMBUZER RIVER

intelligence that the *nabob* had halted at a village six miles distant, and there Clive was advised to fall upon him by surprise. The colonel replied that he should bivouac that night at Plassey, "and advance next day as far as Daudpoor, where, if Meer Jaffier failed to join him, he would make peace with the *nabob*."

The march was resumed before sunset; and having by dint of great exertion dragged the boats and conveyed their stores a distance of fifteen miles, they halted in the grove of Plassey at one in the morning. There they lay under arms, being startled by the sound of gongs, metal *ghurries*, drums, and cymbals, which, as they marked the vicinity of Indian guards, convinced them that they were within a mile of the *nabob's* camp; yet the men, "after the sentinels were duly planted, slept as soundly as soldiers are apt to do even on the eve of a battle." The grove of Plassey, in which the soldiers lay, was 800 yards long by 300 broad, and consisted entirely of mango trees planted in regular rows.

It was surrounded by a slight embankment, and a ditch choked up with weeds, and approached at its north-western angle within fifty yards of the river. A hunting-seat belonging to the *nabob*, which stood upon the bank of the stream, afforded, with its walled garden and enclosures, an excellent point of defence for one of Clive's flanks, as well as a convenient station for his hospital. In the meantime, the enemy occupied an intrenched camp about a mile or a mile and a half in his front, which, commencing at the neck of a peninsula formed by a curvature of the stream, ran directly inland for 200 yards, after which it formed an obtuse angle, and bore away nearly three miles to the northeast.

In this acute angle stood a redoubt on which cannon were mounted; there was also an eminence covered with luxuriant timber 300 yards beyond; while a couple of water-tanks, girt by earthen mounds, offered peculiar advantages, either in advancing or retreating, to the force which should first seize them. All these features of the position became visible to Clive when the brightening dawn enabled him to reconnoitre, and the sun arose of that day which was to decide the fate of Bengal.

Colonel Clive mounted to the roof of the hunting-seat, and with his telescope was examining the *nabob's* camp, when he suddenly beheld a general stir within it. Ere long the heads of glittering columns, all turbaned and attired in many brilliant colours, began to move into

COMBAT AT PLASSEY

the green plain, and in a few minutes the whole imposing array advanced, but slowly.

There came 50,000 infantry, armed with matchlocks, spears, swords, daggers, and rockets; and 20,000 cavalry, all well mounted, and armed with *tulwar*, lance, and shield. There, too, were their fifty pieces of cannon, planted in the openings between the columns. All came on in the form of a semicircle, as if for the purpose of hemming in and completely surrounding the little force that lay in the mango grove.

The mode in which the cannon were moved was not the least remarkable feature in this Oriental warlike show. The guns, chiefly twenty-four and thirty-two pounders, were each placed on a huge wooden stage, raised six feet above the level of the ground; and these cumbrous platforms, supporting guns, gunners, and ammunition, were each dragged forward by forty or fifty bullocks, assisted by an elephant, which pushed in the rear. Four light field-guns acted apart from the rest, and were worked by the French, who took post in one of the tanks near the edge of the grove.

Clive's artillery consisted of eight six-pounders and two howitzers.

He drew up his whole force in one line, with the three slender European regiments in the centre, and just beyond the skirts of the grove. He did this under the impression that if he kept his men in cover, the *nabob*, mistaking prudence for fear, would acquire additional confidence; besides this, he felt that a corps so pliable might at any moment be thrown back, long ere the unwieldy masses of the enemy could interfere with his alignment. He posted three cannon on each flank, and the remaining two, with the howitzers, under cover of a couple of brick-kilns, so as to protect his left; and having ordered his slender force "to keep steady, and neither advance nor retire without orders," he betook himself again to his station on the house-top.

About eight o'clock in the morning a shot from the French artillerists at the tank gave the signal for a general discharge of all their artillery, and a shower of bullets from fifty pieces of cannon tore through the mango trees. The guns of Clive returned this promptly; and for some time, a fire was kept up which made terrible havoc in the ranks of the *nabob*, but from his cannon being placed on platforms, or not properly depressed, it proved harmless to the other party.

By nine o'clock, Clive, finding that several of his men were beginning to fall, directed the whole line to withdraw into the shelter of the grove. Upon this the enemy, mistaking the change of ground for a sudden flight, with yells and tumultuous cries, pushed their artillery farther to the front, and fired with increased ardour; but as the Europeans and *sepoys* crouched behind the trees, they sustained little or no damage, whilst the shot from their light field-guns plunged through the dense masses of horse and foot that were exposed on the open plain, and piled the corpses over each other in ghastly heaps.

So, passed the day till noon; Clive, after duly consulting with his officers, having determined to act on the defensive throughout the action: but a heavy shower of rain having fallen, the ammunition of the enemy became damaged and their fire began to slacken.

Still, however, they kept their ground; but in about two hours after the bullocks were seen to be driven to their stations beside the platforms, and the whole, covered by the horse and foot, moved slowly to the rear, to the astonishment and joy of Clive and his little army. The truth was that the imperious *nabob* had suddenly lost heart on hearing of the fall of one of his most trusted chiefs, Meer Murdeen, whom a ball had mortally wounded.

Overwhelmed by a misfortune so great, he summoned the *vizier* Meer Jaffier, and throwing his turban on the ground, exclaimed—

"Jaffier, that turban you must defend!"

The traitor bowed, and quitted the presence of the *nabob*, to dispatch in all haste a letter to Colonel Clive, acquainting him with what had passed, and requesting him "either instantly to push on to victory, or to storm the *nabob's* camp during the following night."

But the letter was not delivered until the fortune of the day was decided; so that Clive was still in considerable suspense with respect to the ultimate intentions of his secret ally. While the rest of the vast Indian Army fell back, the little party of Frenchmen at the tank, under an officer named Sinfray, kept its ground manfully, and galled the British both with cannon and musketry. Clive at this moment was sound asleep, excessive fatigue having fairly overcome him; but Major Kilpatrick, placing himself, at the head of two companies of Europeans, with a couple of field-pieces, made ready to dislodge the party at the tank, and occupy the latter as a position whence to gall the retreating enemy.

Prior to moving, a correct sense of military discipline induced him first to refer to Colonel Clive, who sharply reproved him for attempting to take such a step on his own responsibility. However, he warmly praised the idea of the proposed movement, and sending Kilpatrick to the rear to bring up the rest of the troops, he took command of the storming party, and captured the tank without the loss of a single life.

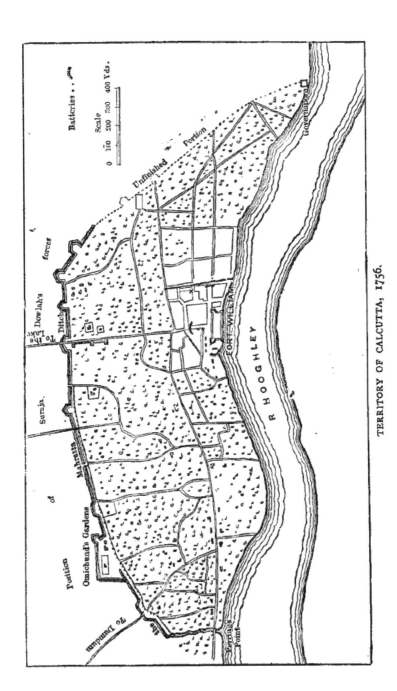

TERRITORY OF CALCUTTA, 1756.

Put in motion by the major, the whole line quitted the grove and advanced. A considerable column was now observed to be extending itself from the right of the enemy, towards the north-east angle of the grove. This was the corps of Meer Jaffier, but being unknown to the British leaders, their guns opened on its ranks at once. The corps halted irresolutely, paused, then broke, and fled with the crowd. On this the detachment under Clive rejoined their comrades, and with loud cheers pushed on for the redoubt, which, as well as the wooded eminence, was stormed and taken. The guns were then run up, loaded with round shot and grape, and a destructive fire was opened on the camp, where a scene of confusion baffling all description soon prevailed.

One corps of the *nabob's* army alone held together, and was soon recognised by its standards to be that of the traitor Jaffier; so, the fact of his adherence to the original secret agreement became proved to Clive and his officers.

"Forward! Push on!" were now the orders, and the camp was entered at the point of the bayonet and almost without any other opposition than that occasioned by abandoned guns and tumbrils, tents half thrown down, and piles of baggage; while thousands of horses and bullocks, with many elephants, overspread the plain, and the broken and discomfited army, which even then might have turned and utterly destroyed its assailants, fled in all directions without firing a shot—fled by tens of thousands. The *nabob* rode among the foremost of the fugitives, mounted on a swift dromedary, an animal now rarely used or seen in Bengal.

Being liberally promised prize-money, the troops remained steadily in their ranks, though surrounded by the gorgeous plunder of an Oriental camp. After a brief halt, which enabled the commissaries to collect as many bullocks and horses as were requisite for the transport of the cannon, the troops advanced in the highest spirits as far as Daudppor, towards which the advanced guard had been pushed for the purpose of observing the enemy's rear; and there the lists of the day's losses were made up. They proved to be singularly small.

Not more than sixteen *sepoys* and eight Europeans lost their lives; while the wounded amounted to forty-eight in all, twelve of these only being English.

Such was the Battle of Plassey, a writer says:

Which belongs to that class of events which defy all calculation previous to their occurrence, and silence all criticism after they have taken place.

The future results of this great victory were not less remarkable than the victory itself. At eight o'clock in the evening Clive halted in Daudpoor, and next morning he saluted the traitor Jaffier as *Subah* or *Nabob* of Bengal, Bahar, and Orissa.

LORD CLIVE.

Sea-Fight off Cape François, 1757

During the war with France our cruisers kept at sea amid all the severity of the winter, for the double purpose of protecting the commerce of the kingdom and annoying that of the enemy. Great were their activity, vigilance, and success; so, the trade of France was almost destroyed. A gallant exploit was performed by a Captain Bray, who commanded the *Adventure*, a small armed vessel, which fell in with the *Machault*, a large privateer of Dunkirk, near Dungeness. He ran on board of her, and lashed her bowsprit to his capstan, and after a close, and hot engagement compelled her to submit. A French thirty-six-gun frigate was taken by Captain Parker, in a new fire-ship of much inferior force. Many privateers of the enemy were taken, burned, or sunk, and a vast number of valuable merchant ships were made prizes.

The great success of our ships of war was not confined to the Channel. In the month of October, 1757, there was a brilliant action fought off the island of Hispaniola, between a French squadron and three ships belonging to the fleet which had sailed for Jamaica under the flag of Admiral Cotes.

Captain Arthur Forest, an officer of distinguished merit, with the *Augusta*, 60 guns, had sailed from Port Royal, accompanied by the *Dreadnought*, 60, and the *Edinburgh*, 64, commanded respectively by Captains Maurice Suckling and William Langdon, with orders to cruise off Cape François, on the northern coast of Hispaniola, in sight of Port Dauphin and the headland of Monte Christo. This service they literally performed in the face of the French squadron, under Admiral de Kersaint, which had lately arrived from Africa, to convoy a number of merchant vessels assembling there for Europe.

Piqued to find himself insulted by the presence of these three ships, De Kersaint resolved to come forth and give them battle, to the end that he might either take, or sink, or drive them out to sea, so as to afford free passage for the merchant shipping in his care. Hence he took every precaution to ensure success. His squadron consisted of seven vessels, as follows:—

L'Intrepide, 74 guns, 900 men, De Kersaint; *La Sceptre*, 74 guns, 800 men, M. Cleveau; *L'Opiniatre*, 64 guns, 680 men, De Moliau; *Greenwich*, 50 guns, 500 men, De Faucault; *L'Outarde*, 44 guns, 400 men; *Le Sauvage*, 32 guns, 300 men; *La Licorne*, 32 guns, 300 men. Total, 370 guns, 3,880 men.

Though he had but three English ships to contend with, carrying in all only 184 guns and 1,232 men, he reinforced his squadron by several store-ships, mounted with guns and completely armed for the grand occasion; he took on board seamen from the merchant ships, and a body of troops from the garrison, and on the 21st of October stood into the offing.

The French were no sooner perceived to be under sail, than Captain Forest held a brief Council of War with the two other captains.

Gentlemen, you know our own strength, and see that of the enemy; it is far more than double ours. Shall we give them battle?

Both officers replied in the affirmative. He said confidently and exultingly:

Then fight them we shall! Return to your ships, and clear away for action.

Without further hesitation, the three British men-of-war bore down on the enemy; and as the latter found their honour at stake, were confident in their vast and superior strength, and knew that the coast was lined with, spectators expecting to see them return in triumph, it is but fair to admit that the French fought with even more than their customary bravery.

By nine in the morning the *Dreadnought*, which had first seen the enemy in motion, according to the dispatches, tacked to join her consorts and prepare for battle.

The *Edinburgh* being to leeward, very properly tacked too, and made a trip to gain her station; while Captain Forest also tacked, reefed his topsails, and made the signal for the line ahead, standing from them under easy sail, just sufficient to preserve the wind, draw them from the coast, and permit them to come up. The French now pursued with great pride, forming a line of seven sail, the tenders plying about their chief; and the whole came up very fast.

The three British ships having fully secured the weather-gage and plenty of sea-room, now hauled up their foresails, letting the enemy see that they awaited them. The moment this little evolution was performed, the French squadron tacked and stood inshore; on which the three British ships bore down upon them under a press of canvas.

Captain Suckling having requested that he might take the lead, it was accorded to him.

In about a quarter of an hour after, the enemy tacked again, and stood towards us to the northward; forming an extensive line as before, with this difference, that their commodore now led. We continued our course till abreast of the third ship, when the squadron wore in a sweep, the *Dreadnought* still keeping the lead, and lasking (*sic*) for the headmost ship.

The smaller sails were now furled, and the three vessels stood on under only their foresails and topsails. M. de Kersaint now ordered his frigates out of the line, and sent *Le Sauvage* ahead.

This last action having left their spaces open a little; their commodore very foolishly brought to with his foretopsail to the mast, and lost command of his ship.

When the *Greenwich* (a captured ship), under Captain de Faucault, shot too near the commodore, she nearly fell on board of him. This caused De Kersaint to fill and let fall his foresail, by which *Le Sauvage* was thrown out of her station, and the *Greenwich*, being compelled to back her sails, made a great gap in that part of the line.

At a quarter-past three the French commodore opened fire on the *Dreadnought*, which sprung her luff in order to steer with him as he set sail. The fore-courses were soon after hauled up on both sides, and being then within musket-shot, the fire was given and returned with equal fury.

Rear-Admiral Cotes wrote to the Admiralty:

Captain Forest, by the opening I have described, was obliged to bear more immediately down upon his opponent, and suffered in the manner the *Dreadnought* might have expected, before she approached near enough to return the enemy's fire. This likewise obliged the *Edinburgh* either to have taken a large sweep, or lie as she did for some time at the beginning of the action, without being able to do all the service she could have wished; so that the *Augusta* had now the whole weight (*i.e.*, fire) of the rear to sustain.

The cannonade soon became general on all sides, and the *Dreadnought* getting on the bow of *L'Intrepide,* kept the helm hard-a-starboard to rake her fore and aft, or, if she proceeded, to fall onboard of her in the most advantageous position possible; but the commodore chose to bear up, and continued to do so during the whole of the action, till his stately seventy-four was disabled and began to drop astern.

The dispatch continues:

By this bearing short upon her own ship, those astern were thrown into fresh disorder, from which they never thoroughly recovered; and when *L'Intrepide* dropped (relieved by *LOpiniatre,* 64), the *Greenwich*, still in confusion, got on board of her, while the *Sceptre* pressing on these, the whole heap were furiously pelted by the *Augusta* and *Edinburgh*, especially *L'Intrepide*, having then flying a signal for relief, lying muzzled in a shattered condition. A frigate soon after endeavoured to take her in tow, but from some cause unknown she was prevented. *L'Outarde,* 44 guns, before this had got into the action, and played very briskly upon the enemy, both upper and lower decks.

The ships were now very close together—muzzle to muzzle in some instances—and we are told that

Never was a battle more furious than the beginning. In two minutes there was not a rope or sail whole in either ship. The French use a shot which we neglect, called *langridge*, which is very serviceable in cutting the rigging.

Captain Forest, on perceiving the shattered condition of the *Dreadnought*, sensible of the damage his own ship, the *Augusta*, had sustained, and satisfied with what the enemy had suffered, thought proper to discontinue the action without pursuing them farther in-shore, since, in the condition of the three British ships, after being subjected to the united fire of so many, it was impossible to take any of them. The lower-masts of the *Dreadnought*, *Augusta*, and *Edinburgh* were all more or less wounded, and the loss of one of these, if any pursuit was attempted, would place the disabled ship completely at the mercy of the enemy's frigates, and also of the *Greenwich*, which was at the close of the action the most serviceable of the enemy's squadron.

VIEW IN JAMAICA.

Captain Forest therefore hailed the *Dreadnought*, as he passed to windward of her, ordering her to make sail, but she continued the engagement for some time after, until she bent some fresh canvas "wherewith to haul up," when her antagonist, *L'Opiniatre*, wore round on the heel and stood away. The *Edinburgh*, after the *Augusta* hauled off, was warmly and closely engaged with the *Intrepide*, *Sceptre*, and *Outarde*, for, nearly half an hour, after which she filled her sails to the yard-heads, at a quarter-past six o'clock, and stood after the *Augusta*; so, the battle and the day ended together.

Our losses and damages in the action were as follows:—The *Augusta* had her first lieutenants and eight men killed, twenty-nine wounded, twelve dangerously; her masts, sails, boats, and rigging rendered almost useless. The *Dreadnought* had nine killed and thirty wounded, twenty dangerously. She had her mizzentopmast, mizzen-yard, maintopmast, and top shot away; every other mast, yard, rope, and sail were rendered perfectly unserviceable by the showers of round, chain, and *langridge* shot that had swept her. The *Edinburgh* suffered least; she had five killed and thirty wounded. She was considerably shattered aloft, and had several shot in her hull.

The *Augusta* and *Dreadnought* were both lightly-metalled ships, and one French seventy-four was considered equal to them both in weight of shot. The French lost in killed and wounded about 600 men.

Our ships were so much damaged that Captain Forest and his consorts were obliged to bear up for Jamaica; and Admiral de Kersaint, finding the sea clear, sailed for Europe with his convoy. In the Channel a dreadful storm overtook his squadron. Many vessels were disabled, and *L'Opiniatre*, *Greenwich*, and *L'Outarde*, having anchored in Conquet Roads, parted their cables, were driven ashore, and totally wrecked. The Greenwich had been taken early in the year by a French squadron in the West Indies, when her commander was Captain Roddom.

It is impossible to close this chapter without referring to the future brilliant services of Captain Forest, before the close of the year 1757.

On the 14th of December, Rear-Admiral Cotes being on a cruise off Cape Tiburon with the *Marlborough*, *Augusta*, and *Princess Mary*, when beating up to windward took two French privateers, from the crews of which he learned that a rich convoy was preparing at Port-au-Prince to sail for Europe, under the protection of two armed vessels.

To ascertain if this was true, he ordered Captain Forest to cruise off La Gonaive, an island on the western side of Hispaniola; to remain there for two days, and if he could see nothing of this convoy, to rejoin him at Cape Nicholas. Accordingly, Captain Forest, in the *Augusta*, proceeded into the bay of Port-au-Prince, with the intention of executing a scheme which he had conceived in his own mind, and the first craft he saw were two French sloops. Lest they should take him for a British cruiser, he hoisted Dutch colours, and disguised the *Augusta* by spreading tarpaulins over some portions of her hull.

Moreover, he forbore chasing. At five in the evening seven more sail were seen steering to the westward; and still to avoid creating suspicion. Captain Forest kept the Dutch ensign flying, and hauled from them till after dark, after which he set all sail and bore towards them. About ten o'clock he sighted two vessels, one of which fired a gun; the other then parted company, and steered for Leogane, a bay in the island of Hispaniola.

Captain Forest now reckoned eight sail to leeward, near another port named Le Petit Goave. Overhauling the ship which had fired the gun, he hailed her, told her captain who he was, and running out two of his heaviest guns, threatened to sink her with all on board if her crew gave the least alarm. They at once submitted. He put a lieutenant with thirty men on board in place of her crew, with orders to steer for Le Petit Goave, and intercept any of the fleet which might attempt to reach that harbour.

He then made sail after the rest, and by daybreak found himself amidst the whole convoy, on each of which he turned his guns in quick succession. They returned his fire for some time, as all the vessels were well manned and armed. At length three struck their colours; prize-crews were put on board, and these aided him in securing five other vessels. Thus, by a well-conducted stratagem, was a whole fleet of vessels taken by a single ship, in the vicinity of five harbours, where they could have found shelter and security. They were as follows:—*Le Mars*, 22 guns, 108 men; *Le Theodore*, 18 guns, 44 men; *La Solide*, 12 guns, 44 men; *Le St. Pierre*, 14 guns, 40 men; *La Marguerite,* 12 guns, 44 men; *Le Maurice*, 12 guns, 30 men; *La Flora*, 12 guns, 35 men; *La Brilliante*, 10 guns, 20 men; *La Monet*, 12 men.

The total capture amounted to 112 guns, 409 men, and 3,070 tons. The prizes were conveyed to Jamaica, and there sold for the benefit of the crew of the *Augusta*, "who may safely challenge history to produce such another instance of success," says Smollett.

Captain Forest served long in the West Indies, and died when commodore, at Jamaica, on the 26th of May, 1770.

St. Cas, 1758

The year 1758 witnessed vigorous preparations for the prosecution of the war with France, and it was resolved to make at least one descent upon the coast of that country. Two squadrons were fitted out, and placed under the command of Lord Anson and Sir Edward Hawke.

A battalion from each regiment of Guards, and the four grenadier companies, formed in one battalion, joined the army, which was composed of sixteen battalions, with 6,000 marines, three companies of artillery, and nine troops of light horse, under Lieutenant-General the Duke of Marlborough. A light, or hussar troop, as it was called, had been lately added to each regiment of heavy cavalry, and these were all selected for this service. The *Weekly Journal* of the 23rd of May, 1758, says:

> The flower of the hussars, is the (Scots Grey) troop commanded by Captain Lindsay, quartered at Maidenhead, where they have been practising the Prussian exercise, and for some days have been digging large trenches and leaping over them; also leaping high hedges with broad ditches on each side. Their captain, on Saturday last, swam his horse over the Thames, and the whole troop was made to swim the river yesterday.

The Guards had now, for the first time on service, steel in lieu of wooden ramrods.

Under Marlborough were Lieutenant-Generals Lord George Sackville, William Earl of Ancrum, K.T, (one of the veterans of Culloden), and four major-generals, Dury, Mostyn, Waldegrave, and Elliot, afterwards Lord Heathfield, the hero of Gibraltar; who led the light horse.

Twelve flat-bottomed boats, each capable of holding sixty-three men in marching order, were prepared; these were to be rowed by

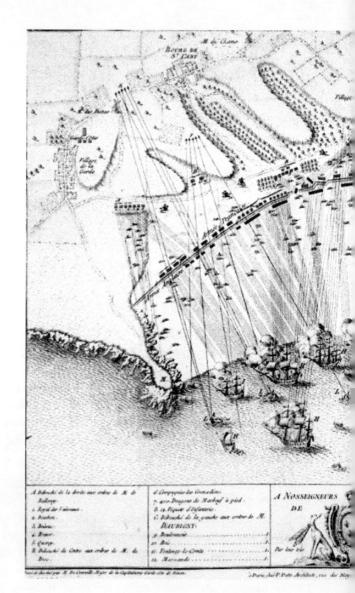

Levé et dessiné par M. De Caresolle Major de la Capitainerie Garde côte de Dinan.

A Paris, chez P. Patte Architecte, rue des Noy

A. Débouché de la droite aux ordres de M. de
    Ruffray.
1. Royal des Vaisseaux.
2. Bourbon.
3. Brienne.
4. Brane.
5. Quercy.
B. Débouché du Centre aux ordres de M. de
    Bric.

6. Compagnies des Grenadiers.
7. 400 Dragons de Marbœuf à pied.
8. La Pique d'Infanterie.
C. Débouché de la gauche aux ordres de M.
    DAUBIGNY.
9. Boulonnois 1
10. Brie 1
11. Penthievre-le-Comte 1
12. Marsande 1

A NOSSEIGNEURS
DE

Par leur très

twelve oars each, and were not to draw more than two feet of water; and a vast quantity of baskets for fascines, sandbags to form batteries, scaling-ladders, and wagons for the conveyance of the wounded, were brought from the Tower to Portsmouth. So great was the enthusiasm in London, that Viscount Down, Sir John Armytage, Sir James Lowther, and many other men of distinction, shouldered their muskets in the fleet and army as private volunteers. In all there were 13,000 fighting men, with 60 pieces of cannon and 50 mortars, destined for this useless invasion of France.

By the 5th of June the whole armament was running with a fair breeze along the coast of Normandy, so close in-shore that the houses, the farms, and even the people, could be distinctly seen without the aid of telescopes; and at two o'clock p.m. the squadron dropped its anchors in Cancalle Bay, on the coast of Brittany, nine miles eastward of St. Malo.

A small battery of only two guns on the shore was soon silenced; when the commodore's ship with three others opened their broadsides to the land, and filled the whole bay with smoke, while for seven hours every rock and mountain echoed to the thunder of a cannonade which was fired on mere speculation at the trees and bushes, as there was a dread that masked batteries might be among them. Under cover of this fire, the flat-bottomed boats, with three battalions of the Guards and eleven grenadier companies of the Line, commanded by Lord George Sackville and General Dury, were rowed inwards and landed safely.

The cavalry and artillery were next disembarked. The infantry, formed in quarter-distance columns, were silent and still, no sound being heard save the uncasing of the colours, and the examination of flints and priming. The night passed without alarm, and the noon of the following day saw the whole army encamped on an eminence, which was crowned by an ancient windmill. The inhabitants of Cancalle fled, according to Entick's *Late War*, and their village was plundered, for which one soldier was hanged, and seven seamen flogged.

On the 7th the Duke of Marlborough began his march for St. Servan and Solidore, publishing as he went a manifesto to the people of Bretagne, that he came, not to make war on them, but on the troops of France. Eight ships, mounting 204 guns, fourteen merchant ships, and many smaller craft, were destroyed by him, together with all the magazines at St. Servan, which may be termed the suburb of St. Malo. The grenadiers, as they advanced alongside the ships, threw fire and

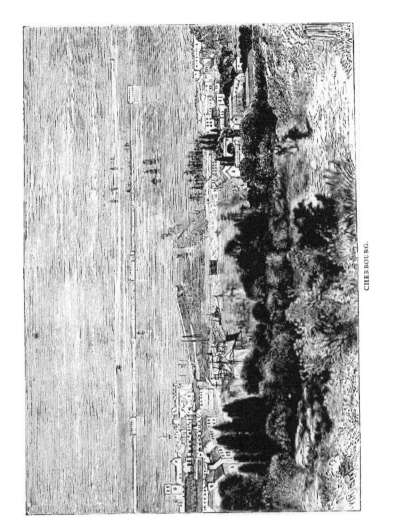

CHERBOURG.

hand-grenades point-blank on their decks and down the open hatchways; but the most destructive missiles were the anchor-balls fired by the artillery.

These were filled with powder, saltpetre, sulphur, resin, and turpentine, and had a grappling-hook, which caught alike the rigging of a ship or the roof of a house; and ere long these sheeted the whole place with flames. £800,000 worth of property was destroyed; and with the loss of only twelve men, who were slain by one random shot from the castle of St. Malo. The Duke of Marlborough, on receiving information that an overwhelming force was gathering to attack him, deemed it prudent to return to Cancalle Bay and re-embark; and after threatening Havre, and actually having all the Guards in the flat-bottomed boats to land amid a wild tempest, he returned to St Helen's on the 30th of June.

But the service of the army was not yet over. It was dispatched to France a second time, under Lieutenant-General Bligh, and the fleet came to anchor in Cherbourg Roads on the 7th of August. The landing was again successful, the troops being quite unopposed, and the fine basin of Cherbourg was completely destroyed. Designed by Vauban, it was noble and spacious. Two piers, one of a thousand, the other five hundred feet in length, had been built; and there were outer and inner basins large enough to contain line-of-battle ships, and closed by gates each forty-two feet in width.

To destroy these, General Bligh had 1,500 soldiers at work making blasts, and so skilful were they in the work of destruction, that the labour of thirty years and the expense of £1,200,000 sterling perished in a few days. All the bastions along the shore, from Fort Querqueville to the Isle Pelee were also blown up; 166 pieces of cannon were dismounted or flung into the sea, while two mortars and twenty-two beautiful guns of polished brass were put on board the flag-ship. Two ships were taken, and eighteen filled with stones were sunk in the harbour, while by beat of drum 44,000 *livres* were levied on the inhabitants. Ruin and desolation reigned around Cherbourg before the Count de Raymond could muster forces to oppose us, as France had then two armies in Germany.

By the 17th of August, after all this havoc, our troops were all on board and the whole armament ready for sea, exulting in having destroyed what was styled in the prints of the time "that most galling thorn in the side of British commerce," our loss being only Captain Lindsay, of the Scots Greys, twenty-four others killed, and about thirty wounded in several of the skirmishes that occurred with out-parties of the enemy.

On the 19th of August the armament came to anchor in Portland Roads. The colours and brass guns taken at Cherbourg were exhibited in Hyde Park, and conveyed through the streets in triumph to the Tower, as the spoil of humbled France, whose time of vengeance was soon to come, when the Ministry, on the 29th of the same month, resolved to pay her another filibustering visit—for these most injudicious and ill-planned descents on the French coast, were little better than such—and on the 1st day of September, once more the fleet, with the army on board reduced to 6,000 men, appeared off St. Malo, and came to anchor in the bay of St. Lunaire, where the whole forces disembarked and encamped at a short distance from the shore. General Bligh at once dispatched 500 grenadiers to the small town of St. Briac, where they burned twenty vessels and destroyed some batteries.

A Council of War was held, when the admiral stated the impossibility of co-operating against the strong and beautiful castle of St. Malo, which is flanked with towers, that with four great bastions and the ramparts around the town render it a place of strength, while on the north it is quite inaccessible.

All attempts on it were therefore abandoned; and as there was no safe anchorage in St. Lunaire Bay, the ships removed to that of St. Cas, a few leagues to the westward, while it was resolved to march the troops into the interior, taking care to proceed in such a manner as to keep communication with the fleet open. A poor French shepherd was compelled to act as a guide on this occasion, and purposely misled the Coldstream Guards, who were somewhat in advance. For this Colonel (afterwards General) Vernon ordered him to be hanged. Colonel Mackinnon says:

> That officer, used to relate that he never witnessed a more affecting sight than the efforts made by the shepherd's dog to interrupt the men as they proceeded to put the rope round his master's neck.

The general added:

> But, John Bull is a poor creature when it comes to a pinch. I would not find it in my heart to put the stubborn fellow to death for his patriotism, and after well frightening him, and almost breaking his heart by threatening to have his dog destroyed, I let him go, and the faithful creature with him.

Lieutenant-General Bligh marched on the 8th of September for St. Guildo, nine miles distant; and next day some armed peasantry, with shouts of "St. Malo for Bretagne!" by a fire from behind some hedges and houses, seriously annoyed the troops while crossing a stream at low water. The general sent a message by the *curé* of the village, intimating that unless "they desisted their houses would be reduced to ashes."

No regard being paid to this intimation, they were set on fire as soon as the troops had formed their camp, about two miles beyond the village. On reaching Matignon, two battalions of the French line were discovered, and dislodged by the artillery. When General Bligh, who had made somewhat of a circular movement, was encamped three miles from the bay of St. Cas, he was informed that the Duke d'Aiguillon, Lieutenant-General of Bretagne under the Duke de Penthièvre, at the head of twelve battalions of infantry, six squadrons of horse, two regiments of militia, with eight mortars and two pieces of cannon, was within five miles of him, and meant next day to avenge the destruction which had ensued at St. Malo and Cherbourg.

A Council of War was held, and it was resolved that the British troops should embark early that evening; however, by delays, they did not reach the beach until past nine next morning.

The bay of St. Cas was covered by an entrenchment which the enemy had thrown up to prevent or oppose any disembarkation; and on the outside of this work there was a range of sandhills which could have served as a cover for the enemy, and whence they might have annoyed the troops in reembarking. For this reason, a proposal was made to the general that the embarkation should take place on the fair open beach between St. Cas and St. Guildo; but the advice was rejected, and indeed the whole operations of the little army savoured of rashness and blind security. Had the troops decamped quietly in the night, in all probability they would have reached the beach before the French had any idea that they were in motion; and in that case the whole might have got on board without interruption.

But instead of proceeding thus cautiously, Bligh ordered all his drums to beat at two in the morning as if he intended to apprise the enemy, whose drums instantly responded; but so great were the delays and interruptions on the short march, that the beach was not reached, as we have said, till nine o'clock, and by that time the French were in possession of an eminence which fully commanded it, and from where their ten pieces of cannon and eight mortars opened a fire with the most disastrous precision, under an officer named M. de

Villepatour.

Even then the embarkation might have been successfully achieved, had the transports lain near the shore and received the men as fast as the boats could take them off, without distinction; but many of the ships were anchored at a great distance, and every boat, with a punctilio absurd in such an emergency, carried the men rigidly to the transport to which they belonged, and by this, much time was lost. Smollett records that had all the cutters and small craft belonging to the fleet been properly occupied in this service, the terrible disasters of the day could not have occurred.

The battery on the eminence fired round shot and grape alike on the troops and on the boats, and many of the latter were dashed to pieces and sunk with all on board. It is related that little Prince Edward, afterwards Duke of York (brother of George III.), then a youth serving on board Lord Howe's ship, attempted to go on shore to assist in bringing off the troops, as he had become maddened by the scene of helpless slaughter presented along the whole line of beach. He was caught dropping from a porthole into a boat alongside, when he was stopped by the commodore from going on a service so desperate.

The battalions of the Duke d'Aiguillon now began to march down the hills, partly concealed by a hollow way on the British left, with the intention of gaining a wood, where they might form and extend themselves along the British rear; but in their descent, they suffered extremely from the cannon and mortars of the shipping, which made great havoc in their ranks, and threw them into dire confusion. Their line of march for a time was staggered; then, deploying over a hill to their left, they advanced along a hollow way, whence they suddenly rushed, full of fury and vengeance, to the attack.

By this time the greater part of the British troops, including the Coldstream Guards, had got on board; but the grenadiers of the Guards and half of the 1st Regiment of Guards, in all about 1,500 men, under Major-General Dury, remained to cover the embarkation, but having fired away all their ammunition, they found themselves placed between the sea on one side and the overwhelming masses of the Duke d'Aiguillon on the other, without a cartridge in their pouches.

General Dury, a brave and resolute officer, formed them in grand division squares of two companies each, and in this order they prepared, with the bayonet alone, to meet the great force that was rushing against them.

Under a dreadful fire of cannon and musketry, those splendid

English guardsmen stood for two hours and a half, according to the French account (for only five minutes according to Smollett), unaided by sea or land.

General Dury was severely wounded, and, rushing into the sea, perished in attempting to reach a boat.

An officer who was present says:

> At length the Guards gave way. The grenadiers soon followed; and as there was no place of retreat for them in an enemy's country, most of them plunged into the sea and endeavoured to swim to the ships; several were killed in the water, and all who could not swim were drowned. At one o'clock the firing ceased, and the French sang '*Te Deum.*'"

On an insulated rock one little band stood shoulder to shoulder, and surrendered at discretion. There fell Sir John Armytage, Baronet, of Kirklees, and with him more than one thousand chosen officers and men. Captain Schomberg, in his *Chronology*, reduces the number to 822; but among the slain were many officers who belonged to other regiments than the Guards, and who disdained to embark while a private remained on the beach.

Of the Guards there were killed Captains Walker and Rolt, and Ensign Cox; and there were taken Lord Frederick Cavendish, Lieutenant-Colonels Pearson and Lambert, Captains Dickens, Hyde, and Pownal, and Ensign Sir Alexander Gilmour, of Craigmillar, with 39 other officers and 800 men, who were treated with great humanity by the Bretons, whose conduct deserves every praise, as it cannot be denied that during their stay in the country the British had been guilty of great excesses.

The French account of St. Cas says that:

> Great numbers were killed while endeavouring to reembark. Three boats full of their soldiers were sunk; and many more were slain in the boats on their way to the fleet. About 1,900 were left on shore 3 among them were several officers of distinction. We have taken upwards of 600 men and 39 officers, some of whom are of the best families in England. This body of troops is totally destroyed.

Sir William Boothby, of the grenadiers, swam two miles before he was picked up. He died a major-general, in 1797.

After the action was over, some civilities by flag of truce passed between the Duke d'Aiguillon and the British commanders, who were favoured with a list of the prisoners, among whom were four captains of the Royal Navy. Some other matters being adjusted, Commodore Howe returned with the fleet to Spithead, where the troops who survived this most disastrous encounter (which so closely resembled that of Camaret Bay, in 1694) were disembarked at Cowes.

And so, ended the last of those most injudicious descents upon the coast of France; but for many weeks after, triangular beavers bound with gold or white braid, powdered wigs, &c., and red-coated corpses, gashed and mutilated by shot, and others otherwise disfigured by fish, after being the sport of the waves, continued to be tossed by them on the rocks of St. Malo, the sands of St. Cas, and the bluffs of Cape Frehel.

Disaster in the Bay of St. Cas

Ticonderoga, 1758

Amid the most beautiful scenery on the western shore of Lake Champlain stand the now lonely and grass-covered, ruins of the once great fort of Ticonderoga, whose trenches have been so often traced in blood during the French, British, American, and Indian conflicts in the State of New York. The remains are still considerable, the stone walls being in some places thirty feet high, (as at 1892). They are situated on a green eminence, just north of the outlet into Lake Champlain from Lake George, which was named by the Indians of old the Horican, by the Pilgrim Fathers the Lake of Sacrament; for, charmed by the limpid purity of the water and the sylvan beauty of the scenery, it had been selected by them, and more especially by the Jesuits, as a place for procuring the element of baptism.

Mount Defiance lies about a mile south of the fort, and Mount Independence about half a mile distant, on the opposite side of the lake, around which are wooded hills that in some places rise to a thousand feet in height.

During the progress of the Colonial War with France, about the disputed boundaries, in the summer of 1758, Lieutenant-General (afterwards Lord) Amherst proceeded with the expedition against Cape Breton; and the 42nd Highlanders, with other troops, under Major-General Abercrombie, were detached to attack Ticonderoga, which was strongly fortified and garrisoned.

In addition to the Black Watch, or *Freicudan Dhu,* as they loved to style themselves, several other Highland regiments, whose names will occur from time to time, had now been added to the British Army, and it was the best public service of the great Pitt when he first rallied round the British throne the soldiers of those warlike clans who had been so long the foes of the House of Hanover, he said:

I sought for merit wherever it was to be found, it is my boast that I was the first minister who looked for it and found it among the mountains of the north. I called it forth, and drew into your service a hardy and intrepid race of men, who, when left by your jealousy, became a prey to the artifice of your enemies; and who, in the war before the last, had well nigh overturned the state. These men in the last war were brought to combat by your side; they served with fidelity, as they fought with honour, and conquered for you in every part of the world.

At this period the officers of the Highland regiments wore a narrow gold braiding round their jackets; but epaulettes were not as yet adopted, and all other lace was laid aside, to render them less conspicuous to the French-Canadian riflemen. The sergeants laced their coats with silver, and still carried their native weapon, the terrible Lochaber axe, the head of which was fitted for hewing, hooking, or spearing an enemy. Many of the officers and men of these corps had, but twelve years ago, drawn their swords for the House of Stuart.

The troops under General Abercrombie consisted of the 27th, or Inniskilling; the 42nd Highlanders, 44th, 46th, 55th, the first battalion of the Royal American (now 60th Rifles), Colonel Gage's Light Infantry, and eight battalions of Provincials. In all he had 15,391 men, who were embarked, with their artillery and stores, on board 900 *batteaux* and 135 whale-boats, the guns to cover the landing being mounted on rafts. The strongest regiment under his orders was the Black Watch, to which three additional companies, under the son of Lord George Murray, Stewart of Urrard, and Stirling of Ardoch, had just been added, making up its strength to 1,300 bayonets.

These forces sailed down Lake Champlain on the 5th of July, and landed near the extremity of that beautiful sheet of water on the following day, and began their march through a thickly-wooded country, in four columns, upon Ticonderoga; but their guides mistook the route through the then trackless forests, and caused the greatest confusion, the columns being broken by unexpectedly falling upon each other among the trees. Lord Howe, of the 55th, being advanced at the head of the right-centre column, fell suddenly on a French detachment which had also lost its way, and some warm bush-fighting ensued. The enemy was driven in, with the loss of 300 killed and 150 taken; but in this encounter Viscount Howe was killed among the first, and his loss was deeply regretted by the whole army.

The troops suffered severely owing to the nature of the ground

ATTACK ON THE TICONDEROGA FORT

they had to traverse, having literally to force their way through a dense primeval forest; and, to make matters worse, provisions became scarce, as many had thrown away their rations to lighten the weight they had to carry.

On the forenoon of the 7th, Lieutenant-Colonel Bradstreet, with the 44th Regiment, six companies of the Royal Americans, and a body of Rangers and Provincials, advanced to take possession of a sawmill within two miles of Ticonderoga; into which a body of the enemy retired, after firing the mill and breaking down a bridge that led thereto. The advanced pickets were now in sight of the fort, which was built in 1756, and had all the advantages that nature and art could give it, being girt on three sides by water, which is full of rocks, and partly on the fourth by a deep swamp; and where the latter failed the French garrison had dug a trench, and thrown up a breastwork nine feet in height, and the approach to it was rendered difficult by felled trees, having their branches turned outward.

The prisoners taken in the forest were unanimous in stating that the garrison consisted of eight battalions, and some Canadians and Colonial troops; and that a reinforcement of 3,000 Canadians, besides Indians, was expected, under the command of M. de Levy, who was to have made a, diversion on the side of the Mohawk river, but, upon receiving tidings of our approach, had been recalled. It was thought advisable to make an attack at once, as this fort barred the way to Crown Point, and had to be taken before our troops could march there.

Great difficulty being experienced in getting the artillery to the front, and Mr. Clark, the engineer, an officer of the 27th Regiment, having reported that the works might be carried by storm, Major-General Abercrombie resolved to hazard the attempt without cannon.

The general wrote in his dispatch:

Upon his, Mr. Clark's, return, and favourable report of the practicability of carrying these works before they were finished, it was agreed to storm them that very day. Accordingly, the Rangers, light infantry, and the right wing of the Provincials were ordered immediately to march and post themselves in a line out of cannon-shot of the intrenchments; the right extending to Lake George, and their left to Lake Champlain, in order that the regular troops destined for the attack of the intrenchment might form on their rear. The pickets were to begin the attack, seconded by the grenadiers, and they by the battalions; the

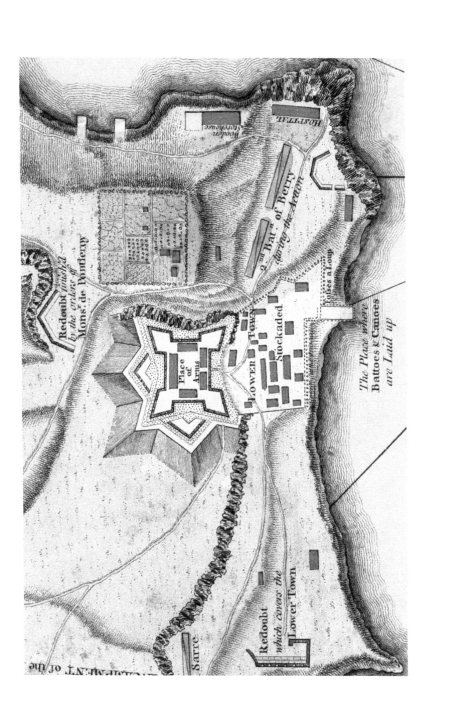

Modern Storehouse

HOSPITAL

Redoubt finished by the orders of Mons.r de Pontleroy

2.nd Bat.n of Berry during the Action

Fort a Loup

The Place where Battoes & Canoes are laid up

Place of Arms

LOWER TOWN

Stockaded

Redoubt which covers the Lower Town

Sarre

...MENT of the

whole were ordered to march up briskly, rush upon the enemy's fire, and not give theirs till they were within the breastwork.

The 42nd Highlanders were to form the reserve of the attacking force.

The troops advanced with incredible ardour, making a fierce rush at the works, which proved to be infinitely stronger than the engineer had reported; for more than 100 yards before the nine-feet breastwork, over which the French were pouring in security a deadly fire of musketry and swivel guns, they had covered the whole ground with an abattis of trees, logs, stumps, and brushwood, amid which the stormers got helplessly entangled, and were shot down in heaps. Amid that abattis officers and men fell in hundreds. Struggling on at the head of their men. Colonel Donaldson and Major Proby, of the 55th, were killed on the very summit of the trench. Regiment after regiment rushed on, but only to lose in killed or wounded half its number ere it reached the breastwork, to be hurled back breathless and in disorder.

An officer of the Rangers writes:

About three o'clock, just as the regulars were retreating, out regiment and those of the left threw in a very heavy fire, intending to retire likewise very soon, and indeed some had already began to retreat, which it is supposed the enemy observed, for they hoisted English colours, clubbed their arms, showed themselves on their breastwork, and tauntingly beckoned us to come up. On this the whole advanced briskly; but coming within fifteen or twenty yards of the enemy, the latter struck their colours, and threw in upon us a most terrible and heavy fire, such as we had not yet experienced, which killed multitudes, and obliged us to retire, to recover ourselves from the disorder into which we were thrown.

When the stormers began to fall back, the Royal Highlanders, infuriated by the slaughter they witnessed, the branches and confusion of the abattis full of dead and dying men, amid whom the showers of lead were still falling, broke from their position in the reserve, and, with cries of vengeance, advanced to the attack, as an officer of the 55th described it, without orders, "and like roaring lions breaking from their chains."

They cut a passage through the fallen trees by their claymores, sprang through the trench, and made a gallant effort to carry the

Montcalm at the victory of Ticonderoga

breastwork by storm; the *Regimental Record* says:

> Climbing on one another's shoulders, and placing their feet in holes made in the face of the works with their swords and bayonets, no ladders having been provided.

Captain John Campbell and a few men succeeded in getting up, and rushed sword in hand, in the old Highland fashion, at the foe; but they were speedily overpowered and shot down. After a succession of these gallant but unavailing efforts had been continued for several hours, and most serious loss had been sustained in killed and wounded, General Abercrombie ordered the whole to retreat; but so exasperated were the Highlanders by the slaughter of so many comrades and kinsmen, that the order had to be given to them three times before they would obey it, and they were consequently the last to withdraw from this unequal contest.

The British retired to their camp on the south of Lake George, and the French did not venture to pursue.

General Abercrombie reported the loss in killed, wounded, and missing in his entire force at 1,944 of all ranks; of these 119 were officers. The engineer whose fatal report led to the attack was among the first killed.

On no regiment did the slaughter fall so heavily as on the Black Watch, which had a ghastly roll of 647 killed and wounded, of whom 26 were officers belonging to some of the best families in the Highlands.

When the tidings of Ticonderoga, months afterwards, were carried, with many an exaggeration doubtless, to the remote glens and fastnesses of the clans, a strong sentiment of vengeance was excited among the Highlanders; and so many recruits poured in for the regiment, that not only were all the casualties speedily replaced, but the surplus was found to be so numerous that the king immediately issued letters of service to form them into a second battalion for the 42nd Foot, and such it continued to be until 1786, when it was constituted the 73rd Highlanders, and is now called the Perthshire Regiment.

Censure always attends miscarriage, and it did not spare the character of General Abercrombie, whose attack was denounced as rash, and his retreat as timidity. Smollett says:

> How far he acquitted himself in the duty of a general, we shall not attempt to determine; but if he could depend upon the courage and discipline of his forces, he surely had nothing to

fear after the action from the attempts of the enemy, to whom he would have been superior in number, even though they had been joined by the expected reinforcement. He might, therefore, have remained on the spot, to execute some other enterprise when he should be reinforced in his turn.

CAPE BRETON.

Cape Breton, 1758

We left General Amherst proceeding with his troops against Cape Breton. Scenes of great importance were now about to be acted in North America, where, exclusive of the fleet and marines, our Government had assembled 50,000 men, 22,000 of whom were our regular infantry of the Line. The Earl of Loudon having returned to Scotland, the command of these troops devolved on Major-General Abercrombie; but as the objects of operation were various, the forces were divided into three columns, under three different leaders.

About 12,000 were destined to undertake the siege and reduction of Louisbourg, on the island of Cape Breton.

The general reserved some 16,000 for the reduction of the fort at Crown Point; while 8,000, under Brigadier-General John Forbes, were detailed for the conquest of Fort Duquesne, near the Ohio; and a considerable garrison was left at Annapolis, in Nova Scotia. The reduction of Louisbourg, being an object of immediate consideration, was undertaken with the utmost dispatch.

Major-General Amherst, on being joined by Admiral Boscawen, embarked his column at Halifax, on the 28th of May, when the whole fleet, consisting of 157 sail, put to sea. These two officers were on board the *Namur*, 90 guns; Sir Charles Hardy, Rear-Admiral of the White, had his flag flying on board the *Royal William*, 84 guns; and Commodore Philip Darell had the *Princess Amelia*, 80 guns. There were twenty-five sail of the line, eighteen frigates, and many bomb-ketches and fireships.

The troops were the 1st Royal Scots, 15th, 17th, 22nd, 28th, 35th, 40th, 45th, 47th, 58th, two battalions of the 60th, or Royal Americans, the old 78th, or Fraser Highlanders, and the New England Rangers. The brigadiers were Lawrence, Monkton, Whitmore, and the gallant James Wolfe, whom we last heard of at Culloden, as major of the 20th

Foot.

The armament came to anchor in Gabarus Bay, seven miles from Louisbourg, then an important and flourishing city, which had been captured by our fleet and forces in 1745, but was restored to France by the Treaty of Aix-la-Chapelle. The garrison, under the Chevalier de Drucourt, consisted of 2,500 regular infantry, 600 militia, and 400 Canadians and Indians. Six ships of the line and five frigates protected the harbour, which is more than half a mile from east to west in breadth, and six miles in length.

The ruins of Louisbourg are now, (1892), covered by turf and moss, and a few fishermen's huts alone mark the site of its great square and fortifications. On the north side of the former, while possessed by the French, stood the governor's house and the church. The other three sides were occupied by bomb-proof barracks, in which, on the appearance of our ships, the women and children were immediately secured; and three of the frigates were sunk at the harbour's mouth to bar entrance.

The fleet was six days off the coast—days of fog, wind, and a heavy surf bursting on the shore—before landing was attempted; but on the 8th of June the violence of the weather abated, and the troops left the fleet in three divisions. That on the left, which was destined for the real attack, was commanded by Wolfe, and was composed of the flank companies of the army, with the Fraser Highlanders, whose equipment is described by General Stewart as consisting of:

A musket and broadsword, to which many of the soldiers added the dirk at their own expense, and a purse of badger's skin. The bonnet was raised or cocked on one side, inclining down to the right ear, over which were placed two or more black feathers.

Before daybreak the troops were all in the boats; the centre division was led by Brigadier Lawrence, the right by Brigadier Whitmore. The *London Gazette* says:

The enemy acted very wisely, they did not throw away a shot till the boats were close inshore, and then directed the whole fire of their cannon and musketry upon them. The surf was so great that a place could hardly be found to get a boat on shore. Notwithstanding the fire of the enemy and the violence of the surf, Brigadier Wolfe pursued his point, and landed just at the left of the cove, took post, attacked the enemy, and forced them to retreat. Many boats overset, several were broke to pieces, and

20TH REGIMENT OF FOOT

all the men jumped into the water to get on shore.

The place where the flankers and Highlanders landed was occupied by 2,000 French infantry, under Colonel St. Julien, intrenched behind a work armed with eight pieces of cannon and ten swivel-guns. The fire of the latter knocked many of the boats—fully one hundred of them—to pieces; thus, numbers of men were killed or drowned before they could reach the shore.

As they struggled through the surf, Captain Baillie and Lieutenant Cuthbert, of the Highlanders, Lieutenant Nicholson, of Amherst's Regiment, and thirty-eight men, were killed, and fifty-nine of all ranks wounded:

> But nothing could stop our troops when led by such a general. Some of the light infantry and Highlanders got first ashore, and drove all before them. The rest followed, and being encouraged by the example of their heroic commander, soon pursued the enemy to the distance of two miles, when they were checked by a cannonade from the town.

The latter enabled the general to prove the range of the enemy's guns, and to judge of the exact distance at which he might make his camp for the investment. The regiments marched to the various points assigned, and lay all night on their arms; but as the wind blew a gale, nothing could be obtained from the fleet. In the pursuit about seventy prisoners were taken; a French officer, several privates, and an Indian chief were killed. The latter had at his neck a crucifix and medal, representing the King of France in a Roman dress, shaking hands with an Indian, and the legend "*Honor et Virtus.*"

Seventeen pieces of cannon, two mortars, and fourteen swivels were taken after St. Julien was routed.

For a few days the offensive operations proceeded very slowly. The continued violence of the weather retarded the landing of the stores and provisions, and the nature of the ground, which in some places was very rocky, and in others swampy, presented many serious obstacles.

On the 11th the six-pound field-pieces were brought on shore by the artillery, who numbered 300 men; and three days after a squadron of the fleet, under Sir Charles Hardy, was fairly blown out to sea. On the 19th a French frigate, *L'Echo,* 32 guns, which had crept out of the harbour in the night, intending to reach Quebec, was taken by His Majesty's ships *Juno* and *Scarborough.* On board of her were found Madame de Drucourt and many other ladies, with all their plate, jewels, and most valuable effects.

By the 24th Colonel Bastide, the chief engineer, had thirteen twenty-four-pounders and seven eighteen-pounders in position against the place. The first operation had been to secure a point called the Lighthouse Battery, the guns from which could play on the ships and on the batteries on the opposite side of the harbour. This duty was assigned to Wolfe, who executed it with his usual vigour and activity, at the head of the flank companies and Highlanders, with very small loss. On the 25th the fire from this post silenced the island battery immediately opposite. An incessant cannonade was, however, kept up from the other batteries and shipping of the enemy. On the 9th of July the latter made a furious sortie in the night, on the brigade of Lawrence, General Amherst says:

> And though drunk, I am afraid they rather surprised a company of grenadiers of Forbeses, commanded by Lord Dundonald, posted in a *flèche* on the right.

In repulsing them, William seventh Earl of Dundonald was killed, and there were twenty-one other casualties. Captain the Chevalier de Chauvelin, who led the French, was also killed, with seventeen of his men.

On the 16th, Wolfe pushed forward some grenadiers and Highlanders, and took possession of the hills in front of the Barasay Battery, where a lodgement was made, despite the guns of the town and ships. One of the latter, a line-of-battle ship, caught fire on the 21st, and blew up. Her burning brands ignited other two, which burned to the water-edge, and these events nearly decided the fate of Louisbourg. The batteries there were almost silenced, and the fortifications shattered to the ground; but to effect the capture of the harbour one decisive blow yet remained to be struck. For this purpose, the admiral sent 600 seamen in boats, with orders to take or burn two ships of the line that remained, resolving, if they succeeded, to send in some of his larger vessels to bombard the town from the harbour.

This enterprise was most gallantly executed by Captain (afterwards Admiral Sir John) Laforey, and Captain George Balfour, an officer who lived till 1794. They succeeded in cutting-out *Le Bienfaisent* and *La Prudente*, two sixty-four-gun ships. While the boats' crews were about this desperate service, General Amherst reports:

> I ordered all the batteries at night to fire into the enemy's works

as much as possible, to keep their attention to the land. The miners and workmen went on very well with the approaches to the covered way, though they had a continued and very smart fire from it, and grape shot and all sorts of old iron from the guns on the ramparts. We continued our firing without ceasing. The boats got to the ships at one in the morning, and took them both. They were obliged to burn the *Prudente*, as she was aground; and they towed off the *Bienfaisent* to the north-east harbour.

For this gallant service Captains Balfour and Laforey were posted, and Lieutenants Affleck and Bickerston were made masters and commanders. Both in future years were knighted, and died admirals of the Royal Navy.

Six ships were to have been sent in next day to bombard Louisbourg from the water, when articles of capitulation arrived from the Chevalier de Drucourt, as the works were ruined, and out of fifty-two pieces of cannon on the walls, no less than forty were now broken, dismounted, or otherwise unserviceable.

The terms agreed upon were that the garrison should become prisoners of war; that all artillery and warlike stores should be delivered to His Britannic Majesty's troops; that all merchants and inhabitants should be conveyed to French soil in British ships; and the prisoners should be transported to England, until exchanged.

Louisbourg was surrendered on the 26th of July, and the gate called Porte Dauphine was given up to the troops of General Amherst Next day Andrew Lord Rollo of Duncrub, colonel of infantry, marched in and took formal possession of the town, where the garrison was drawn up under arms, with colours flying. The latter, to the number of eleven, with all the arms and stores, were surrendered.

There were here taken twenty-four companies of marines, of the usual garrison, and two of artillery; the 2nd battalion of the *Voluntaires Etrangers de Clermont-Prince*; a battalion of the Regiment of Artois, or 31st of the Line; another of Cambise, 62nd of the Line; another of Bourgoyne, 43rd of the Line: the total number of prisoners being 5,637 men and officers, with 18 mortars, 120 pieces of cannon, and 7,500 stand of arms.

Save Lord Dundonald, no officer of rank was killed, and our total losses were 525 in all. Eleven French ships of war, mounting in all 498 guns, were sunk, burnt, or taken.

Fronteniac and Duquesne, 1758

To further complete the subjugation of the French territories in America, General Abercrombie had detached Lieutenant-Colonel Bradstreet, with a body of 3,000 infantry, chiefly Provincials, to execute a plan which this officer had conceived against Caradaqui, or Fort Fronteniac, which was situated on the north side of the river of St. Lawrence, just where it takes its origin from the Lake of Ontario.

According to the colonel's dispatch, it was a square fort, measuring about a hundred yards each way, armed with sixty pieces of cannon and sixteen mortars; and garrisoned by 110 Frenchmen and a body of Indians.

He landed his troops at the point of land on which the fort was built, in the dusk of the evening of the 25th of August, about one mile distant from the fort, where they were protected from its cannon by a rising eminence.

Next morning, he got his guns into position at 500 yards' distance from the fort, and opened fire upon it; but their metal seemed too light to affect the solid wall or rampart of the place, which was ten feet-high. Some shells were thrown which did considerable damage, and Colonel Bradstreet resolved to draw nearer to the fort that night. With this view he took possession of an old intrenchment, which had been formerly made as a species of outwork to the fort itself; and a party of his troops stole silently into it in the dark.

As some addition to the work was found necessary, the clink of the pickaxes and shovels used by his men was heard in the fort; a fire of cannon and small-arms was opened on the place; but as it was done at random, no man was killed, and only five were wounded. By sunrise this advanced party was under cover, and having got the true elevation with their mortars, they threw in shells, every one of which did execution; and by their cannon soon silenced those in the fort, where the French colours were pulled down in token of surrender.

Immediately on this the Indians issued forth, and fled with yells into the nearest forest; while a large brig, which they had captured from us at Oswego, slipped her cable, in order to sail for Niagara.

Colonel Bradstreet now turned his guns on her; several of the men on board were killed, the rest fled in their boats, and left the brig together with a schooner adrift. The terms given to the little garrison in the fort were that they were to retain their money and other property, but to be prisoners of war.

Colonel Bradstreet demolished the walls of the fort, destroyed all the stores by fire, and seven vessels in the harbour by the same means, and brought away all the cannon and small-arms. The next enterprise of this eventful year was one of greater magnitude, being that undertaken against Fort Duquesne, which stood on a point of land at the confluence of the Alleghany and Monongahela Rivers, and on the slope of a green eminence.

The troops detailed for this expedition consisted of 1,284 men of Montgomery's Highlanders, or the old 77th Foot, raised by Major Montgomery, of the house of Eglinton, in January 1757, and disbanded in America at the conclusion of the war; 554 of the 60th Royal Americans, and 4,400 Provincials—in all 6,238 men, with 1,000 wagoners, wood-cutters, and other camp-followers.

The whole were commanded by Brigadier-General Forbes, of Pittencrief, in the county of Fife, who had served in the Scots Greys and on the staff during the wars in Germany. He had been lastly serving under the Duke of Cumberland, in Flanders, when he was ordered to America, the *Westminster Journal* has it as:

> Where, as by a steady pursuit of well-concerted measures, he, in defiance of disease and numberless obstructions, brought to a happy issue a remarkable expedition, and made his own life a willing sacrifice to what he valued more—the interest of his king and country.

With his little army. General Forbes began his march in the beginning of July, from Philadelphia, for the banks of the Ohio, through a vast tract of wild country, then but very little known, destitute of military roads, and where the paths, such as they were, traversed steep mountains, great morasses, and dense old forests, that in some places were almost impenetrable. Smollett says:

> It was not without the most incredible exertions of industry,

that he procured provisions and carriages for this expedition, forming new roads as he marched, extending scouting parties, securing camps, and surmounting innumerable difficulties in his tedious route.

Having brought the main body of his forces as far as Ray's Town, at the distance of ninety miles from Fort Duquesne, he sent forward Colonel Bouquet, with 2,000 men, chiefly Highlanders, to a place called Loyal Henning. This officer in turn detached 838 men of Montgomery's regiment to reconnoitre the fort and its outworks.

These were commanded by Major James Grant, of Ballindalloch, who died a general, a brave but exceedingly rash officer. When he came within eight miles of the fort, he sent forward a subaltern with a few Indians to reconnoitre. These men lay on a hill near it all night, and saw many Indians in canoes paddling across the Ohio to join the enemy.

Before these scouts could return. Major Grant had again begun his march, and came within two miles of the fort, where he received the report of the subaltern. He now halted, left his baggage under a guard, and proposed that night to attack an encampment which the scouts alleged to be outside and in front of the fort. For this purpose, and to distinguish his men, he ordered them to wear white shirts over their uniforms—a useless precaution, as they were all in the kilt, and the attack was to be made with the claymore.

Finding the alleged camp did not exist, when the dawn drew near, he marched steadily against Fort Duquesne, with all his pipes playing and drums beating, as if he was about to enter a friendly town.

The French stood instantly to their arms; but instead of opening a fire upon the advancing Highlanders, they threw their gates open, and, accompanied by more than a thousand Indian warriors, armed with musket, knife, and tomahawk, yelling like so many fiends, they flung themselves like a torrent upon the soldiers of Grant, but were immediately repulsed.

General Stuart says:

The major ordered his men to advance sword in hand. The enemy fled on the first charge, and rushed into the woods, where they spread themselves; being afterwards joined by a body of Indians, they rallied, and surrounded the detachment on all sides.

Being themselves concealed by a thick foliage, their heavy and

WASHINGTON RAISING THE BRITISH FLAG AT FORT DUQUESNE

destructive fire could not be returned with any effect. Major Grant was taken in an attempt to force his way into the wood where the fire was thickest. On losing their commander, and so many officers being killed and wounded, the troops dispersed. About 150 of the Highlanders got back to Loyal Henning.

The bayonet, the axe, and the scalping-knife speedily disposed of the rest. The French infamously gave a premium for every scalp brought them; and we are told that when Lord Rollo in that year took possession of the island of St. John, in the Gulf of St. Lawrence, he found in the governor's quarters a vast number of them stored up like trophies.

Of Montgomery's regiment, there fell before Fort Duquesne Captains Munro and Macdonald, and Lieutenants W. Mackenzie, R. Mackenzie, A. Mackenzie, and two Macdonalds. Three other officers of the 60th and some of the Provincials were slain, while nineteen were taken prisoners with Grant.

This check, however, did not dispirit General Forbes, who pushed forward with fresh expedition, and soon came before Fort Duquesne. There the garrison, dreading a siege, abandoned it as soon as his troops appeared, and fled down the River Ohio to their settlements on the Mississippi.

This was on the 24th of November, 1758, and next day it was in possession of the British. Brigadier Forbes, having fully repaired it, changed its name from Duquesne to Pittsburg, secured it with a garrison of Provincial troops, and concluded treaties of alliance and friendship with the Indian tribes around it.

On the then bleak point, where the solitary stockaded fort looked down on the lonely waters of the Ohio, there now stands the town of Pittsburg, second only in importance to Philadelphia, with its flourishing manufactures, and its spires and chimneys overhung by a perpetual cloud of black smoke, as the surrounding country is rich in bituminous coal.

General Forbes, soon after capturing the fort, returned to Philadelphia:

Where he died, universally lamented and respected, as one of the most accomplished and able officers then in America.

TROIS RIVIÈRES

Before turning to the war being waged elsewhere against France,

157

TROIS RIVIÈRES.

we may relate the following episode of the strife in America.

Midway between Montreal and Quebec, on the north side of the river St. Lawrence, and about 200 miles from Crown Point, stands the city of Trois Rivières, which was then fortified. Its name was derived from the circumstance that the entrance into the river St. Maurice, at the confluence with the St. Lawrence, is separated by two islands, which thus form three channels.

Opposite to this place was the village of St. François, in which 300 well-armed Indians had taken up their residence, and whence they made hostile and predatory incursions on all sides. As it was necessary to cut them off, General Amherst issued the following order to Major Rogers, a famous officer of Provincials, who accomplished his purpose by means so very different to the common practice that Simes says in his *Military Guide:*

> I cannot help paying a compliment to his abilities, for carrying on a war against this barbarous people, of which art we were totally ignorant when General Braddock, at the beginning of our late dispute with the French, led on his troops to unthought-of destruction.

Sir Jeffery Amherst's orders to the major ran thus, and they read unpleasantly like King William's doubly-signed warrant for the infamous Massacre of Glencoe:—

> Sir,—You are this night to set out with the detachment as ordered yesterday (*viz.*, of 200 men), and proceed to Mississquey Bay, from whence you will march and attack the enemy's settlements on the south side of the River St. Lawrence, in such a manner as you shall judge most effectual to disgrace the enemy, and for the success and honour of His Majesty's arms.
>
> Remember the barbarities that have been committed by the enemy's Indian scoundrels, on every occasion when they had an opportunity of showing their infamous cruelties on the king's subjects, which they have done without mercy. Take your revenge; but do not forget that though these villains have dastardly and promiscuously murdered the women and children of all ages, it is my orders that no women or children be killed or hurt
>
> When you have executed your intended service, you will re-

159

turn with your detachment to camp, or join me wherever the army may be.

Yours, &c.,   Jeff. Amherst.

Camp at Crown Point, Sept. 13, 1759

The difference between the above order and that of William is, that the latter made no exception in favour of either women or children.

The major, with 200 men, chiefly of the 1st Royal Scots, sailed in *batteaux* down Lake Champlain. On the fifth day after his departure, by the explosion of a keg of gunpowder. Captain Williams, of the Royals, and several of his men, were injured; and as they required others to convey them to Crown Point, the detachment of Rogers was reduced to 142 bayonets.

Proceeding on his journey, the major landed at Mississquey Bay on the 10th of September, and concealed his boats in deep woody creeks, with provisions sufficient to take him back to Crown Point; and left with them two trusty rangers, who were to lie in concealment near the *batteaux* till his party returned, unless the Indians discovered them, on which they were to pursue the track of the troops, and give him the earliest intelligence.

On the second evening after, the rangers, breathless and weary, overtook Major Rogers, with tidings that 400 French soldiers and some Indians had discovered the *batteaux*, which had been carried off by fifty men, while the rest were pursuing him with all speed.

As he received this information privately, he did not deem it wise to let all his party know of it; but he immediately directed Lieutenant Macmullen, with eight soldiers and the two rangers, to make their way, if possible, to Crown Point, and inform General Amherst of what had happened, and to request that he would send provisions to Cohoas, on the Connecticut River, by which route Rogers intended to return.

He now resolved to outmarch his pursuers, and cut off the Indian village of St. Francois before they could overtake him; and accordingly continued to push on till the 4th of October, when, about eight in the evening, he came within sight of the doomed village, and when it was completely dark, he took with him two Indians who could speak the language of the enemy, and, dressing himself in the Indian manner, with a hunting-shirt, *moccasins*, knife, pouch, &c., he deliberately went to inspect the place.

He found the inhabitants in "a high frolic," as it was named, and engaged in singing and dancing. At two in the morning he rejoined his detachment, and by three had marched it to within 500 yards of the village enclosures, and there halted, the strictest silence being enjoined. At four, while thick darkness yet rested on the forests and river, the Indians broke up from their dance and retired to rest. By daybreak all were buried in sleep, when a vigorous attack was made upon them from several quarters at once, before they had time to make the least resistance effectually.

Out of 300 men, 200 were shot or bayoneted on the spot, as they came rushing from their *wigwams*; twenty only were taken prisoners, and five Englishmen who had been captives of the tribe were rescued.

The provisions and weapons were all secured; the village was then set in flames, and by seven o'clock it was burnt to ashes. When the detachment mustered, it was found that six soldiers were slightly wounded, but that only one was killed.

After refreshing his party, the major began his march for Crown Point, leaving to his pursuers the task of burying the dead. He was, however, harassed on his march, and several times attacked in the rear; till, being favoured by the dusk of evening, he formed, an ambuscade upon his own track, and furiously assailed the enemy when and where they least expected it. After this he was permitted to continue his march without further annoyance, and reached headquarters in safety, with the loss of very few men.

The 1st Royals were elsewhere employed in many such expeditions against the Cherokees, among the then wild forests of South Carolina, their orders being simply to kill all but the women and children.

Colonel Grant, wrote in a narrative of these transactions published in the *South Carolina Gazette*, remembering probably the barbarities he had seen in his native glens after Culloden.

I could not help pitying them. Their villages were agreeably situated, their houses so neatly built and well provided, having abundance of everything. They must be pretty numerous, for Estatoe and Sugartown consisted of at least 200 houses, and every other village of at least 100 houses. After killing all we could find, and burning every house, we marched to Keower, and arrived on the 2nd of June, after a march of sixty miles without sleeping, at Fort Prince George. This service was performed with the loss of four men killed, and Lieutenants Marshal and Hamilton of the Scots Royals wounded.

Minden, 1759

From such disasters as that at St. Cas, and the subsequent one by the shore of Lake Champlain, we gladly turn to the glories that were won by the British infantry on the plains of Minden in the following year.

Early in the spring of 1759, operations were commenced in Germany, and the Allies gained some advantage; but when the French forces were assembled they possessed so great a superiority in numbers that Prince Ferdinand was obliged to fall back as they advanced. A series of retrograde movements brought the allied army to the vicinity of Minden, situated on the bank of the Weser, in Westphalia.

The French Army, commanded by the Marshal de Contades, took possession of Minden, and occupied a strong position near that city, which in ancient times had been the favourite residence of several of the early German emperors.

Prince Ferdinand of Brunswick, who commanded the Allies, manoeuvred. He detached one body of troops under his nephew, the hereditary prince, and appeared to leave another exposed to the attack of the whole opposing army. Hence the destruction of this corps was resolved upon by the French commander, who put his whole army in motion for that purpose. While the French were on the march, Prince Ferdinand advanced with the allied army; and early on the morning of the 1st of August, as the leading column of the enemy attained the summit of an eminence, it was surprised to discover, instead of a few weak corps, the whole allied army formed in order of battle, in two long lines, with a reserve.

Thus, the French marshal suddenly found himself compelled to fight upon unfavourable ground; and after some delay he began to form his columns in line to the front. Some authorities make the French 60,000 strong, and the Allies only 34,000; but Prince Ferdi-

Battle of Minden

nand had in the field 86 battalions and no squadrons. Of these, 12 battalions and 28 squadrons were British troops, with forty-eight twelve-pound guns and four mortars.

The right of the first line was led by Lord George Sackville, and the left by the Prince of Holstein.

The centre of the second line was led by General Sporken; the right wing by the famous Marquis of Granby, the left by General Imhoff; while Major-General Prince Charles of Bevern led the corps de reserve, consisting of the Black Hussars, under Colonel Redhaezle, the Hessian Militia, the Hanoverian Hunters, the volunteers of Prussia, and other mixed corps.

The morning of Minden is recorded as having been one of great beauty; and the dense old forests that cast their shadows on the Weser, the watery barrier which the French had undertaken to defend, and which the Allies were to force at all risks, were in the fullest foliage of summer.

The allied army was formed on the plain called Todtenhausen, in front of the town of Minden, which occupies the left bank of the Weser; and the embattled walls and Gothic spires of which, the Catholic and the Lutheran, could be seen shining in the morning sun as the troops advanced. In Minden there was a strong French garrison, the guns of which commanded its famous bridge, 600 yards in length.

At five in the morning the battle began. The 23rd Fusiliers, under the command of Lieutenant-Colonel Edward Sacheverel Pole, with the 12th and 37th British regiments, followed by Wolfe's old corps, the 20th, the Edinburgh, and 51st, under Major-Generals Waldegrave and Kingsley, flanked by two battalions of Hanoverian Guards, and the Hanoverian corps of Hardenberg, supported by three regiments of Hanoverians and one of Hessian Foot Guards, advanced with great boldness and rapidity to attack the left wing of the French army, where Marshal de Contades had posted the *élite* of his cavalry—the *Carbineers*, the *Gensdarmes*, and the Black and Grey *Mousquetaires*—under the queen's brother. Prince Xavier of Saxony, leader of the Household Cavalry of France.

In their advance these regiments were covered by a fire from the British artillery, which was admirably served by Captains Phillips, Macbean, Drummond, and Foy. On the other hand, the guns of the enemy opened a tremendous fire, which rent terrible chasms in the brigades of Waldegrave and Kingsley; while the *Carbineers* and *Mousquetaires Gris et Rouges*, so well known for the splendour of their

THE MARQUIS OF GRANBY.

costume and their headlong valour, come on with great éclat to the charge, with their accustomed fury; but a rolling volley met them as they came on. Men and horses fell over each other in hundreds. The survivors reined up in confusion and uproar, wheeled round, and galloped to the rear, their artillery recommencing its fire as the repulsed squadrons withdrew. The Hanoverian Brigade now formed up on the left of the 12th, 23rd, and 37th, and the three other British regiments on the right.

This formation was barely completed when another line of French cavalry, in gorgeous uniforms and in great strength, came rapidly forward, with all their brandished swords flashing in the sun, and with loud defiant cries; the *Records of the 23rd* says:

> But, they were struck in mid-onset by a tempest of bullets from the British regiments, broken, and driven back with severe loss.

Pressing on again with growing ardour, the three united brigades became suddenly exposed to a fire from infantry on their flanks, but nothing could stop them. Encouraged by past success, and confident in their own prowess, they followed up their advantage, and fairly drove the boasted cavalry of France out of the field.

> Notwithstanding the loss they sustained before they could get up to the enemy (to quote the *Campaigns of Prince Ferdinand of Brunswick*); notwithstanding the repeated attacks of the enemy's cavalry; notwithstanding a fire of musketry well kept up by the enemy's infantry; notwithstanding their being exposed in front and flank; such was the unshaken firmness of those troops that nothing could stop them, and the whole body of French cavalry was routed.

The brunt of the battle was unquestionably sustained by these six noble regiments of British infantry and the two of Hanoverians. After repulsing the cavalry, they were next opposed by a column of Swiss, with whom they exchanged several thundering volleys at twenty yards' distance; but shoulder to shoulder they stood, closing in from the flanks as the dead and dying fell, the rear rank filling up the gaps in front, and never pausing in their fire save to wipe their pans, renew their priming, or change their flints.

The French now brought up several *batardes*, as they termed their eight-pounders; and the range of these extended to the cavalry of the second line, on the extreme right of which were the 3rd Dragoon

3RD REGIMENT OF DRAGOONS

Guards, 10th Dragoons, and the Scots Greys led by the aged Colonel Preston, who had been their kettle-drummer in the wars of Queen Anne, and still wore a buff coat—the last ever seen in the service.

The Swiss, who were formed in two brigades, were quickly broken and dispersed. A body of Saxons next made a show of coming down upon the conquering British infantry, but they were soon put to flight; and the brigades of Waldegrave and Kingsley continued their splendid advance, in spite of all opposition.

The aim of the French Marshals De Contades and De Broglie was to drive in or destroy either flank of the Allies; but in this they signally failed, while a terrible slaughter was made of their men.

On the left the Hessian and Hanoverian cavalry, with some regiments of Holstein and Prussian dragoons, performed good service, as also did the artillery, under the Grand Master the Count de Bukebourg, compelling the enemy to make a precipitate retreat, which speedily became general along the whole line.

The cavalry of the right had no proper opportunity given them for engaging. Smollett says:

> They were destined to support the infantry of the third line. They consisted of the British and Hanoverian horse, commanded by Lord George Sackville, whose second was the Marquis of Granby. They were posted at a considerable distance from the first line of infantry, and divided from it by a scanty wood that bordered on a heath.

It was at the instant the whole French left gave way, and the flight along the line became general, according to another historian:

> Prince Ferdinand of Brunswick, sent orders to Lord George Sackville to advance to the charge. If these orders had been cheerfully obeyed, the Battle of Minden would have been as that of Blenheim; the French army would have been utterly destroyed, or totally routed and driven out of Germany. But whatever was the cause, the orders were not sufficiently precise, were misinterpreted, or imperfectly understood.

For this miscarriage. Lord George Sackville, after being victimised by the public press, had to appear before a general court-martial. By ten o'clock, after five hours of incessant firing, the whole French Army literally fled in the greatest disorder, with the loss of forty-three pieces of cannon, ten stand of colours, and seven standards.

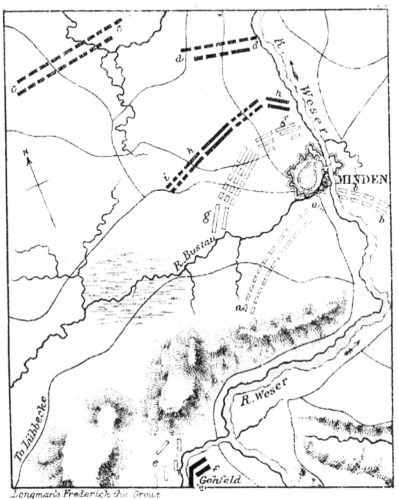

Longman's Frederick the Great

BATTLE OF MINDEN
August 1. 1759.

a a, French Army behind Minden, July 31.
b b, Broglio's detachment.
c c, The Allied Army, July 31.
d d, Wangenheim.
  e, The Duc de Brissac.
  f, The Hereditary Prince.
g g, French Army in battle order, August 1.
h h, Allied Army about to attack, August 1.
  i, Cavalry under Sackville.

On the field there lay 1,394 officers and men of the six British infantry regiments alone. The loss of the French was immense, between six and seven thousand. The Prince de Camille was among the slain, together with the Prince de Chimai and M. de la Fayette, colonels of the Grenadiers of France; and among those taken were the Count de Lutzelbourg, and the Marquis de Monti, two *marechaux de camp.* Colonel de Vogue, and many others. The rather obscure Memoirs of Sir James Campbell of Ardkinlass, who rode on Prince Ferdinand's staff that day, and who died at Edinburgh so lately as 1836, among the slain enumerates Prince Xavier of Saxony and the colonel of the *Mousquetaires Gris,* whose body he saw lying naked on the ground.

The passage of the fugitives across the Weser was a scene of unexampled horror. Beside the stone bridge already mentioned, their engineers had chained two pontoons, which broke in succession under the weight of the crowding passers; thus, many wagons full of wounded officers were swept away by the current, and the flower of the cavalry, the *Carbineers* and *Mousquetaires,* were almost destroyed; and amid their shrieks and cries were heard the exulting hurrahs and scattered shots of the advancing Allies.

The town of Minden surrendered, with 5,000 men, one-half of whom were wounded. The light troop of the Scots Greys, with some Prussian hussars, remained on the field, to protect the wounded from "death-hunters," and oversee the working parties of 2,000 peasants who buried the dead; while all the rest of the cavalry went in pursuit of the foe, and on this duty, none was so active as the aged colonel of the Greys, who actually took his regiment 200 miles from the scene of the battle, and captured a vast number of prisoners. Part of the military chest, with all the splendid equipages of the Prince of Condé and Marshal de Contades, fell into his hands. An officer who served under him records that at the capture of Zerenburg old Preston received more than a dozen sword-cuts, which fell harmlessly on "his buff jerkin."

In the General Orders of the following day, it was stated that His Serene Highness desired his greatest thanks to be given to the whole army for their bravery, particularly to the British infantry and the two battalions of the Hanoverian Guards. His Serene Highness also declared publicly that, next to God, he attributed the glory of the day to the intrepidity and extraordinary behaviour of the troops.

The British regiments had the king's authority to bear on their colours the word "Minden," and in the third corner thereof the White

Horse, which is still borne on the royal shield of Hanover, the badge alike of the Old Saxons in Germany, as it was of those in Kent in the earliest ages of English history.

From Minden the Allies followed the retreating army with great energy; ascending precipices, passing morasses, overcoming many difficulties, and with so much resolution, that several French corps were nearly annihilated, and many prisoners, with a vast quantity of baggage and other plunder, taken.

Sir James Campbell says:

"At Minden, a sergeant of the 51st, who had served in the wars in Flanders, made me observe on the day after the battle, when the dead bodies were stripped by the ruthless followers of the army, that the places might be distinguished where the troops of different nations had fought, by the colours and complexions of the native dead; the French in general being brown, the English and Germans fairer. This old sergeant at the same time pointed out to me several heaps of corn, which had been pulled up for the purpose of covering some object underneath. He told me it was a practice with the French soldiers, that when one of their comrades fell from a severe wound, in a field of grain, they immediately pulled and covered him over with part of it; and, to convince me of the truth of what he said, he took up a man's arm which was lying near to one of these heaps, observing that probably it belonged to the person underneath. His conjecture proved to be correct, for on uncovering the heap, we found a miserable object in the agonies of death, and beyond the reach of any human assistance."

GENERAL MAP
OF THE
SCENE OF OPERATIONS

Lemförde

Rahden

Hunte

Osterkappeln

Levern

Gr. Aue

Osnabrück

Wittlage
Pr. Oldendorf

Lübbe

Wissingen

Wiehen

Tecklenburg

Hasbergen

Hase

Buer

Melle

Else

Kirchlengern

Lengerich

Iburg

Hankenberg

Bünde

Ems

Greven

Glane

Glane

Kuttenvenne

Dissen

Borgholzhausen

Herford

Teutoburger

Bever

Versmold

Halle

Heepen

Werse

Telgte

Sassenberg

Bielefeld

Münster

Oerlinghausen

Wolbeck

Warendorf

Harsewinkel

Angel

Freckenhorst

Gütersloh

Oel B.

Verl

Sendenhorst

Rhoda

Wiedenbrück

Ems

Drensteinfurt

Oelde

Forth B.

Rietberg

Ahlen

Werse

Beckum

Wadersloh

Delbrück

Werne

Lippe

Hamm

Lippe

Paderborn

Vellinghausen

Hovestadt

Lippstadt

Salzkotten

Aasse

Geseke

Alme

Kamen

Erwitte

Werl

Soest

Unna

Anrochte

Büren

Afte

Ruhr

Mohne

Fürstenberg

Menden

Honne

Neheim

Rüthen

Menden

Hüsten

Warstein

Kallenhardt

Iserlohn

Arnsberg

Brilon

English Miles

0   5   10   15

Eversberg

Bigge

Dier

Kilometres

0   5   10   15   20   25

Meschede

Ruhr

Uchte
Stolzenau
Neustadt
Gr. Burgwedel
Rehburg
Steinhuder Meer
Steinhude
Bohnhorst
Wunstorf
Sachsenhagen
Petershagen
Leine
Linden
Hannover
Stadthagen
Weser
Rodenberg
Dohren
Bückeburg
Bücke B.
Deister G.
Wennigsen
Pattensen
Weser
Rinteln
Munder
Springe
Innerste
Geb.
Oldendorf
Varenholz
Eldagsen
Hohenhausen
Exten
Koppenbrugge
Hildesheim
Hameln
Elze
Lauenstein
Gronau
Bosingfeld
Aerzen
Salzhemmendorf
Lemgo
Brake
Alverdissen
Saale
Grohnde
Duingen
Pyrmont
Alfeld
Detmold
Blomberg
Lugde
Ottenstein
Emmer
Delligsen
Polle
Eschershausen
Schwalenberg
Stadtoldendorf
Steinheim
Lippe
Altaxen
Holzminden
Nieheim
Einbeck
Dassel
Salzderhelden
Hoxter
Leine
Driburg
Weser
Solinger Wald
Ilme
Brakel
Nethe
Northeim
Moringen
Dringenberg
Beverungen
Uslar
Willebadessen
Karlshafen
Hardegsen
Nethe
Borgholz
Helmarshausen
Bodenfelde
Sauer
Gottsbüren
Bovenden
Borgentreich
Sielen
Rein-
hards
Wald
Adelebsen
Diemel
Göttingen
Warburg
Veckerhagen
Liebenau
Hofgeismar
Dransfeld
Reinhausen
Volkmarsen
Münden
Arolsen
Wilhelmsthal
Hedemünden
Mengeringhausen
Werra
Fulda
Zierenberg
Wolfhagen
Cassel
Witzenhausen

Quebec, 1759

The autumn of this eventful year witnessed the battle on the Heights of Abraham, and the capture of Quebec, which left the British masters of the princely dominion of Canada.

On the 12th of January, 1759, James Wolfe, was appointed, when in his thirty-third year, Major-General and Commander-in-Chief of the forces to be employed in a projected expedition against Quebec; for which place he sailed on the 17th of the subsequent month, accompanied by three young brigadiers and his *aide-de-camp*, Captain Bell, afterwards of the 5th Foot. They were on board the *William and Anne*, a vessel that was still ploughing the ocean so lately as 1855. The fleet which accompanied him consisted of twenty-one sail of the line and other ships, having on board 7,000 troops, to reinforce those already in America.

The proposed plan was, that while General Wolfe assailed Quebec with these forces. Sir Jeffery Amherst, with 12,000 men, should reduce Ticonderoga, and march from Lake Champlain to the River St. Lawrence, and then co-operate with the young general in his attack upon the capital of the Canadas; that Brigadier Prideaux, after investing the fort at Niagara, should capture Montreal, and also join Wolfe—a scheme of operations by which it was confidently hoped the whole of the French possessions in America would be conquered.

Accordingly, the expedition departed from Louisbourg, under the convoy of Admiral Saunders, whose entire fleet consisted of forty sail, with artillery, provisions, and horses. Captain Cook, the famous navigator, master of the *Mercury*, sounded ahead of the fleet.

The troops on board were the 15th, 28th, 3Sth, 43rd, 47th, 48th, 58th, and 60th Regiments, with the Master of Lovat's Fraser Highlanders, or old 78th, disbanded in 1763.

Towards the end of June these forces were landed on the Isle of

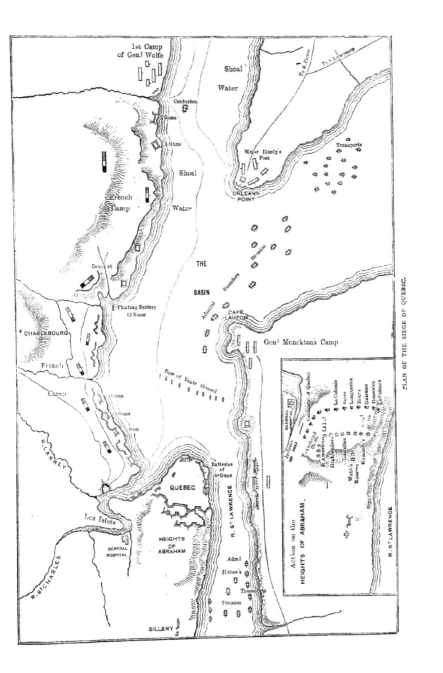

1st Camp
of Gen¹ Wolfe

Shoal

Water

To S¹ Lawrence
To S¹ Pierre

Centurion

Guns

Guns

Major Hardy's
Post

Transports

French

Camp

Shoal

ORLEANS
POINT

Water

Devonport

THE

BASIN

Division

Saunders

Admiral

Floating Battery
12 Guns

CAPE
LAUZON

CHARLESBOURG

Gen¹ Monckton's Camp

French

Camp

Row of Boats Moored

Guns

Guns

Gun

R. LA HREY

QUEBEC

Batteries
of 20 Guns

R. S¹ LAWRENCE

Les Islets

GENERAL
HOSPITAL

HEIGHTS
OF
ABRAHAM

R. S¹ CHARLES

Adm¹

Holme's

Transports

Division

SILLERY

Action on the
HEIGHTS OF ABRAHAM.

GENERAL HOSPITAL

Quebec

Infantry

La Colonie

Royal Roussillon

Sarre

Kanaskatia I.I.I.I.

Languedoc

Highlanders

Webb's

Bearn

Bragg's

Guienne

Reserve

Ayde

Royal

La Colonie

Roussillon

Kennedy

R. S¹ LAWRENCE

PLAN OF THE SIEGE OF QUEBEC.

Orleans, which is formed by two branches of the River St Lawrence, where the shore slopes gradually to the beach. This was but a few leagues below the city of Quebec, and there Wolfe, with Brigadiers Monckton, Murray, and Townshend, published a manifesto, in vindication of the war undertaken against the French colonies, by referring to the armaments prepared in France for the invasion of Britain; pointing out the hopelessness of the Canadians resisting the armies now in the field against them; and offering to them "the sweets of peace amidst the horrors of war." He concluded:

> General Wolfe flatters himself that the whole world will do him justice, if the inhabitants of Canada force him, by their refusal, to have recourse to violent methods.

But this document produced not the slightest effect on the French Canadians in general, or the citizens of Quebec in particular.

Strong by nature, the latter city is built upon a steep and lofty line of rocks, rising on the northern bank of the St. Lawrence, and almost insulated by the River St. Charles. On its north rises Cape Diamond, to the height of 345 feet. In rear of the city is a chain of hills that are rugged in outline—the famous Heights of Abraham—the scene of Wolfe's last and greatest exploit.

Across the peninsula between the two rivers just named lay a line of fortifications; and these the Marquis de Montcalm, King Louis' general, was prepared to defend at the head of the regiments of La Sarre, Royal Roussillon, Languedoc, Guienne, and Beam (respectively the 24th, 27th, 53rd, 68th, and 72nd of the old French Line), with some colonial troops, making 10,000 bayonets in all; while a garrison under the Chevalier Ramsay, the governor, a Scottish Jacobite refugee, occupied the city. Louis Joseph, Marquis de Montcalm and de St. Veran, was a lieutenant-general, and a man of high spirit, with many accomplishments; and his heroic temperament rendered him worthy of being the opponent of James Wolfe.

He was born at the Château de Candiac, near Nismes, in 1712; and when colonel of infantry had distinguished himself at the battle of Plaisance, where he was thrice wounded. He received two more wounds at the subsequent combat of Exilles; and became brigadier and camp-master of a regiment of horse, named after himself. In 1758 he was gazetted *marechal de camp*, and commander of all the troops sent by France for the defence of her American colonies.

Several movements necessarily preluded the deadlier encounter

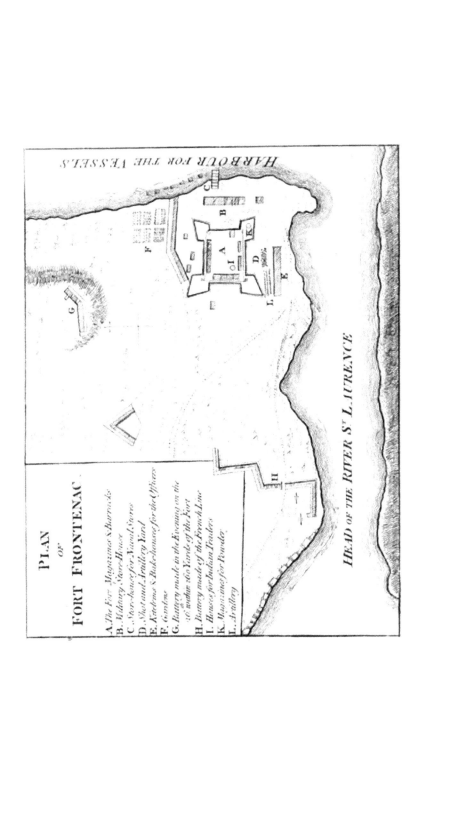

PLAN
OF
FORT FRONTENAC.

A. The Fort, Magazines & barracks
B. Military Store-House
C. Store-house for Naval Stores
D. Naval and Artillery Yard
E. Kitchens & Bake-houses for the Officers
F. Gardens
G. Battery made in the Evening on the
   16 within 160 Yards of the Fort
H. Battery made of the French Line
I. Houses for Indian Traders
K. Magazines for Powder
L. Artillery

HARBOUR FOR THE VESSELS

HEAD OF THE RIVER ST. LAURENCE

before Quebec. General Wolfe ordered Brigadier Monckton, with four battalions, to possess himself of Point Levée, which rises precipitously within cannon-shot of the city. The brigadier, in obedience to this order, crossed the river in the night, and captured the post indicated, his advanced guard driving in the French as it proceeded. He then erected a battery of artillery and mortars, which opened upon Quebec at once.

Colonel Carleton had in the meanwhile been dispatched to seize the western point of Orleans; and now Wolfe learned with great chagrin that he could obtain no assistance from Sir Jeffery Amherst, and that he must cope alone with the veterans of Montcalm, in a city rendered so strong by art and nature that she was then named the "Gibraltar of the Western World."

Yet, though the enemy so far outnumbered him, he did not lose heart, but resolved to proceed; "for," as he wrote in one of his letters to the Premier:

A brave and victorious army finds no difficulties.

Every day now made time more precious, as a Canadian winter, with all its snow and severities, would soon be at hand; and after having vainly endeavoured to bring the veterans of the marquis to a general action, he determined to pass the river Montmorency, and, with six companies of grenadiers and a part of the 60th Regiment, to attack a redoubt the glacis of which was washed by the water, while Generals Monckton and Murray effected a crossing higher up.

The grenadiers, though strictly ordered not to advance until the 1st brigade was ready to support them, rushed cheering, with fixed bayonets, in a tumultuous manner on the enemy, whose steady fire, thrown in point-blank, and almost at pistol-range, drove them back in such disorder that Wolfe was compelled to recross the river, and retreat, during a dreadful thunderstorm, into the Isle of Orleans; and, but for the headlong bravery with which the Fraser Highlanders covered the rear, facing about at times with musket and claymore, his whole force had been cut to pieces.

A deep and mournful impression was made on the ardent mind of Wolfe by this unforeseen disaster. He knew how capricious was the humour of the people at home, and how keenly they had resented disasters elsewhere, even to sacrificing Admiral Byng on his quarterdeck; and he thirsted for some achievement to wipe out the dishonour he conceived himself to have suffered at the Falls of Montmorency,

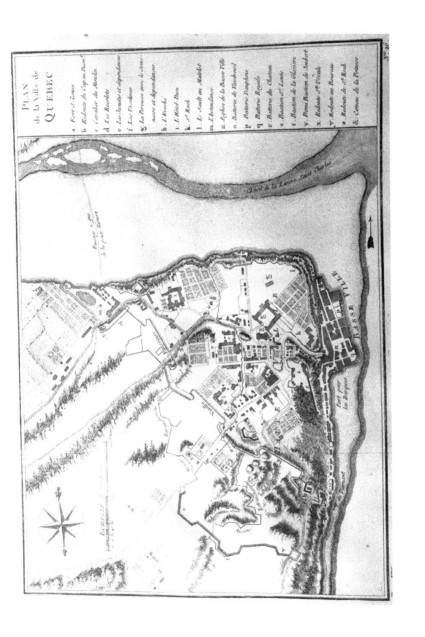

PLAN
de la Ville de
QUEBEC

a Fort S. Louis
b Redoute du Cap au Diam.ᵗ
c Citadelle du Moulin
d Les Recolets
e Les Jesuites et dependances
f Les Ursulines
g La Paroisse avec le Sem.ʳᵉ
  naire et dependances
h L'Evêché
i L'Hôtel Dieu
k S.ᵗ Roch
l Le S.ᵗ.te au S.ᵗhiste
m L'Intendance
n Eglise de la Basse Ville
o Batterie de Vaudreuil
p Batterie Dauphine
q Batterie Royale
r Batterie du Château
s Bastion S.ᵗ Louis
t Bastion de la Glacière
v Petit Bastion de S.ᵗ Louis
x Reduite S.ᵗ Ursule
y Redoute au Potevin
z Reduite de S.ᵗ Roch
& Cotteau de la Potasse

BASSE VILLE

Cliniè de la Rivière Saint Charles

Pointe à feu
de la petite Rivière

ECHELLE

and by many officers who shared his confidence he was often heard to declare—

I will never return home to be exposed, as other unfortunate commanders have been, to the censure and reproach of an ignorant and ungrateful populace.

A Scottish officer, named Lieutenant Macculloch, is said at this time to have suggested to him the daring but brilliant idea of attempting that which the French conceived to be impracticable—the scaling of the Heights of Abraham—and thus gaining the lofty ground which overlooked the city at a part where its defences were most weak.

Macculloch had personally examined the mountains; and the boldness of the plan gave Wolfe new health and heart, and roused him from a bed of sickness, on which the fever of his spirit had thrown him; and he resolved that at midnight, on the 11th of September, he would make the grand attempt, or perish in it.

Before moving, with some of his favourite officers, he had a farewell carouse in his tent, and sang to them that noble old military song beginning—

How stands the glass around?
For shame, ye take no care, my boys! &c.

It was long known by his name, but can be traced to an old broadsheet of 1710.

Exactly at one o'clock in the morning, amid silence and obscurity, the Master of Lovat's Highlanders, the Louisbourg Grenadiers, and four battalions of the Line began to cross the river in flat-bottomed boats, under Brigadiers Monckton and Murray, two officers whose ages were about the same as that of their leader. With the tide and the river's flow, the boats dropped down; but such was the rapidity of the current that most of them landed a little below the point of disembarkation proposed by Wolfe, whose daring plans were nearly baffled by two circumstances beyond his anticipation,

Two French deserters, taken in the twilight of the September morning, were brought on board of the vessels belonging to the fleet of Admiral Saunders. His ship lay at anchor near the northern shore; and they told him that "the Marquis of Montcalm was that night to receive a convoy of provisions in boats from M. de Bougainville, whose command was at a distance." These men, on perceiving the leading boats full of the Highlanders and grenadiers beginning to

CLIMBING THE HILL

cross the river, asserted that they were the convoy referred to. The captain, Richard Smith, who was ignorant of Wolfe's plans, had his guns run out to open fire, when the general came alongside in person, having detected some commotion on board, and thus arrested a discharge of cannon that would have raised the whole city in arms. The only naval captain named Smith in Saunders' squadron commanded the Stromboli, fire-ship.

The second episode, as given by Smollett and others, is perhaps more extraordinary.

A line of sentinels had been posted by Montcalm along his bank of the river, with orders to challenge all passing craft, and to keep each other on the alert. The first boat, crowded by Fraser Highlanders, was just approaching the wooded shore, when from amid the darkness the challenge of a French sentinel rang out—

"*Qui vive?*"

"*La France!*" responded a Highland officer, with great presence of mind, who having served in Holland, and being master alike of the French language and their camp discipline, knew in an instant the necessary reply.

"À *quel régiment?*" demanded the wary sentinel once more.

"*De la Reine,*" replied the Highlander, who by a lucky accident, knew that this regiment was actually under the command of Bougainville, and thus might form part of the convoy.

"*Passe, monsieur!*" cried the soldier, uncocking his musket, and supposing the boats to be certainly the convoy, he questioned them no more; but lower down the stream another sentinel, who was probably more wary, after the same challenges and responses, suddenly exclaimed—

"*Pourquoi est ce que vous ne parlez pas plus haut?*" ("Why don't you reply with an audible voice?").

"*Mon camarade, tais toi,*" replied the Highlander; "*nous serron entendus!*" ("Hush, we shall be overheard!").

So, the boat with its kilted freight drifted peacefully on to the place now called Wolfe's Cove.

The first who sprang ashore was Wolfe; and on looking at the precipice which towered away above them into obscurity, he turned to the Highland officer, and said—

I do not believe, sir, there is any possibility of getting up, but you must now do your best.

And the escalade of the heights immediately began. On this duty it was remarked that one of the most active was an old Highland gentleman, Malcolm Macpherson, of Phoiness, who, when verging on his eightieth year, accompanied the Frasers as a volunteer. Ruined by a lawsuit, he had been driven in extreme old age to become a soldier of fortune; and the fury with which he handled his broadsword in the subsequent battle so delighted General Townshend, that through Mr. Pitt, says General Stewart, of Garth, he received a commission from the king.

Slinging their muskets, and climbing, some with their swords in their teeth, the Frasers scrambled up the steep and woody precipice, grasping the roots of trees, the tufts of grass, the rocks, and whatever might aid their ascent, till the summit was won; and rushing on, claymore in hand, they dislodged a captain's guard which manned a battery near it, and possessed themselves of a narrow path which enabled their comrades of Louisbourg and the Line to reach all the sooner the plateau which stands 250 feet above the flowing river.

Following the Highlanders, Wolfe was soon on the plateau of the precipice, and with ardour he formed his troops in contiguous columns of regiments as they came toiling up; and ere the rising sun began to gild the spires and ramparts of Quebec and the far-stretching bosom of the mighty St. Lawrence, he had his whole force marching in battle array along the famous Heights of Abraham, with colours flying and all their bayonets glittering. To keep the redoubt taken by the Frasers, to cover the landing-place, and to act as a rear-guard, he left two companies; and at once began to descend from the green slopes towards the city.

The Marquis of Montcalm, whose force by various contingencies had become greatly diminished, was now aware that a battle could no longer be avoided, and he felt, too, that on its issue rested the fate, not only of Quebec, but of all Canada; yet he came boldly to the front from his camp at Montmorency, while the British halted about three-quarters of a mile from the ramparts, with their right flank resting on the edge of a steep precipice that overhangs the river.

The regiments of Bearn and Guienne formed the centre of the French line; the right wing consisted of the regiments of the Royal Roussillon and La Colonie; another battalion of the latter, with those of La Sarre and Languedoc, formed the left. These regiments all wore the then uniform of the French Line—white coats, with scarlet vests and gilt buttons. A twelve-pound gun was planted on each

Surrender of Louisburg to the British

flank; among the bushes and underwood that fringed the front of his line were posted five companies of grenadiers, 150 Canadians, 230 dragoons, and 870 militiamen. His second in command was Brigadier Senzenerques; and M. Beauchâtel, major of the 24th Regiment, was his third.

The British line was composed of the Louisbourg Grenadiers, the Fraser Highlanders, the 15th, 28th 38th, and 58th Regiments. The light infantry covered the left wing, while the precipice already mentioned rendered the right perfectly secure. Peregrine Lascelles' regiment, the 47th, formed in grand divisions, was the small reserve. There was only one field-piece; all the troops entered the action with their bayonets fixed.

Precisely at eleven o'clock the firing began, when the dusky Indians and the hardy Canadian Sharpshooters, clad in hunting-shirts and moccasins, began to dart from bush to bush, on the woody banks that overhung the St. Charles, and filled all the valley with reports of irregular musketry. The bright scarlet uniforms of the British officers rendered them fatally conspicuous to these riflemen, and in the lulls of the firing their French commanders were frequently heard to say—

Soldats, marquez bien les officiers!

By the express command of Wolfe, his whole line retained its fire until within forty yards of the enemy's bayonets, when it suddenly poured in a close, deadly, and running volley upon the French, whose advance was at once arrested, their movements paralysed by the sudden heaps of killed and wounded that fell over each other, and caused great gaps in the ranks.

By a sudden movement Montcalm now menaced the British left; but on being roughly repulsed, a vibration seemed to pass along his whole line, and his troops began to waver. It was at this most critical moment that Wolfe was mortally wounded, while standing on the extreme right flank, near the head of the 28th Regiment. There the conflict was both close and desperate; and his position, somewhat in front of the line, rendered him fatally conspicuous.

A shot from a Canadian rifle struck him in the wrist. Wrapping a handkerchief round the shattered limb to staunch the blood, he hastened to head a bayonet charge of the Louisbourg Grenadiers, when a second shot pierced his abdomen, and a third his breast. With the blood pouring from three wounds, he found himself no longer able to stand, and staggering back towards the 28th, he leaned his head on the shoulder of Captain Currie of that regiment; but even then, when in the agonies of death, he could not forget his anxiety or the fate of the day.

"My eyesight and strength fail me," said he to the officer who supported him.

Then it was that, infuriated on seeing him fall, the whole line simultaneously advanced to the charge, the Highland regiment raising a loud yell.

"Claymore! claymore! Dirk and claymore!" was their cry; the same wild shout that had rung in a thousand clan battles now echoed along the Heights of Abraham.

Flinging down their muskets in the old Highland fashion, the Frasers rushed on with their basket-hilted swords and armpit daggers, making a dreadful slaughter among the French, whom Montcalm was vainly striving to rally, nine ranks deep.

Every medical assistance was meanwhile bestowed upon General Wolfe, who was borne to the rear, where he was laid upon the sward; and there he lay dying, with his sorrowing friends around him, and the roar of the battle in his ear.

"They run! See how they run!" exclaimed Captain Currie, who still supported him.

"Who run?" asked he, seeking to prop himself on his elbow.

"The French—they are giving way in all directions!" said those about him.

"What! Do they run already?" exclaimed the dying hero. "Then go, one of you, to Colonel Burton, and tell him to march Webb's regiment to the River St. Charles, to secure the bridge and cut off the retreat of the fugitives. Now, praised be God, I die happy!"

He then turned, with a spasm, on his left side; and expired in the arms of Fraser, his favourite Highland orderly, who was weeping over him.

By this time Brigadier Senzenerques on one side, and Monckton on the other, had been borne wounded from the field; and the gallant Marquis of Montcalm, when in the centre of his retreating line, had a thigh smashed by a shot.

The *Scots Magazine* for 1807 states:

Captain John Macdonell, the officer who rescued the French commander-in-chief, Montcalm, when sinking under his wounds, by the interposition of his own body between him

DEATH OF WOLFE.

and the bayonets of our soldiers, when roused to madness by the loss of their beloved general," died in his eighty-fifth year. Captain of Invalids at Berwick, leaving five sons in the service.

The marquis fell, but was borne by his fugitive troops into Quebec, to the gates of which they were followed by the kilted Highlanders, who, leaving all behind in the pursuit, made dreadful havoc among them, losing, however, many of their finest officers, among whom were the three Macdonalds, of Boisdale, Keppoch, and Lochgarry; Ross, of Culrossie; and Roderick Macneil, of Barra. The letter of an officer, in the *Edinburgh Chronicle* says:

Our regiments that sustained the brunt of the action were Bragg's, Lascelles', and the Highlanders; the two former had not a bayonet, or the latter a broadsword, untinged with blood.

Another writes:

When these Highlanders took to their broadswords, my God, what havoc they made! They drove everything before them, and stone walls alone could resist their fury.

The Marquis of Montcalm, just before he expired, dictated to General Townshend, who succeeded to the command of the British, a letter, bequeathing to his care the wounded and prisoners. When it was ended, he exclaimed—

Thank Heaven, I shall not live to see the capitulation of Quebec! I have got my death fighting against the bravest soldiers in the world, at the head of the greatest cowards that ever carried muskets!

He expired on the 14th of September, and his remains were interred in a hole which had first been partly made by the explosion of a shell, thus forming, as a French writer has it, a characteristic tomb for a brave soldier who died on the bed of honour.

Four days after, Quebec was formally surrendered by the governor, M. de Ramsay, on a promise that all the rights and liberties of the inhabitants should be respected, and that all prisoners taken should be sent home to old France. The loss of the British in killed, wounded, and missing was only 57 officers and 591 soldiers; whilst that of the French was about 200 officers, and 1,200 men of other ranks.

In Quebec and near it there were taken 298 brass and iron guns, howitzers, and mortars, with two petards and 1,100 bombs.

MONUMENT TO GENERAL WOLFE.

On board the *Royal William*, 80 guns, the body of Wolfe was sent home to England; and Pitt wept when he pronounced a eulogy upon the fallen hero in the House of Commons.

His father had survived him but two months, and his grave at Greenwich had barely been closed when the remains of the victor arrived at Portsmouth, on the 12th of November; and amid deep silence, much ceremony and sorrow, surrounded by a mighty multitude, they were interred in the parish church at Greenwich, his mother attending as chief mourner.

A noble monument at Westminster, a cenotaph on the heights of Abraham, and another in his native village of Westerham, have been raised to perpetuate the memory of the soldier to whom Britain owed the conquest of Canada.

Sir Henry Smith, Bart, one of his *aides-de-camp*, died, in his seventy-seventh year, in 1811, at Elmswell; and an artilleryman who supported him in the field died in the following year, at Carlisle; while it is recorded that Lieutenant Macculloch, the officer according to whose suggestion he first conceived the idea of turning the French flank by scaling the Heights of Abraham, died a pauper in Marylebone Workhouse, in the year 1793.

Hawke and Conflans, 1759

Early in June, 1759, Admiral Sir Edward Hawke sailed from Spithead to cruise off the Soundings, with a powerful fleet, consisting of forty-three sail. He detached several squadrons to watch the coast of France, and more particularly Brest. Though the weather proved very tempestuous. Sir Edward persevered in cruising near that seaport, till a storm forced him to take shelter in Torbay, early in November. The Marquis de Conflans, Marshal of France, and *Vice-Amiral des Armées Navales*, being now convinced that the coast was clear, put to sea on the 14th of November, and on the same day the British fleet sailed out of Torbay.

On the 15th, Captain M'Cliverty, in the *Gibraltar*, joined the fleet, and reported that he had seen the French armament about twenty-four leagues north-west of Belleisle, steering to the south-east. On this Sir Edward Hawke immediately shaped his course for Quiberon Bay, in the district of the Morbihan; but a gale from the east drove the fleet considerably to leeward. On the 19th the wind shifted to the westward, when the Maidstone and Coventry, frigates, were ordered ahead, to look out for the enemy; and next morning at eight o'clock they let fly their topgallant-sails, the exciting signal that the French fleet was in sight.

The whole force proved to be in pursuit of Captain Duff's squadron, then stationed in Quiberon Bay, blocking up in the Morbihan those transports destined for a projected invasion of Britain.

The moment the Marquis de Conflans perceived the British fleet, he recalled the leading ships that were in chase, and, after, some manoeuvres, formed all in order of battle; while Sir Edward Hawke drew his fleet into line abreast. In the battle that ensued, one of the most brilliant in our annals, the strength engaged was as follows:—

The French fleet consisted of twenty-five sail, all save three ships of

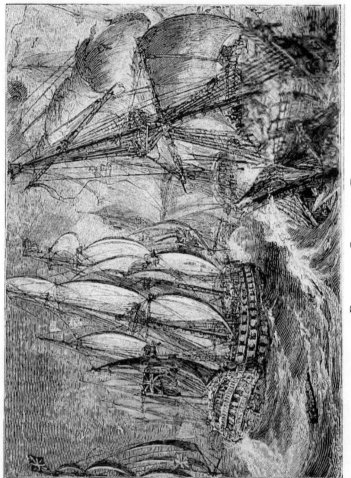

Battle in Quiberon Bay

the line, manned by 15,200 men, and mounting 1,598 guns.

The British fleet mustered twenty-three sail, all, or nearly all, of the line, with 13,295 seamen and marines, and carrying 1,596 guns; hence the enemy outnumbered Hawke's force by 1,905 men.

As they drew nearer. Sir Edward changed his plans, and (according to Campbell, in his *Lives of the Admirals*) told his officers that he did not "intend to trouble himself with forming lines, but would attack them in the old way, and make downright work with them."

Accordingly, he threw out a signal for seven of his ships to chase, in order to provoke battle. As these neared the French, the weather became rough, black, and squally; and Conflans, who at first seemed boldly to offer or accept the gage of battle, suddenly changed his mind and stood away inshore, right before the wind, with as much sail as he dared to carry.

Before our headmost ships could get up with his rear, and the *Warspite*, 74 guns, Captain Sir J. Bentley, with the *Dorsetshire*, 70 guns. Captain Denis, open fire, it was the hour of two in the afternoon; and we are told that the imagination can conceive nothing more grand than the spectacle presented by the hostile squadrons at that time.

In heaven overhead the clouds were black and dense; the darkened sea was rolling in tremendous waves before a stormy gale, and these were lashing themselves into foam on the treacherous rocks and sandy shallows that lie off the coast of Bretagne, and were all unknown to the pilots of the British ships. In the midst of these natural perils, which were calculated to awe or intimidate, two hostile fleets of vast power and strength, trusted each with the defence and the glory of their respective countries, were preparing for battle. Campbell says:

"It was a moment, as if Nature had resolved to contrast the tameness of physical terror with the grandeur of heroism, and to show how much more sublime are the moral sentiments of a collected mind than all the awful phenomena of the heavens darkened, the ocean agitated by a tempest, with the multifarious dangers of secret rocks and unknown shoals."

In a good offing, Conflans might have risked engaging without the imputation of rashness, as his force was numerically superior to that of Hawke; but, like a prudent commander, he sought to avail himself of the advantages that arose from the local knowledge of his pilots, who were well acquainted with the shallows and perilous rocks that stud the sea about the coast of Brittany, and he ordered them to steer in such a manner as to decoy the British upon certain reefs. But, in the execution of this proceeding, which was deemed both treacherous and disreputable, he was luckily disappointed, as our leading ships, by their swift sailing, came up with his rear before the fleet was well ready for action.

Le Formidable, a French eighty-gun ship, commanded by Rear-Admiral M. de St. André de Verger, a man of great courage, behaved in the most heroic manner. Broadside after broadside was poured into him by the British ships, as, with all their sails set, they passed successively onward to reach the van of the enemy, and her crew, consisting of 820 men, returned their fire with a promptitude that excited the admiration of both fleets.

In the meantime, the *Royal George*—the same noble ship, of 100 guns, which was afterwards fated to sink in Portsmouth Harbour—with Sir Edward Hawke on board, was approaching *Le Soleil Royal*, 80 guns, which carried the flag of the Marquis de Conflans. As if intent only on securing her prey, she passed without heeding the booming shot of the other ships, with the angry sea flying in sheets of snowy foam over her bows as she came rapidly on, under a press of spreading canvas.

Seeing the breakers foaming on every side, her pilot said to the admiral, "Sir Edward, we cannot carry on farther without the greatest danger from shoals."

"You have done your duty in pointing out the risk," replied Hawke; "but lay me alongside of the *Soleil Royal*."

The pilot bowed in token of obedience, and gave the requisite orders. The crew of *La Superbe*, 70 guns, perceiving the intentions of the British admiral, generously interposed her hull between her commander and the *Royal George*, whose fatal broadside had been intended for the marquis. The thunder of the explosion was instantly followed by the wild shrieks of all on board, mingled with the cheers of the British tars, as they ran back their guns to reload. But almost immediately their triumph was checked by another emotion, for when the smoke rolled away before the gusty wind, the masts only of *La Superbe*, with her colours flying, were visible above water; in another moment they were covered by the black waves of the rolling sea, as, with her crew, consisting of 650 men, she went down into the deep.

By this time Rear-Admiral de Verger had 200 of his men killed. Viscount Howe, in the *Magnanime*, 74 guns, attacked the *Thésée*, 74 guns, commanded by Captain de Kersaint; but the *Montague* running foul of the former with a dreadful crash, so much disabled her that she fell astern. Captain the Honourable A. Keppel, in the *Torbay*, 74 guns, then turned his guns on the *Thésée*; but soon after this combat began, as the lower-deck ports of the latter were not shut down, and the waves were rolling very high, she suddenly careened over, filled, and went down, amid the despairing cries of her crew, which when the battle began mustered 700 men.

Lord Howe having now got clear of the *Montague*, bore down, and, heedless of rocks and shoals, attacked *L'Heros*, 74 guns, commanded by the Vicomte de Sanson, and soon forced her to strike; but the weather was too boisterous for us to take possession of her, and, being thoroughly disabled, she drove ashore in the night and was totally lost.

Darkness and obscurity coming on with great rapidity, the remainder of the enemy's ships fled, and no less than seven, all of the line, hove their guns overboard and ran into the River Villaix. About as many more, in a shattered condition, escaped to other ports.

The wind continued to blow furiously from the north-west; and there being no pilots in the fleet sufficiently qualified to take charge of the ships, the admiral gave over the pursuit, and come to anchor under the lee of the Isle of Dumet. There the fleet remained during the night, burying the dead and attending to the wounded; and as the tempest continued to increase, and the ships to strain madly at their anchors, the darkness wag occasionally broken by the red flashes of cannon, and the hoarse roar of the breakers on the beach was augmented in horror by the booming of those signals of distress, which, says Captain Schomberg, our seamen were unable to distinguish whether they came from friends or foes.

> This action, more memorable, on account of the terrific circumstances in which it was fought, than any other of equal magnitude in the annals of heroic achievement, was duly appreciated by the whole of Europe; and the celebrated Voltaire did honour to the gallantry of his nation, in admitting that there were natural circumstances which gave superiority to the English mariner, in all ages, over that of France (Campbell).

In the morning, when day broke, the *Resolution* and *L'Heros* were seen to be ashore and totally wrecked on the Foue Bank. In ignorance of where he was, amid the darkness and horror of the midnight storm, the French admiral, in the *Soleil Royal*, had come to anchor in the very heart of the British fleet!

The moment he discovered his singular position, he cut his cable and drove his ship ashore a little to the westward of Crozie. The *Essex*, 64 guns, Captain Lucius O'Brien, was ordered to pursue her, and in the execution of this duty struck upon a shoal and perished. On the 22nd, Sir Edward Hawke sent the *Portland*, the *Chatham*, and *Vengeance* to destroy the *Soleil Royal* and *L'Heros*. The first, on seeing the approach of our ships, was fired and abandoned by her crew; and the latter shared the same fate at the hands of our own people; while *Le Juste*, 70 guns, was totally wrecked at the mouth of the Loire.

In this most memorable victory the French lost seven ships of the line, and the number of slain and drowned was never ascertained; but if we may judge of the former by the carnage on board the *Formidable*, it must have been very great. The British fleet had only 300 killed and wounded. Among the former there was only one officer, Lieutenant Price, of the *Magnanime*.

Captain John Campbell, of the *Royal George* (afterwards Vice-Admiral of the Red), was dispatched to Britain with the news of the victory. This officer, a man of acknowledged bravery, who had originally been pressed into the service when an apprentice boy on board of a Scottish coaster, was taken to the palace in the carriage of Lord Anson, with whom he had sailed round the world in the *Centurion*.

"Captain Campbell," said the old admiral, on the way, "the king will probably knight you, if you think proper."

"Troth, my lord," replied Campbell, who retained the Scottish accent to the time of his death, in 1789, "I dinna ken o' what use that will be to me."

"But your lady may like it," urged his lordship.

"Then His Majesty may knight her, if he pleases," was the blunt response of Campbell.

By the king he was very graciously received, and was presented with five hundred guineas to purchase a sword.

On the return of Sir Edward Hawke he received the thanks of Parliament, and had a yearly pension of £2,000 assigned him on the Irish establishment, for his life and the lives of his sons. He was afterwards raised to the peerage, as Baron Hawke of Towton; and amid other augmentations to his coat armorial was a *chevron erminois* between three boatswain's whistles.

It is worthy of note that during this war we took or destroyed twenty-seven French ships of the line and thirty-one frigates; two of their great ships and four frigates perished; so that their whole loss was sixty-four sail: whereas the loss to Great Britain did not exceed seven sail of the line and five frigates. Thus, it may easily be conceived how the French marine, at first greatly inferior to ours, must have been affected by this dreadful balance to its detriment.

OFFICER WITH GORGET, AND FUSIL AT THE "CARRY,"
MARCHING PAST (A.D. 1759).

Cape Lagos, 1759

A little time prior to the Victory of Sir Edward Hawke, the British fleet had achieved another off the coast of Portugal.

Admiral Edward Boscawen, son of Viscount Falmouth, an officer who had displayed great bravery in the *Namur* in the action of 1747, who had commanded in the Indies, America, and at the capture of Louisbourg, was employed in blocking up the harbour of Toulon, where lay a French squadron, under M. de la Clue, designed, it was believed, to assist in the projected descents upon the coast of Great Britain. Having in vain displayed the British flag in sight of the mouth of the Moselle, by way of defiance to M. de la Clue, he ordered three ships of the line—the *Conqueror, Culloden,* and *Jersey,* under Captains Smith, Harland, and Barker—to enter, and burn two vessels that lay close to the harbour mouth.

They bore in accordingly, but met with a very warm reception from certain batteries, of whose existence their commanders had been ignorant. Two of these they attempted to destroy, and cannonaded them for some time with great vigour; but overmatched by the guns on shore, and the wind dying away, so that their canvas flapped against the masts, they sustained great damage, and in a somewhat shattered condition were towed out by their boats.

Admiral Boscawen, in consequence of this, sailed for Gibraltar to refit them; and M. de la Clue took the opportunity to steal out of Toulon and put to sea, in hope of passing the Straits unobserved with his squadron, which consisted of twelve ships of the line and three frigates.

Admiral Boscawen, who had under his flag fourteen sail of the line, two frigates, and several fireships, having almost refitted, detached the *Lyme*, 20 guns, to cruise off Malaga, and the *Gibraltar*, also of 20 guns, Captain M'Cliverty, to hover between Estepana, on the coast of Granada, and the peninsula of Ceuta, with orders to "keep a sharp look-out," and give him timely notice of the approach of the enemy.

At eight in the evening of the 17th of August, the *Gibraltar* discovered the French squadron close in on the Barbary coast, creeping towards the mouth of the Straits, through which De la Clue no doubt hoped to pass in the night. Captain M'Cliverty immediately stood over to Gibraltar Bay and reported the circumstance.

At this crisis the fleet was by no means in a state to proceed to sea; most of the ships were in process of refitting, many having actually their sails unbent and their topmasts struck: but so great were the exertions of the officers, and so enthusiastic were the crews on learning that the enemy were at hand, that by ten at night the whole force was clear of Gibraltar Bay, and out at sea.

At seven next morning Admiral Boscawen got sight of seven of the French squadron, and made signal for a general chase. M. de la Clue at first mistook the British fleet for a part of his own, from which he had been separated in the night. He hoisted a private signal, and on finding that no response was made, crowded all sail to get away.

The British now displayed their colours, and spread every inch of canvas in pursuit. The squadrons were yet so far apart, that even then M. de la Clue might have escaped, had he not been compelled to back his mainyard occasionally and wait for *Le Souvrain*, 74 guns, which was a dull sailer.

The wind, which had blown a fresh gale all the morning, died away about noon; and although Admiral Boscawen had made signal to chase and engage in a line of battle ahead, it was not until half-past two that his leading ships could overtake those of the enemy's rear.

Without waiting to return the fire of the sternmost, which he received as he passed, Boscawen bore on under a press of canvas, intent only on coming up with the *Ocean*, an eighty-gun ship, which carried the flag of De la Clue. He passed her to windward, and then suddenly altering his course, about four in the afternoon, ran right athwart her hawse, and poured in a dreadful broadside from his own ship, the *Namur*, 90 guns. De la Clue soon got his broadside to bear, though the raking fore and aft occasioned terrible confusion in his ship, and the action began with equal fury on both sides; but it proved of short duration. In about half-an-hour her mizzen-mast, and fore and main-topsail-yards were wounded and fell crashing on her decks. She dropped astern, while, with cries of triumph and derision from her crew, the *Ocean* bore away.

The *Centaur*, 74 guns. Captain Sabian de Grammont, the sternmost of the enemy's ships, was so much damaged from having received the broadside of every ship that passed her in succession, that she was compelled to strike; but not until her commander and 200 of her crew lay killed or wounded about their guns.

Admiral Boscawen now shifted his flag on board the *Newark*, an eighty-gun ship, and leaving the *Edgar* in charge of the prize, pursued the flying French ships all night. Under favour of its obscurity, the *Souvrain* and the *Guerrier* altered their course, and deserted their commander. At daybreak the latter, whose left leg had been fearfully shattered by a cannon-shot, finding that the British squadron was still following him inexorably under a cloud of canvas, resolved to burn or blow up his ships, rather than permit them to become the prizes of the victors.

Already the friendly shore was in sight, and the rising sun brightening the hills of Algarve and the Pinhao of the citadel of Lagos. The bay there is six miles wide from east to west, three from north to south, and defended by several batteries on the Point Nossa Senhora de Piedade; and if once anchored there, De la Clue believed he should be safe in neutral waters. But it was not so.

Three of his squadron came to anchor in the bay, but the *Ocean* got among the breakers, and ran ashore six miles from Lagos, near the fort of Almadona, the commander of which, as a warning that was unheeded, fired three shotted guns at the pursuers.

The moment the *Ocean* struck, her masts went by the board. Though wounded and helpless—almost dying—De la Clue and another French captain endeavoured to get their crews ashore by the boats; but there was a heavy gale from the seaward, and the breakers were rolling roughly and in foam upon the beach, hence disembarkation proved a difficult and dangerous process. The captains of the *Téméraire* and *Modeste*, MM. De Castillon and De Lac Montvert, instead of destroying their ships according to orders, anchored as close as they could to the forts of Xavier and Lagos, hoping to receive protection from their guns; but in that hope, they were disappointed.

M. de la Clue having been landed, the command of his shattered ship devolved on the Count de Carne, who, on receiving a single broadside from the *America*, a sixty-gun ship, commanded by Captain Kirk, at once struck her colours, and the ship—one of the finest in the French navy—became the prize of the conquerors.

Captain Bentley, of the *Warspite*, an officer who had served under

Lord Anson, and who had greatly distinguished himself by his courage on the preceding day, attacked the *Téméraire*, 74 guns, and brought her off with little damage; while Vice-Admiral Brodick, the second in command, in the *Prince*, burned the *Redoubtable*, a seventy-four-gun ship, which lay bulged among the breakers, and had been abandoned by her officers and men. By this time, the little Bay of Lagos was one arena of flames, smoke, and wreck. He also made a prize of the *Modeste*, which had been but little injured during the engagement. The *Ocean* was found to be so fast ashore, that Captain Kirk took the crew out of her, and set her on fire. Ere long she blew up with a crash, scattering blazing brands on every side.

The combat was now over, and the victory was obtained at a very small expense of men—in the British squadron there were only 56 men killed and 196 wounded. The loss of the enemy is unknown, but it must have been considerable, as Admiral de la Clue, in his letter to the French ambassador at Lisbon, owned that on board his own ship, the Ocean, 100 men were killed and 70 dangerously wounded; but the most severe circumstances of his disaster were the loss of four great ships of the line, two of which were destroyed, and two brought in triumph to England, "to be numbered," adds Smollett, "among the best bottoms of the British Navy."

The *Gentleman's Magazine* states that the *Modeste* had only been launched in the preceding year, 1758, and carried thirty-two-pounders on her lower deck; her quarter-deck guns were brass, and her poop was mounted with brass swivels. The *Téméraire*—a. name that afterwards became famous in our naval annals—carried forty-two-pounders below, eight brass guns abaft her mizzen-mast; and ten on her quarter. Both vessels had not above twenty shot in their hulls.

Admiral de la Clue did not long survive his defeat, as he died soon after of exhaustion and mortification, at Lagos. Not one of our officers lost his life in the engagement.

Captain Bentley, whom Admiral Boscawen sent to England with his dispatches, was knighted by the king; and, like Captain Campbell, who bore those of Admiral Hawke, received five hundred guineas wherewith to purchase a sword, in commemoration of the battle off Lagos cape and bay.

Martinique and Guadaloupe, 1759

Having now detailed the glories won in this year on the plains of Minden, on the heights of Abraham, and on the ocean by Hawke and Boscawen, we have to relate the achievements of our troops in the tropics, more particularly the expedition to the Leeward Isles, under the command of Major-Generals Hopson and Barrington—the latter an old and experienced officer—with Colonels Armiger, Haldane, Trapaud, and Clavering (afterwards General Sir John Clavering, K.B.) serving under them as brigadiers.

The troops detailed for this expedition consisted of the 3rd Buffs', 4th (or King's), 6th, 63rd, 64th, seven companies of the 42nd Highlanders, 800 marines, and a detachment of artillery; in all 5,560 men. They sailed from England under convoy, and after a three weeks' voyage came to anchor in Carlisle Bay, Barbadoes, where they were joined by Commodore Moore, who was to command the united squadron, amounting to ten ships of the line, besides frigates and bomb-vessels. Ten days were spent supplying the fleet with wood and water, in reviews, and beating up for volunteers. Every ship had forty sturdy negroes put on board, to assist in drawing the artillery; and on the 13th of January the armament put to sea.

It is worthy of remark that the Highlanders with this force were mere recruits, being the 2nd battalion of the Black Watch, formed at, Perth in the preceding, August, as we have elsewhere related, to revenge the slaughter of the 1st battalion at Ticonderoga.

Next morning the squadron sighted the mountains of Martinique, the highest of which, Mont Pelée, was then a dormant volcano, covered with woods, which continually attracted the clouds. The chief stronghold of this valuable island was the citadel of Fort Royal, a regular fort, garrisoned by four companies, 36 bombardiers, 80 Swiss, and 14 officers. One hundred barrels of beef constituted their chief

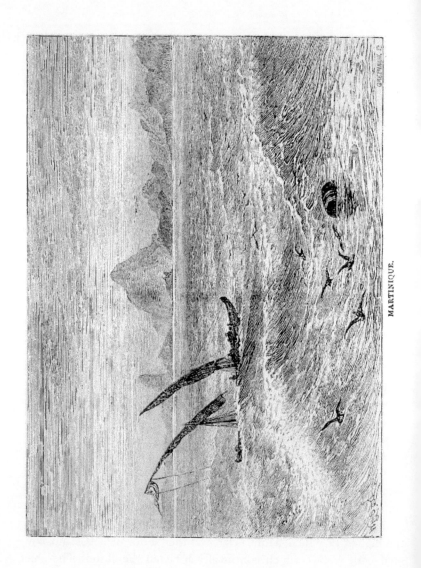

MARTINIQUE.

provisions; their cisterns were destitute of water, and their stores were without wadding, matches, or *langridge* shot for their cannon. They were very short of other ammunition, and their walls were ruinous; but they formed some intrenchments at St. Pierre and a place called Casdenaviers, where they thought the landing would be attempted.

On the 15th the squadron entered the great bay of Fort Royal, where some of the ships were exposed to the fire of a battery erected on the little Isle de Raniereo, halfway up the inlet. At their first appearance, the *Florissant*, 74 guns, with two frigates, drew close in towards the citadel, and came to anchor in the careenage, under shelter of the fortifications; but one, named *La Vestale*, made her escape in the night, through the transports, and sailed for European waters, where she was afterwards taken by Captain Hood.

Next day three ships of the line were ordered to attack Fort Negro, a battery three miles distant from the citadel, the guns of which they soon silenced; and it was soon after taken by a body of seamen and marines, who landed from their boats, scrambled up the rocks and masses of mangroves, till they reached the embrasures, which they entered with bayonets fixed, while the enemy fled with precipitation. The Union Jack was immediately hoisted, amid loud cheers; the guns were spiked, the carriages broken, the powder destroyed, and the detachment remained in possession of the battery.

The battery at Casdenaviers was next silenced. The French troops, reinforced with militia, had marched from the citadel to oppose any landing; but on seeing the whole British squadron, with the transports full of red-coats, and Fort Negro already in possession of the marines, they retired to Fort Royal, leaving the beach open; and there next morning the whole army landed, quietly and leisurely, as if going to exercise.

By ten o'clock, the grenadiers, the King's Regiment, and the Highlanders moved forward, and soon fell in with some parties of the enemy, with whom they maintained an irregular fire, till they came within a little distance of Morne Tortueson, an eminence in rear of Fort Royal, and the most important post in the island. There they maintained a sharp skirmish, during which it was said of the Highlanders, that:

Although debarred the use of arms in their own country, they showed themselves good marksmen, and had not forgotten how to handle their weapons.

In this skirmish sixty-three men and officers were killed or wounded.

About two in the afternoon. General Hopson gave the commodore to understand that he could neither maintain his ground nor attack the citadel unless the squadron would supply him with heavy guns. But as the latter must have been landed at a level green savannah, where they, with the boats' crews and negroes, would have been exposed to a fire from the fort, it was found necessary to relinquish the idea of having a battering-train; and after a Council of War was held, the troops were recalled from Morne Tortueson, and after burning the sugar-canes, and desolating the country in their retreat, all were re-embarked that evening.

The inhabitants of Martinique could scarcely credit their senses when they suddenly saw themselves delivered from all fear, at a time when they were overwhelmed with dismay and confusion, when all their leaders had resigned the thought of resistance, and were actually assembled in the public hall of Fort Royal to send deputies to General Hopson, with proposals for capitulation and surrender.

The majority of the sea and land officers constituting the Council of War having given their opinion that it might be for the public service to attack St. Pierre, the fleet proceeded to that part of the island, and entered the bay on the 19th. The commodore told General Hopson that as the town was open, it could be reduced with ease; but as the ships might be so disabled in the attack as to become unfit for more important duties, it was proposed that more attempts on Martinique should be relinquished, and the conquest of Guadaloupe was suggested. General Stewart says:

> There might be very good grounds for this preference, although it does not appear how any service of this nature can be accomplished without running a risk of disabling and diminishing the arms employed.

Accordingly, soon after the squadron was close in-shore, and the ships were ranged in a line with the Basse Terre, or western portion of Guadaloupe. Here stands the metropolis of this Caribbean Isle, defended by the citadel and other fortifications. Guadaloupe, which is about seventy miles in length by twenty-five in breadth, is divided in two by a channel called La Rivière Salée, about eighty yards broad. Its elevated hills consist chiefly of coral rocks, some of which are a thousand feet in height, and one. La Souffirin, rises to an altitude of 5,115 feet above the level of the sea. It is a mountain of sulphur; and though Martinique was an island of much more importance than Guadaloupe, the latter, at the time of which we write, made a much greater quantity of sugar than the former, and equipped far more privateers against British commerce.

It was resolved to make a general attack upon the citadel and other fortifications. Accordingly, the ships took up their various stations, and at nine o'clock on the morning of the 23rd of January the action began by Captain Trelawney turning the broadside of the *Lion* against a nine-gun battery, while the rest of the fleet continued to place themselves abreast of the other batteries, and the citadel, which was armed with forty-two guns and two mortars.

In a very short time the action became general. The booming of the cannon echoed with incessant reverberations among. the wooded mountains and on the shore, while the roar of the small-arms from the ships and batteries filled up the intervals of sound. For several hours this was continued with unabated vivacity; while the commodore, who had shifted his broad pennant from the flagship to the *Woolwich*, frigate, that he might watch the operations with ease, and apart from the smoke, gave his orders with the greatest deliberation. Save once before, in the attack on Carthagena, this expedient had never been resorted to by a British commander; but it was necessary on this occasion for the commodore to do so, that he might consult with the general, the brigadiers, and the engineer officers, on the various plans they had in view.

In opposing the batteries, every captain fought his ship with remarkable bravery, but more particularly Louis Leslie, of the *Bristol*: Thomas Burnet, of the *Cambridge*, 80 guns; Clark Gayton, of the *St. George* (an admiral in after years); Edward Jekyll, of the *Ripon*; Sir William Trelawney, of the *Lion*, who died Governor of Jamaica; and Molyneaux Lord Shuldam, of the *Panther*, "who, in the hottest of the engagement, distinguished themselves equally by their courage, impetuosity, and deliberation."

The *Burford* and *Berwick* being blown out of range by the rising wind, Captain Shuldham, in the *Panther*, was left unsustained; and two batteries turned all their fire upon the *Ripon*, which by two in the afternoon silenced all the guns of one, called the Morne Rouge, but at the same time she ran aground. On perceiving this disaster, the exulting French assembled in vast numbers on an adjacent hill, and lining a breastwork, opened therefrom a rolling fire of musketry; while the militia, with an eighteen-pounder, raked the helpless ship fore and aft for two consecutive hours.

Captain Jekyll returned the fire as well as he could, though his crew were perishing fast on every hand, till all his grape shot and wadding were expended, his rigging cut to pieces, and, to add to his misfortunes, a case containing 900 cartridges blew up on the poop, and set the ship on fire.

Jekyll threw out a signal of distress, but it was unseen amid the smoke. The flames, however, were extinguished; and Captain Leslie, of the *Bristol*, seeing the utterly helpless situation of the ship, ran in between her and the battery, laid his maintopsail to the mast, and opening fire upon the shore, made an immediate diversion in favour of Captain Jekyll, whose ship did not float till midnight, "when she escaped from the very jaws of destruction."

It was singular that the *Burford*, though she was fearfully mauled in her hull, and had her rigging cut to pieces and many of her guns dismounted, had not one man killed on board. But in other ships the casualties were severe, and many men were fated to find their last home among the long tangle-weed, the coral branches and rocks, at the bottom of the deep green Caribbean Sea.

By seven in the evening, all the other large ships having silenced the guns to which they had been respectively opposed, joined the rest of the fleet; and now in the darkness that so suddenly follows twilight in the tropics, four bomb-ketches anchored near the shore began to hurl their red hissing bombs and flaming carcasses into the town, which was speedily set on fire in all quarters, while ever and anon a magazine of powder blew up with a terrible explosion.

At two o'clock in the afternoon, next day, the fleet came to anchor in Basse Terre roads, where the flaming hulls of many vessels were to be seen, set on fire and abandoned by the enemy. Several ships attempted to escape and get to sea, but were taken. At five o'clock the troops began to land without opposition, and taking possession of the half-ruined town and empty citadel, encamped quietly in the vicinity.

For several days nothing took place but the establishment of some small posts on the hills nearest the town. On one of these Major Robert Melville, of the 38th—in after years a general officer and eminent as an antiquary—took up a position over against some intrenchments formed by Madame Ducharmey, a lady of high spirit, who, despising the French governor, the Chevalier Nadau d'Estriel, had armed her negroes and servants for resistance to the last. But of this more *anon*.

From a Genoese deserter the general learned that the French troops, before retiring, had laid a train to blow up the powder magazine in the citadel after ours had entered it; so, one of the first measures executed was to cut off the train and secure the magazine. The nails by which they had spiked their cannon were drilled out by the *matrosses*. A panic seemed to have possessed the French here. It is remarkable, says a foot note to Smollett, that the apprehension of cruel usage from the British, who are undoubtedly the most generous and humane enemies under the sun, not only prevailed among the French soldiery during the war, but even infected officers of distinction, who ought to have known better and to have been of a more liberal turn of thought; and to this emotion has been attributed the timid conduct of D'Estriel, the governor of Guadaloupe, who, when the British attacked the citadel and batteries, instead of remaining to animate and lead the defenders, retired to a distant plantation, and tamely watched the course of events.

The inhabitants continually harassed the scouting detachments by firing upon them suddenly from the thick woods and plantations of sugar-cane. These were set on flames in all directions, yet the bush fighting was incessant, and the French Creoles and armed negroes proved very expert at it. The beautiful scenery of Guadaloupe seemed to undergo a change as this strife went on. Instead of the bustle observable amid the peaceful sugar plantations, the working of mills, the driving of bullock-carts, the cutting of canes, and boiling of sugar, while the negroes sung and chorused, black clouds of smoke rolled over the green savannahs and curled among the long avenues of palms and the waving branches of the cocoa-nut trees.

Everywhere the pretty little dwellings of the negroes, the villas and mills of the planters, were destroyed. Ever and *anon* the musket-shot rang sharply out among the coral cliffs, while Creoles and negroes fled from bush and tree, followed by British marines and kilted Highlanders. Three hundred more of the latter had come from Scotland in the *Ludlow Castle*, just before the landing of the troops in Guadaloupe.

Madame Ducharmey, at the head of her armed slaves, having made many furious attacks upon the post of Major Melville, and intrenched them on a hill in his vicinity, he was under the necessity of attacking this Amazon sword in hand, and carrying her works by storm. She made her escape, but her houses and plantations were destroyed. Some of her people were killed, and a number taken. Of the major's party, twelve were killed and thirty wounded, including three officers, one of whom lost an arm. The latter was Lieutenant Maclean, of the 42nd Highlanders.

General Stewart says:

> It would appear, that this very noisy and unpolite intrusion on a lady's quarters did not injure Lieutenant Maclean in the esteem of the ladies of Guadaloupe; for we find that, although he got leave from General Barrington to return home for the cure of his arm, he refused to leave the regiment, and remained at his duty. He was particularly noticed by the French ladies for his gallantry and spirit, and the manner in which he wore his plaid and Scottish regimental garb.

Fevers invaded both the land and sea forces. Five hundred sick were sent to Antigua; and the total reduction of Guadaloupe appearing somewhat impracticable, the general resolved to transfer the seat of operations to the eastern part of the isle, called Grand Terre, which was protected by a strong battery, named Fort Louis. Accordingly, on the 13th of February, after a six hours' cannonade from the ships, a column of marines and Highlanders landed in boats. Their progress towards the shore being arrested by long trailing plants and mangrove roots, they leaped into the water, which rose above their girdles, attacked Fort Louis, and carried it at the point of the bayonet. In a few minutes the French colours were torn down and the Union Jack hoisted in their place.

> No troops could behave with more courage than the Highlanders and marines did on this occasion.

By this time 1,800 men and officers were dead or in hospital. General Hopson having died of fever, the command devolved upon General Barrington, who resolved to prosecute the reduction or the island with vigour; and in a few days all the batteries in and about Basse Terre were blown up. The detachments were recalled from the advanced posts, and the whole army re-embarked, except one battalion which was left under Colonel Debrissay, an accomplished and experienced officer, in the citadel of Basse Terre.

The enemy no sooner perceived the squadron under weigh than they descended from the hills in force, and endeavoured to take possession of the town, from which they were driven by a fire from the citadel. They now threw up a battery, from which they hurled shot and shell, and began to attempt a regular attack, but were repulsed

The taking Fort Louis

by a sally from the castle. In the midst of these operations, the gallant Colonel Debrissay, Major Trollop, a lieutenant, two bombardiers of the artillery detachment, and a number of soldiers, were blown up and destroyed by the explosion of a powder magazine. During the confusion caused by this catastrophe, the enemy made a vigorous attack, but were repulsed successfully; and General Barrington, on learning the fate of Debrissay, sent Major Melville to assume the command and repair the fortifications.

Meanwhile Commodore Moore, having received certain intelligence that the French Admiral de Bompart had arrived at Martinique with eight sail of the line and three frigates, with a battalion of Swiss and other troops on board, sailed, oddly enough, not to that island, but to the bay of Dominique; leaving General Barrington on that division of Guadaloupe known as Grand Terre, with only one ship of forty guns to protect the fleet of transports.

Colonel Crump was now ordered, with 600 bayonets, to attack the towns of St. Anne and St. Francis, and they were captured before sunrise, in a most gallant manner; and, notwithstanding a heavy fire from some trenches and batteries, the losses were trifling, and only one officer, Ensign Maclean, of the Highlanders, fell in the assault.

Pushing forward. Colonel Crump on the following day drove the enemy from another position, and stormed a battery of twenty-four-pounders. General Barrington now formed a scheme to surprise Petit Bourg and St. Marie's, on the Capesterre side, and this duty he assigned to Brigadiers Clavering and Crump; but, owing to the darkness of a most tempestuous night, when the wind howled amid palm and cocoa-nut trees, and the lightning flashed among the mountains, thus exciting the terror of their negro guides, the attempt failed, and the general was compelled to do that by force which he intended to have done by stratagem.

He now ordered the same commanders to land near the town of Arnonville, and they did so unopposed by the enemy, who retreated to a strong position on the banks of the Licorn. Save at two narrow passes, this river, rendered inaccessible by a morass covered by mangroves, was fortified by a redoubt and intrenchment mounted with guns.

Despite these disadvantages, the brigadiers determined on an assault, confident that their active Highlanders might surmount any natural obstacle. Under cover of a fire from their field-pieces, the Black Watch advanced to the attack, supported by the regiment of Duroure, or 38th. As they pushed on, the enemy began to waver. Then we are

212

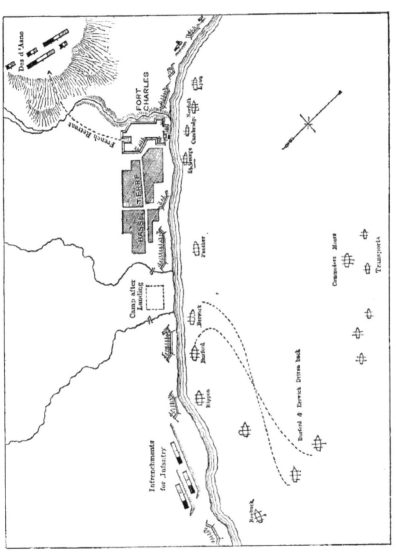

PLAN OF THE ATTACK ON THE ISLAND OF GUADALOUPE.

told, in *Letters from Guartaloupe*, that, slinging their muskets:

> The Highlanders drew their swords, and, supported by part of the other regiment, rushed forward with their characteristic impetuosity, and followed the enemy into the redoubt, of which they took possession.

Like the rest of the troops, they had endured intolerable heat, continual fatigue, the air of a climate to which they were unaccustomed, and the toil of climbing lofty mountains and steep precipices.

In storming this work, 65 men and officers were killed or wounded. Other works and towns being carried or captured elsewhere, they pushed on to Capesterre, amid the most lovely tropical scenery, and captured from one planter alone 870 negroes, who, being saleable, were then as valuable as prizemoney. There Colonel Clavering was met by MM. de Clairvilliers and Duquerny, deputed by the inhabitants of the island to know what terms of surrender would be granted to them.

They were conducted to General Harrington, who, considering the smallness of his force, which was diminishing daily by fever and the bullet, the chance of the enemy being succoured from Martinique, and the unaccountable absence of the commodore, resolved to settle the terms without delay; and they were barely signed when a messenger came with tidings that General Beauharnois had landed at St. Anne's with succour from Europe, with the squadron under M. de Bompart. But on learning that the capitulation was complete, these forces returned to Martinique.

Siege of Pondicherry, 1760-1

In every quarter of the globe where France had territory, war was waged against her at this time, and nowhere more successfully than in India.

The chief strength of the French there was at Pondicherry, on the Coromandel coast of Hindostan, a place which, while yet a village, with a slip of land about five miles long, had been purchased by King Louis from the Rajah of Bejapore. After being taken by the Dutch, and restored at the Peace of Ryswick, it speedily became populous; and fifty years of tranquillity enabled the French to construct a handsome and regular town—the capital of their settlements in India—with strong fortifications, from which, unaided by European arms, the natives could never have expelled a garrison.

The lofty bastions and ramparts were armed with formidable artillery; and, from its situation, Pondicherry could not be bombarded from the sea. Round this centre French influence extended over various parts of the vast peninsula, and France soon had colonies or factories at Ballasor, Cossimbazar, Masulipatam, and other places. Their power almost overshadowed ours; and, like us, they were soon drawn into alliances with native princes, and from being merchant-traders became soldiers.

When the tide of European war flowed from the West to the East, there were in India, on the British and French sides, men of eminent ability and romantic courage. If we had Clive, Hastings, and Eyre Coote, they had Lally, La Bourdonaye, and De Bussy.

On the declaration of war, in 1756, the Count de Lally, an Irish soldier of fortune in the French service (son of Captain O'Lally, of Tulloch-na-Daly, in Galway), was sent out as lieutenant-general and commander-in-chief of the French forces in India—a distant, and to

Europeans, but little-known land in those days, and only to be reached by long and perilous voyages round the stormy Cape.

In support of this expedition, the Court destined six millions of *livres*, six battalions of infantry, and three ships of war. The Chevalier des Soupirs was the second in command to Lally, who embarked at Brest, accompanied by his brother Michael. After various encounters, with varying success, in India, the Governor and Council at Calcutta, hearing that Lally meant to threaten Trichinopoly, determined that Colonel Eyre Coote, who had recently come from Europe, should take the field against him with about 700 European infantry, 7,000 *sepoys*, 370 horse, and 14 guns. Lally began his march at the head of 2,200 Frenchmen and 10,000 native troops.

Among the latter were 1,800 *sepoys*, called the Regiment de Marquis de Bussy, 300 Caffres, and 2,000 cavalry furnished by a Mahratta chief with whom Lally was in alliance. They were all clothed and armed after the brilliant and picturesque fashion of their country, and were led by a *rissaldar*, or commander of independent horse. Lally had with him twenty-five pieces of cannon.

He came in sight of the British on the banks of a sandy river, the Poliar, then quite dry, though in the usually rainy month of October. There they hovered in sight of each other, till Lally suddenly invested Vandevash, a fortress of the Carnatic, against which his batteries opened with such effect that in three days there was made a practicable breach in the outer bastion; but about the very time that Lally, a fiery and energetic officer, was about to lead the assault, Coote, with. 1,700 Europeans and 3,000 *sepoys*, fourteen pieces of cannon, and one howitzer, came suddenly upon his rear, to relieve the garrison.

Lally now found himself between two fires; but turning, like a lion at bay, he drew off from the trenches, and, on the 21st of January, 1760, formed in order of battle. While the lines were threequarters of a mile apart, the cannonading began on both sides, and was continued, with fatal precision till noon, when Lally's French horse began to charge the left wing of Coote, who sent a few companies of *sepoys* (whose name is derived from *sepahe*, the Indian word for a military tenant) and two guns, and these soon drove the troopers to the rear of their own army; and as the adverse lines still continued approaching, by one o'clock the roar of musketry rattled from flank to flank, and the broad green plain on which the unclouded sun was shining became shrouded in snow-white smoke, Lally now placed himself at the head of his line of infantry, and leading on in person the Regiment of Lorraine, impetuously fell on that part of the British line where Coote was dismounted at the head of his troops to receive him.

Two distinct volleys of musketry were given and received, after which the Regiment of Lorraine—which has been sometimes styled *Les Gardes Lorraines*—raised by Prince Thomas of Savoy in 1643, rushed on to the charge with incredible fury. Sword in hand, Count Lally was in front. The bayonets clashed and crossed, and the British line was broken.

Broken, but for three minutes only. Then ensued a brief but terrible and bloody series of single combats, and. the Regiment of Lorraine was hurled back in confusion and defeat, over ground strewn with its own dead and dying; while the explosion of a tumbril in the rear added to the disorder, of which Coote took instant' advantage, by ordering Major Brereton, with Sir William Draper's Regiment, to fall on the French left, and seize a fortified post which they were about to abandon. This service was performed gallantly; the French left was routed, and hurled by the bayonet on its centre.

Draper's Regiment was the 79th, not the present Cameron Highlanders, which were raised in 1805 by Sir Alan Cameron, of Erroch, but an older corps, which was disbanded in 1763, Confusion now reigned supreme among the enemy; but Major Brereton, a gallant and accomplished officer, fell mortally wounded.

"Follow—follow!" he exclaimed to some of his soldiers, who were affectionately disposed to linger near him. "Follow your comrades, and leave me to my fate!"

He expired soon after, but, led by Major Monson, the regiment advanced with increased ardour and fury; and, after a vain and desperate attempt made by the Marquis de Bussy, with Lally's regiment of the Irish Brigade, to repel it, the French and their allies were by two o'clock in the afternoon routed in every direction. The Irish regiment was almost cut to pieces; De Bussy had his horse shot under him, and was captured by Major Monson, to whom he presented his sword.

Lally brought up his cavalry to cover his retreat from a field where he left 1,000 men killed or wounded, and 50 taken prisoners, including the marquis, his quartermaster-general, Le Chevalier de Gadville, Colonel Murphy, many other officers, and nearly all his cannon.

Coote lost 260 in killed and wounded. Marshal Grant, Vicomte de Vaux, asserts that the losses were equal on both sides. Ultimately the campaign ended gloriously for Britain, by the conquest of Arcot, a most extensive maritime district of Hindostan, and by hemming up the Count de Lally in the fortifications of Pondicherry, which ere long was fated to be the last scene of his long and brilliant career. The approach of the, rainy season, together with the well-known reputation for skill, valour, and resolution enjoyed by the Irish general of the now all but ruined French East India Company, caused a regular siege to be deemed almost impracticable for a time. Other measures therefore had to be tried.

"It was resolved," says the Sieur Charles Grant, "to block up the place by sea and land."

Lally had now only 1,500 French troops with him. These were the remnants of nine corps of the King's and Company's services; the cavalry, artillery, and invalids of the latter; the Creole Volunteers of the Isle of Bourbon; the Artillery du Roi, the Regiment de Mazinis, and those of Lorraine and Lally (which were numbered respectively the 30th and 119th of the French Line), with the Battalion d'India,

The British armaments were much more considerable than those of their opponents. On the land they had four battalions of the Line; at sea were seventeen sail of the line, carrying 1,038 pieces of cannon, the smallest vessels in the fleet being three fifty-gun ships.

The fortress of Pondicherry being as strong as art and nature could make it, Colonel Coote was perfectly aware that it could only be reduced by famine. Moreover, he was of opinion that, with such an antagonist as Lally, a siege with regular approaches and assaults might prove futile; as, in addition to his French comrades, the Irish count had a strong body of armed *sepoys*, and a vast store of ammunition and arms, including 700 pieces of cannon and many millions of ball cartridges. Independent of mortars, 508 pieces armed the walls, which were as much as five miles in circumference. There were thirteen great bastions and six gates. Though there was an overplus of population, the first care of Lally had been to victual the place completely, alike for the garrison and inhabitants.

A number of petty forts surrounded Pondicherry; but these were speedily reduced, and the whole surrounding country fell into the hands of the British.

On the 17th of March the fleet of Sir Samuel Cornish came to anchor in the roadstead; and while Coote drew nearer by land, Lally fell back on the fortress, disputing bravely every yard of ground, until in front of Pondicherry he formed those famous lines, which, with a skill and valour that were admirable, he defended for twelve weeks, thus giving sufficient time to have the town fully victualled, and also

A British advance

to conclude a treaty with the Rajah of Mysore, who pledged himself to continue a supply of provisions—a pledge he forgot to fulfil.

On the 2nd of September, 1760, Lally made a fierce sortie on the advanced posts of Coote, but was driven back with great loss, while seventeen of his guns were taken. Eight days subsequently the last work of the fortified boundary was stormed, and the French were fully enclosed in Pondicherry. Coote had 110 killed and wounded. Among the latter was Major Monson, who had a leg torn off by a cannon-shot.

A body of the 89th Highland Regiment, which had been raised among the Gordon clan in the preceding year at Badenoch, were landed from the *Sandwich*, East Indiaman, and behaved with their usual gallantry. Pressing onward, they burst from the rear, through Draper's grenadiers, in their eagerness to get at the enemy. Tossing aside their muskets, they raised a wild cheer, and with their bonnets in one hand and claymores in the other, threw themselves upon the soldiers of Lally, and cut many to pieces. They were only fifty in number, and were commanded by Captain George Morrison. From that time the operations of Lally were confined to the ramparts of Pondicherry. Several of his cannon were taken by the brave little band of Highlanders. Seven of these were found to be eighteen-pounders, loaded to the muzzle with all sorts of projectiles—bars of iron, jagged metal, stones, and bottles.

As the naval *chef d'escadre*, Count d'Ache, seemed, by sailing elsewhere, to have completely abandoned Lally to his fate, a fifty-four-gun ship, a thirty-six-gun frigate, and four Indiamen, all under the French flag, were left shut up hopelessly in the roadstead.

In the month of October five sail of the line remained to blockade Pondicherry from the seaward, under Captain Robert Haldane, of the *America*, (who died on service there); while Colonel Coote enforced the investment by land. By their dispositions and vigilance, the dense population soon became deeply distressed for want of food, while the incessant rains rendered closer operations impracticable. These abated on the 26th of November, and Coote then directed his engineers to erect batteries for the purpose of enfilading the works of the garrison. Failure of provisions now compelled Lally to expel from the town a vast number of native women and children; and as Coote sternly drove them back again, great numbers of these poor creatures were killed or wounded by the fire of the batteries, which were all the time in full operation.

About this time there died of fatigue in the trenches Sir Charles Chalmers, of Cults, a Scottish baronet, who served in the artillery. He possessed only the title, his estates having been forfeited after the Battle of Culloden, fourteen years before.

The English force still continued on the aggressive. On the night of the 7th of October, the boats of the squadron pulled into the harbour with muffled oars; and, under the muzzles of Lally's guns, cut out a frigate and Indiaman, with the loss only of thirty men and officers.

By the 25th of September Coote's force amounted to 3,500 Europeans and 7,000 *sepoys.* The scarcity within the guarded circle of Pondicherry increased daily, till at last the stock of provisions ran out, and the soldiers and citizens were compelled to devour the flesh of elephants, camels, horses, dogs, cats, and even rats. Lally was frequently implored to surrender; but to no purpose, for his lofty pride and resolute spirit had made him vow that he would perish amid the ruins of the place, yet never surrender it.

The price of a small dog was twenty-four *rupees,* and in some instances reached as much as twelve crowns; and by the 9th of November, when Coote erected a ricochet battery at only 1,400 yards' distance from the glacis, all hope had died away in Pondicherry.

Four other batteries were now erected—one at 1,100 yards' distance, called Prince William's Battery, mounted with two guns and one mortar, to destroy the cannon on the redoubt of San Thomé; a second, called Prince Edward's, faced the southern works, at 1,200 yards' distance, to enfilade the streets from north to south; a third, called the Duke of Cumberland's Battery, was thrown up 1,000 yards from the north-west bastion, to enfilade the counter-guard; and a fourth, called the Prince of Wales's Battery, was formed near the sea-beach, on the north, to enfilade the great street which intersects the White Town.

All these began firing at once on the night of the 8th of December; and, personally animating his troops, Lally responded by a simultaneous cannonade. A fifth battery, called the Hanover, armed with ten guns and three mortars, opened at 450 yards' distance against the counter-guard and curtain on the 26th of January, 1761; and now driven frantic by their sufferings, all in Pondicherry clamoured loudly for its surrender.

Thoroughly dissatisfied with the state of Indian affairs, enraged at his desertion by the faithless Rajah of Mysore, and, more than all, by the disorderly conduct of his troops, Lally exclaimed with passion—

Hell has thrown me into this country of wickedness, and, like Jonas, I await until the whale shall receive me into its belly. I shall go among the Caffres rather than remain longer in this place.

On the 5th of January Coote attacked the Redoubt of San Thomé, sword in hand, at the head of his grenadiers and the 89th Gordon Highlanders, captured it, and silenced all its guns; but on the 7th Lally retook it, at the head of 300 Frenchmen, from the *sepoys* who had been left in charge. Six days afterwards, Coote sent 1,100 men, under a field-officer, to erect a sixth battery, for eleven guns and three mortars. Though its formation proceeded under the clear splendour of a brilliant moon, in their sullen despair the soldiers of Lally never offered any opposition, and never even fired to retard the workers, till by the 14th the ravelin of the Madras Gate was beaten down, and a great breach effected, while the cannon of Pondicherry were effectually silenced.

The siege was now over. On the evening of the 15th the French drums beat a parley, and four envoys came from among the ruined walls with proposals for capitulation.

These were, that the garrison, being in a state of starvation, would surrender as prisoners of war; that the people of Pondicherry should retain all their civil and religious rights; that Coote might take possession of the Villenour Gate on the morrow.

Lally asked:

I demand from a principle of justice and humanity, that the mother and sister of Raza Sahib (then in the city) may be permitted to seek an asylum where they please; or that they remain prisoners among the English, and not be delivered into the hands of Mohammed Ali Khan, which are red with the blood of the husband and father, to the shame of those who gave him up to him.

With regard to respecting the churches and permitting free exercise of the Catholic emancipation, Colonel Coote, in the spirit of those pre-emancipation times, declined to reply; and at eight o'clock on the morning of the 16th of January, Lally, with a bitter heart, ordered the white standard of France to be hauled down on Fort Louis; and at the same hour Coote's grenadiers received the Villenour Gate from the Irish regiment of Lally, while the men of the 79th Regiment took possession of the citadel.

Thus, fell the capital of the French Indies, after a siege which the skill and valour of Lally protracted, amid a thousand difficulties, for eight months, against forces whose numbers were treble in strength to those he commanded.

On the 17th he marched out at the head of his famished garrison, the strength of which stood thus, officers included:—Artillery of Louis XV., 83; the Regiment of Lorraine, 237; the Regiment of Lally, 230; the Regiment of the Marine, 295; Artillery of the French India Company, 94; Cavalry and Volunteers of Bourbon, 55; Battalion d'India and Invalides, 316.

One of their first acts before marching out was to cut their commissary to pieces. The quantity of military stores delivered over to Coote is incredible. There were 671 guns and mortars, 14,400 muskets and pistols, 4,895 swords, 1,200 pole-axes, and 84,041 common shot, with powder in proportion. The whole plunder amounted to £2,000,000 sterling.

The 89th Highlanders formed the new garrison. On the same day that Lally surrendered, his Scottish compatriot, Law de Lauriston, nephew of the famous financier, on whose assistance he had long relied, was defeated by Major Carnac, at Guya, and taken prisoner, with sixty other officers in the service of France.

Most miserable was the future fate of Lally. After all his exertions, wounds, and services, he was surrendered by the contemptible Court of France as a victim to popular clamour. He was detained for four years in a close prison, and was repeatedly tortured, according to the barbarous law then in force in France. On the 4th of May, 1763, he was removed from the Bastille to the prison of the *Conciergerie*, at Paris, and his cross and red ribbon were taken from him.

"My God!" he exclaimed, as he clasped his hands. "Oh, my God! is this the reward of forty years' faithful service as a soldier?"

On the 9th of May, 1766, he was ultimately drawn on a hurdle to the place of execution, or the Place de Grève; a gag was put in his mouth to prevent him from addressing the people, and he was hastily —almost privately—beheaded in the dusk of the morning.

So, perished one of Ireland's bravest soldiers of fortune.

The old 79th (or Draper's) Regiment, lost at the siege of Pondicherry thirty-four officers, whose names were inscribed on a beautiful cenotaph, erected on Clifton Downs by Colonel Sir William Draper, and which he inscribed thus:—

Sacred to the memory of those departed warriors of the 79th Regiment by whose valour, discipline, and perseverance the French land forces in Asia were first withstood and repulsed.

SURRENDER OF PONDICHERRY

The Defeat of Thurot, "The Corsair", 1760

During the continuance of this war, the greatest scourge of our mercantile commerce, particularly off the coast of Scotland, was Commodore Thurot, usually known as "The Corsair," whose name was a terror and by-word from south of Berwick to north of Caithness; who actually swept our shipping from the North Sea, and captured Carrickfergus, taking prisoners there nearly the whole of the 62nd Regiment of the Line, at the head of troops composed, according to the *Edinburgh Chronicle*, of drafts from the Scots and Irish in the French service, and who, after a long series of daring exploits, in the course of which he had inflicted immense damage upon the commerce of this country, was eventually doomed to find his last home in the ruined chapel of Kirkmaiden, on the eastern shore of the Bay of Luce, in Galloway.

Smollett says:

> This man's name became a terror to the merchants of Britain, for his valour was not more remarkable in battle than his conduct in eluding the British cruisers who were successively detached in pursuit of him through every part of the German Ocean and the North Sea, even to the Islands of Orkney. It must be likewise owned, for the honour of human nature, that this bold mariner, though destitute of the advantages of birth, was remarkably distinguished by his generosity and compassion to those who had the misfortune to fall into his power; and that his deportment in every respect entitled him to more honourable rank in the service of his country.

A memoir of Francois Thurot appeared in 1760, by Père J. F. Durand, but it is unworthy of credence. His true history is, that he was born at Nuitz, then a village of Burgundy, in 1727, where his father was a surveyor; and after being educated by the Jesuits at Dijon, feeling a vocation for the sea, he travelled secretly to Dunkirk, and at the age of sixteen shipped on board a privateer, which in her first trip was taken by the British. After a few more voyages, on reaching manhood, the *armateurs*, as they were called, or privateer outfitters, of Dunkirk, had no hesitation in confiding to him their vessels; and this trust he rewarded by the capture of valuable prizes, taken while he was a "*corsair*," which in France means a rover without a commission, while "*armateur*" meant one commissioned by the royal authority, yet not a naval officer.

The peace of 1748 found him compelled to become a merchant captain, and the maker of many successful voyages. In one of these, when at London, he became acquainted with a beautiful young girl who lived at the then remote village of Paddington, and who eloped with him in his ship to France.

The war of 1755 saw him at sea in an armed privateer of his own; and so great were his achievements that Louis XV. made him a captain in the Royal Navy, and with *La Friponne*, corvette, he had special orders to cruise in the Channel. His favourite emblem or cognisance was a hound pursuing a pack of deer, and this he had engraved on the blade of a long dagger that he constantly wore, and which is now preserved in the Museum of the Scottish Antiquaries at Edinburgh.

With *La Friponne*, he captured upwards of sixty of our merchant ships. The Marshal Duke de Belleisle now gave him two frigates and two corvettes, with orders to intercept some ships then coming from Archangel. On this expedition he was attacked by one of our frigates, but handled her so roughly that she was compelled to bear away for Plymouth to refit.

So alert were the privateers of France, that between the 1st of March and the 10th of June, 1757, they captured 200 British vessels; and the whole number taken by them between the 1st of June, 1756, and the 1st of June, 1760, amounted to 2,539 sail. In the same space ours took 994 sail, including 242 privateers.

In May, 1758, Thurot infested the coast of Scotland, which since the Union had been left in a very defenceless state. When almost within sight of Edinburgh, he heard of four sail being seen to the seaward; and supposing that they must be merchantmen, he went in search, but found them to be all heavily armed, and two rated as frigates. They proved to be the *Solebay*, Captain Robert Craig, and the *Dolphin*, Captain (afterwards Admiral) Benjamin Marlowe, each carrying twenty-eight guns. Thurot was alone, having only the *Belleisle*, 46 guns and 500 men, yet he hesitated not to engage those four vessels which had left Leith in search of him.

The battle began about seven o'clock in the morning, off the Red Head of Angus, a lofty and rocky cape, chiefly remarkable as being the point northward beyond which, until 1793, coal could not be carried without paying an enormous duty.

Thurot was first assailed by the *Dolphin*, which fought for an hour and half, when the *Solebay* came up, and all three fought with great bravery till noon, when the Frenchmen sheered off, leaving our two frigates so crippled that they were barely able to creep into Leith. The *Dolphin* had her masts wounded, her main, sprit, and topsail-yards shot away, her sails and rigging torn to pieces, and sixteen of her men killed or wounded. The *Solebay* had her main, maintopsail, and maintopgallant yards shot clean away; her sails and rigging rendered totally unserviceable, and eighteen killed or wounded; among the latter her captain. The *Belleisle* had eighty killed and wounded.

During the whole of that year, in the North Sea he caused enormous loss to British, and more particularly to Scottish, commerce, till the 3rd of December, when he anchored safely at Dunkirk, covered with wounds and glory. He was presented by Louis XV. to Madame de Pompadour, at Versailles, and all France resounded with the name of François Thurot.

The French Ministry having consulted with him as to the best means of annoying us, an armament was carefully fitted out at Dunkirk. It was to consist of five frigates and a corvette. Of these Thurot had the sole command, with orders to make descents upon the Irish coast, and thus, by distracting the attention of the Government, facilitate the enterprise of M. de Conflans elsewhere. Favoured by a dense fog, he crept out of the roads of Dunkirk on the 15th of October, 1759; and in the evening, after eluding the watchfulness of Commodore Boys, he came to anchor off Ostend with his little squadron, which consisted of the *Marechal de Belleisle*, 46 guns, with, 226 sailors and 430 soldiers on board; *La Blonde*, 36 guns. Captain La Kayce, 200 seamen and 200 soldiers; *Le Terpsichore*, 24 guns. Captain Desraudais, *L'Amaranthe*, 24 guns, and *La Bezon*, 36 guns, each with about 170 seamen and 170 soldiers—in all, our account says, 700 seamen, and 1,270 soldiers, under Brigadier Flobert, 230 having been left on the sick-list.

On the 16th he again put to sea, and in the night, came upon his old antagonist, the *Solebay*, then commanded by Captain (afterwards Admiral) John Dalrymple; but he ordered all the poop-lights to be put out, and stood on his course in the dark. A few days later saw him menacing Aberdeen.

Along all the coast of Scotland the forts were put in a state of defence; the ancient war beacons were re-erected, muster-places appointed, and, by the request of the Convention of Royal Burghs, 200 stand of arms were issued to every town north of the Tay. The alarm spread to Liverpool, on the west coast, and there twenty companies, each one hundred strong, were enrolled, and a fifty-gun battery erected.

Commodore Boys ploughed the North Sea in vain—he could nowhere find the ubiquitous Thurot, who lost *La Bezon*, which foundered with all hands on board; and, sorely battered by winds and tempests of rain and snow, on the 24th of January, 1760, his diminished squadron threatened the town of Deny in Ireland, but a storm blew him into St. George's Channel, where *La Blonde* had to cast all her guns overboard.

In February, with starving crews, he was in the Sound of Jura, where he procured some cattle and potatoes by a treaty with Campbell of Ardmore, at whose house he and his officers first heard of the terrible defeat sustained by Conflans off Brest. Op the 21st of February he sailed straight for the Bay of Carrickfergus, where he made every preparation for a resolute and hostile landing. In the forenoon his ships were off the Isle of Magee, about two miles and a half from the castle; and, with all their ports open and guns run out, came to anchor at eleven o'clock, within musket-shot of Kilrute Point.

The garrison at this time consisted of only four companies of General William Strode's Regiment (the present 62nd Foot), formed from the 2nd battalion of the 4th or King's, which had landed from Minorca in the preceding year. These companies, however, were raw recruits, and were actually at instruction drill, half a mile distant on the Belfast road, when the boats of Thurot suddenly landed the French infantry. The alarm spread rapidly, as the peasantry were seen flying in all directions. The guards were turned out; the sentinels doubled, and the troops got under arms in the marketplace, under Lieutenant-Colonel Jennings, of the 62nd, who sent his adjutant, Lieutenant Benjamin Hall, to reconnoitre. That officer soon returned to report that eight boats were landing French troops, who were getting into position on rising ground, bordered by walls, dykes, and hedges.

Colonel Jennings ordered detachments to secure the gates of the town; but at first the troops had only blank ammunition in their pouches, and ultimately a very small quantity of ball cartridge could be secured for them and the militia, who now got under arms, and were dispatched to Belfast with all the French prisoners, of whom there were many in the castle of Carrickfergus.

By this time the enemy, under Brigadier Flobert, were in full march for that place, preceded by a few hussars mounted on horses picked up in the fields, for which they had brought saddles and harness ashore. The detachments at the Scotch and North Gates, and along Lord Donegal's garden wall, were now fiercely attacked, but maintained their posts till their pouches were empty, on which Colonel Jennings, by sound of bugle, drew the whole into the ancient and half ruinous castle; but before its gates were closed and barricaded, the French infantry poured through the market-place and assailed them with the bayonet. An entrance was soon forced, but Colonel Jennings, William Knollys, then Viscount Wallingford (who died Earl of Banbury), Captain Bland, and Lieutenant Ellis, of the 62nd, with some gentlemen volunteers and fifty soldiers, drove them back. Lieutenant Hall states that:

> Here he saw great resolution in a few Irish boys, who defended the gate after it was opened, with their bayonets, and those from the Half Moon, who, after their ammunition was gone, threw stones and bricks.

It is recorded by Smollett that while the troops were hotly engaged in the streets, a little child ran playfully between them, upon which:

> A French soldier grounded his piece, took up the child in his arms, and returning to his place, resumed his musket and renewed his hostility.

Finding himself without ammunition, in an old and defenceless castle, which had a breach fifty feet long in its outer wall. Colonel Jennings beat a parley and requested terms, which were given by Commodore Thurot and Brigadier Flobert, to the following effect:—

That the companies of the 62nd Foot should march out with the honours of war, the officers to be on parole, and the men to be exchanged within a month; the castle not to be demolished, or the town burned, and rations to be provided for the French troops.

The alarm having spread by this time. General Strode began to collect at Newry the regiments of Pole, Sandford, and Anstruther (10th, 52nd, and 58th), together with the 5th Royal Irish Dragoons and Whitby's Light Horse (now 9th Lancers). These tidings, together with the hostility of the people, compelled Thurot to spike the guns, reembark the troops, and put hastily to sea, after taking two vessels, laden chiefly with linen, out of the Loch of Belfast, and having with him as prisoner the unfortunate Mayor of Carrickfergus.

On the morning of the 28th, about four o'clock, his ships were seen by Captain John Elliot (of the house of Minto), who had under his command the *Æolus*, 32 guns; the *Pallas*, 36, Captain Michael Clements; and the *Brilliant*, 36, Captain James Logie, with 700 men all told. Thurot was then hovering near the Isle of Man; chase was instantly given, and by one o'clock his ships hauled up their canvas and shortened sail. Then began a close and desperate action. Infuriated by all he had undergone by wind, waves, and starvation on this last expedition, Thurot fought with the fury of despair, till a musket-ball stretched him on the deck in mortal agony.

By that time all his ships were more or less disabled. The stately *Belleisle* had her bowsprit, mainyard and mizzenmast shot away; her hull was completely riddled, and she was in a sinking state, when the first lieutenant of the *Æolus* sprang on her deck at the head of his boarders, and hauled down her colours with his own hand, on which the other ships immediately struck. The *Blonde* and *Terpsichore* were added to the Royal Navy, as was also the *Pallas*, which, in 1782, was destroyed off the Isle of St. George.

François Thurot expired in his thirty-ninth year, and before the action was quite over, in the arms of his mistress; and, in the confusion of the time, his body, wrapped in a piece of carpet torn from the, floor of his cabin, was cast with other corpses into the sea. The British loss was not above 36 killed and wounded; while that of Thurot, as he had troops on board, amounted to more than 300 men. Captain Elliot carried his prizes into Ramsay Bay; and he and Colonel Jennings received the thanks of the Irish Parliament, with the freedom of the city of Cork, in silver boxes, while the defeat and fall of Thurot was causing great rejoicing in all the northern seaports.

Many corpses were now from time to time washed ashore on the south-east coast of Luce Bay, in Scotland, and among them was one which was at once recognised as that of the terrible Thurot.

It had a ball in the pit of the stomach; it was hastily sewn up in a carpet of silk velvet, and was attired in full uniform, with all the insig-

CARRICKFERGUS CASTLE.

nia of a commodore of the Royal Navy of France. In one pocket was found a tobacco-box of chased silver, with his name, François Thurot, engraved on the lid; in another was his watch, which became the prize of a domestic at Monreith House, and is now, or was lately, in possession of a gentleman at Castle Douglas. His linen bore the initials "F.T.;" and in his belt was his long, ivory-hilted, and single-edged dagger, having graven on the blade his well-known cognisance—a hound pursuing a herd of deer.

The lord of the manor. Sir William Maxwell, Bart., of Monreith, interred the remains with every honour in his own burial-place at Kirkmaiden. The silver box he bestowed upon Captain Elliot, the victor, who died an admiral; and he retained only the sodden carpet as a relic of the French hero, whose dagger, we have said, is now preserved at Edinburgh. Sir William acted as chief mourner, and was attended by the minister of Penninghame, who with others had witnessed the battle from the cliffs above the sea.

Long previous to this battle off the Isle of Man, the father of Thurot, the old surgeon of Nuitz, had been in receipt of a handsome pension from Louis XV., as a reward for the warlike services of his son. The grave of Thurot lies within sound of the waves of the Scottish sea, amid the venerable ruins of Kirkmaiden, which are beautifully embosomed among the Heughs, a wooded hollow, by the base of a steep and solitary hill.

The place is unmarked by a stone; but though almost forgotten, even in his native country, a recent history of Galloway and Wigton tells us that the peasant girls still remember him in their songs as "the gallant and gentle Thurret," for so they pronounce his name.

Belleisle, 1761

While the siege of Pondicherry was progressing in the distant East, and Thurot was cutting up the commerce of the Scots, there was planned and executed an expedition which made much noise in its time, for the capture and reduction of Belleisle-en-Mer, in the Bay of Biscay, on the south-east coast of Brittany, an island about fifteen miles long, and varying from five to twelve miles broad. It had belonged in former times to a line of the house of Fouquet, who exchanged it in 1718 with the King of France, for the Duchy of Gisors.

The naval armament, consisting of thirty-three sail, carrying 1,634 guns, was under the command of Admiral the Hon. Augustus Keppel, who had among his captains, Adam Duncan (afterwards Viscount Duncan of Camperdown); John Harvey (afterwards Earl of Bristol); the Hon. Samuel Harrington, son of the viscount of that name; Sir Thomas Stanhope; Captain (afterwards Admiral Sir Edward) Affleck, who was made a baronet for his valour in 1782; John Storr, a future admiral, who lost a leg in battle with the *Orphée*, French frigate; James Gambier; Clarke Gayton, who fought at Guadaloupe; and George Mackenzie, afterwards commodore at Jamaica.

Admirals Keppel's flag was on board the *Valiant*, 74, Captain Duncan.

The troops, which were under the command of Major-General Studholm Hodgson, were 10,000 strong, and, with some light horse, consisted of the following corps:—Regiment of Major-General Edward Whitmore (9th Foot); Regiment of Lord George Beauclerk, Duke of St. Albans (19th Foot); Regiment of Lieutenant-General William Earl of Panmure (Scots Fusiliers); Regiment of the Hon. J. Stuart, son of Lord Galloway (37th Foot); Regiment of Lieutenant-General Sr John Gray, Bart. (61st Foot); Regiment of Sir Henry Erskine, Bart. (25th or Edinburgh Regiment); Regiment of the Hon.

Charles Colville, son of Lord Culross (69th Foot); Regiment of Lieutenant-General William Rufane (disbanded.)

Five newly-raised independent companies were formed into a small battalion, to be commanded by Lord Pulteney. It was too much the fashion in those days to waste the strength of our army in effecting unwise and partial descents on an enemy's coast, rather than combining for one great effort; but the attack on Belleisle was deemed a grand attempt to harass the French on their own soil.

The expedition sailed from St. Helen's on Sunday, the 29th of March, the transports passing through the Needles—that strange cluster of pointed rocks westward of the Isle of Wight—under the convoy of the frigates, to meet the ships of the line; but it was not until the evening of Tuesday that the various officers were informed that the destination of the armament was Belleisle.

Beating against headwinds, it was not until the 7th of April that the French coast was in sight and the wind became fair. The cutters were sent out to reconnoitre the beach, and at midnight the whole fleet came to anchor, and preparations were made for landing. "The citadel of Palais, the capital of the isle," is in London prints of the day described as:

> A strong fortification, fronting the sea, composed principally of a hornwork, and is provided with two dry ditches, the one next the counterscarp, and the other so contrived as to secure the interior fortifications. This citadel is divided from the largest part of the town by an inlet of the sea, over which there is a bridge of communication. From the other part of the town, that which is most inhabited, it is only divided by its own fortifications and a glacis, which projects into a place called the Esplanade, where the great reservoir is kept. Though there is a fine conveniency for having wet ditches, yet round the town there is only a dry one, and some fortifications which cannot in many places be esteemed of the strongest kind; indeed, the low country which lies to the southward can easily be laid under water.

A descent was proposed at three different places from our fleet, which was moored in the great roadstead of Palais; while a squadron, under Captain Buckle, cruised off Brest, to prevent Belleisle being succoured from thence. At five in the morning the troops began to leave the fleet, just about sunrise.

General Hodgson, in his dispatch says:

The enemy's attention was so distracted with our attempts at landing at different points, where there was the best appearance of our being able to succeed, that it gave Brigadier Lambert an opportunity of climbing up a rock with a corps I had left with him for that purpose.

This rock overhung Port Andeo Bay, on the south-east side of the isle; and Lambert's corps landed under cover of a fire from the *Achilles*, 60 guns, and *Dragon*, 74. The steep nature of the coast at this point had rendered the Chevalier de St. Croix, who commanded in Belleisle, somewhat indifferent to the defence of it; hence the grenadier company of the 19th, led by Captain Paterson, were in full possession of the rocks ere the French were aware of the circumstance. They were soon attacked by a detachment 300 strong, but resolutely held their ground till the rest of Hamilton Lambert's brigade joined them; when the French were speedily driven in, with the loss of three pieces of brass cannon and many killed and wounded, while the British casualties were trifling—only some thirty or so—but Captain Paterson lost an arm.

In this affair a private named Samuel Johnson displayed remarkable bravery. On perceiving a subaltern of his regiment, to whom he felt grateful for some act of past kindness, overpowered by numbers, and about to be bayoneted by a French grenadier, he rushed to his assistance, shot one through the head, then, slinging his musket, he drew his broadsword, slew five more, and, though covered with wounds, carried off the officer, who presented him with twenty guineas, and had him next day promoted to the rank of sergeant.

While this attack and lodgement were going on, another was attempted at a place named Sawzon; but at an hour too late in the day, as the general obscurely states, to do more than give the necessary orders for the landing of the first troops at the rocks.

Lambert having silenced the three-gun battery which commanded the bay, the boats of the fleet, with the 37th and 61st Regiments and a body of marines, were pulled in-shore; but the enemy were seen strongly intrenched on each side of a hill, "which," says the general:

> Was so excessively steep, and the foot of it so scraped (scarped?) away, that it was impossible to get up to the breastwork.

Schomberg has it that "the enemy had taken post on the top of an almost inaccessible mountain where they had strongly intrenched themselves," but that several vigorous efforts were made to dislodge them.

Major Purcell, with the grenadiers of the 61st (200 of the Scots Fusiliers, according to one account), and Captain Osborne, with those of the Edinburgh Regiment, were first on shore, and attacked the enemy with great intrepidity; but being exposed to a dreadful fire from the heights above, they suffered severely. A writer in the *Edinburgh Courant* of that date, who served at Belleisle, states that Captain Osborne drew up his grenadiers in such a position as to enfilade the enemy; but that he was not properly supported by the rest of the troops. In landing, having lost his fusil, Osborne drew his sword, and leading on his grenadiers, got so close to the enemy that, though he received two musket-shots, he exchanged several cuts and thrusts with their officers.

His grenadiers fired a volley and then rushed on with their bayonets; but the intrenchment could not be surmounted, though the officer commanding the French was killed. Major Purcell and Captain Osborne also fell dead, and Brigadier Carlton (afterwards Lord Dorchester) was dangerously wounded. All that followed them shared the fate of the former, or were made prisoners. The flat-bottomed boats and the ships that covered the landing were compelled to draw off, with the loss of 500 men, so terrible was the fire of cannon and musketry from the heights.

All that night and next day the wind blew a gale, damaging many of the boats, and driving some of the transports out to sea. But after the weather abated, and the coast was again reconnoitred by General Hodgson and Admiral Keppel, dispositions were made for another landing on the 22nd of April, at Fort D'Arcy; while, in order to distract the enemy's attention from the real point of attack, two feints were at the same time made on other parts of the island.

Brigadier Lambert once more effected a landing, at the head of the grenadier companies and the marines, and all the rest of the troops speedily followed; their disembarkation being ably covered by a fire from the shipping, which soon silenced the batteries of the enemy, who, after withstanding many resolute attacks, were driven back from all their intrenchments and defences.

As soon as the Chevalier de St. Croix found that the British had made good their landing, he collected his whole forces, and fell back upon the fortified town of Palais, and thus laid open the whole country before it. During this retrograde movement, the enemy made a stand in one or two places, but were compelled to retire by the light cavalry.

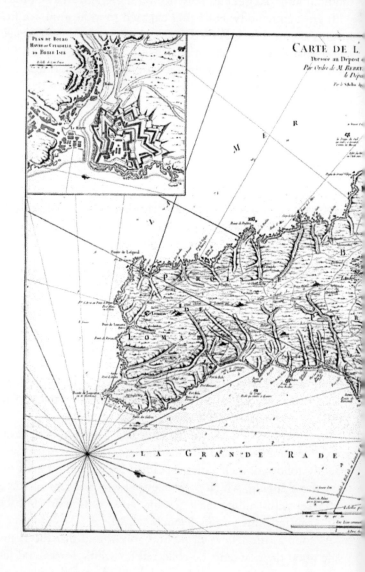

In Palais, St. Croix, hopeless of succour from Brest, was determined to make his last grand stand against General Hodgson, whose chief difficulty consisted in bringing forward his cannon, which had to be dragged up the rocks, and afterwards for six miles along a deep, rugged, and broken road. All this caused a great loss of time. However, the siege was pressed with vigour, and the garrison, inspired by the known bravery of St. Croix, seemed to threaten a long and obstinate defence. Valour and energy were not wanting on either hand.

The French made several furious sallies; and by these a great number of besiegers were killed, wounded, or taken prisoners. Among the latter was Major-General Crawford, who commanded in the trenches; but these severe checks operated only as incentives to fresh energy on the part of the British troops.

The engineers having reported that their works could not be properly advanced unless six redoubts which the enemy had formed to guard the approach to the town were completely reduced, they were accordingly all attacked on the morning of the 13th of May, and were stormed at the bayonet's point, with equal speed and intrepidity, by a battalion of marines, a corps only recently embodied. A great slaughter was made of the enemy, who fled towards the citadel; and such was the ardour of the stormers that they rushed along the streets of Palais pell-mell with the fugitives, and without an hour's delay preparations were made for the reduction of the stronghold. Cormick, in his continuation to Smollett's *History*, says:

This was a place of extraordinary strength, having been built by the famous Vauban, who supplied by art what Nature had left undone to make it almost impregnable; and it was now defended by St. Croix with a show of the most desperate resolution.

Among those who fell in pressing the siege of this place, few were more regretted than Captain Sir William Peere Williams, Bart., of the 16th Light Dragoons, a young man who had shown high talent in Parliament, and had but recently joined the service. In his ardour to examine the works of the citadel, he advanced too near the foot of the glacis, where he was shot dead by a French sentinel. On his body being borne into Palais, St. Croix, suspecting that he was a person of distinction, sent a drummer with a note to General Hodgson, requesting him to send a party for it; but the unfortunate drummer was shot by an ignorant sentinel, who, for this breach of the laws of war, was ordered to be hanged.

BRAVERY OF SAMUEL JOHNSON

St Croix conceiving that there was some mistake, sent forth "another drummer, with a polite intercessory note on behalf of the delinquent, who was pardoned in consequence, and the corpse of Sir William was brought back to the camp." St. Croix sent back with it bills to the amount of £240, drawn on Drummond's Bank, which were found in the pockets of the regimentals.

Parallels were now dug, breastworks thrown up, and batteries constructed. By day and night, the roar of cannon and mortars shook the rocks of Belleisle without intermission, from the 13th till the 25th of May, when the fire of the enemy began most perceptibly to abate. By the end of the month a practicable breach was made in the citadel, and, notwithstanding that the garrison was indefatigable in repairing the damage, the fire of the British increased to such a degree that a great part of the defences were utterly ruined; and by the 7th of June, the Chevalier de St. Croix, having no prospect of relief, and hopeless of his power to repel a general assault, thought it prudent to capitulate, and his drums beat a *chamade*.

Terms being accepted, our troops marched in next day; and, by obtaining the citadel, they were virtually put in possession of the whole island. The garrison of St Croix consisted of 2,600 men, of whom 922 were killed or wounded in the defence; while our losses amounted to 13 officers and 300 men killed, 14 officers and 480 men wounded. The Hon. Captain Barrington, of the Royal Navy, and Captain Rooke, *aide-de-camp* to General Hodgson, bore to London the news of the capture of Belleisle, and each received 500 guineas from George III. on presenting him with the dispatches and French standards. The victory at Belleisle—though it failed in its ultimate aim, which was to draw the French from Westphalia—was celebrated by bonfires and illuminations over all England and Scotland, and it was a subject of no small mortification to France; but the capture "was thought by the most intelligent part of the nation dearly purchased with the lives of 2,000 brave men, besides the immense expenditure of naval and military stores."

The *Brussels Gazette* of the 7th of May accuses Admiral Keppel, on what authority we cannot know now, of having refused to receive on board his fleet 400 British prisoners, whom St. Croix had taken in the first descent, and whom he offered to give up, as they were starving "in a dark and unhealthy prison." But such conduct would be incredible in any British officer, and the accusation is doubtless untrue.

Conquest of Manilla, 1762

The losses at the Havanah, though immense and crashing to Spain, were not the only ones she was fated to suffer through her rash alliance with France. A plan for invading her Philippine Isles, that extensive archipelago in the Eastern seas, north of Borneo, was submitted to the Ministry by Colonel (afterwards Sir William) Draper, K.B., of the 79th Regiment, then stationed in India, and he received permission to put it in execution. No man was better qualified by military talent, and the most accurate local knowledge, to give it effect than this spirited officer, who was that *preux chevalier* who ultimately became a judge paramount in all matters relating to military etiquette, and who, in his celebrated letter to Junius, expressed a hope that he would never see officers pushed into the British Army who had nothing to lose but their swords.

The *Seahorse*, 20 guns, under Captain Cathcart Grant, was first dispatched to cruise off the Philippine Isles, and to intercept all vessels bound for Manilla. On the 21st of July, the first division of the fleet sailed, under Commodore Teddinson; and on the 1st of August, Admiral Sir Samuel Cornish and Colonel Draper followed with the remainder. The armament consisted of fourteen sail, ten of which carried fifty guns and upwards. The admiral's flag was on board the *Norfolk*, 74 guns, her captain being the gallant Kempenfelt, who perished in the *Royal George*.

Under Colonel Draper was his own regiment, the 79th—not the present Cameron Highlanders, but a corps disbanded in 1763. He had also with him an auxiliary force furnished by the gentlemen of Madras, consisting of a company of their artillery, 600 *sepoys*, a company of Caffres, one of Topazees, and one of pioneers. To these were added "the precarious assistance" of two companies of Frenchmen enlisted in their service, and some hundreds of unarmed *lascars* for the use of

243

the engineers and the park of artillery.

At Malacca a great quantity of ratoons were shipped to use as gabions. On the 27th the squadron rendezvoused off the high and woody Isle of Timoan, which is covered with cabbage-palms; and on the 23rd of September came to anchor in the Bay of Manilla, the capital of the Spanish settlements in the Philippine Isles, and which lies on a low sandy point at the mouth of the River Pasig, the water of which is navigable as far as a lake some thirty miles eastward of the town, from which it derives its source, and is prolonged by two long piers into the bay.

In Manilla there was a garrison consisting of the Life Guard of the Governor and Captain-General de los Philippinas; the slender 2nd battalion of the King's Regiment, commanded by Don Miguel de Valdez; a body of Spanish marines; a corps of artillery, under Lieutenant-General Don Felix de Eguilux, whose second in command was Brigadier the Marquis de Villa Medina; a company of irregular Pampangos, or natives of the Isle of Lacon; and a company of cadets. So, a sharp resistance was fully anticipated, though, as at the Havanah, the Spaniards were totally unprepared; and the leaders of the expedition resolved to lose no time in striking an effective blow.

Two miles south of Manilla, which is a town of great extent—most of the houses having great quadrangular courts, but dull streets, the basements being generally warehouses without windows—a convenient place for landing was selected, and three fine frigates, the *Argo*, Captain King, the *Seahorse*, Captain Grant, and the *Seaford*, Captain Pelghin, warped near the shore, with ports triced up, to cover, the descent.

The 79th Regiment, the marines, 274 strong, a detachment of artillery, with three field-pieces and one mortar fixed in the long-boats, assembled in three divisions under their sterns. Colonel Draper led the centre. Major More the right. Colonel Monson the left; and at six in the evening all the boats pushed off steadily for the shore, where a landing was effected with some difficulty, under the direction of Captains Brereton, Kempenfelt, and the future Sir Hyde Parker. A dreadful surf was rolling in from the seaward; the boats in many instances were flung against each other and dashed to pieces, much ammunition was damaged, and many arms were lost, but fortunately no lives.

The enemy had collected, in force, with both cavalry and infantry, to oppose the landing; but, under a brisk cannonade from the frigates, it was successfully achieved: and next day a battalion composed of 632

244

seamen was landed to co-operate with Colonel Draper, under the command of Captains Collins, Pitchford, and Ouvry.

On the 25th of September, a fort named the Polverista, which the Spaniards had abandoned, was seized as a place for arms; while Colonel Monson was detached with 200 men to reconnoitre the approaches to Manilla, the spacious suburbs of which were now sheeted with fire, as the Spaniards had given them to the flames, and the houses of the natives, built of *nipa*, covered with leaves, and raised on wooden pillars ten feet from the ground, blazed like tar-barrels.

The Hermita Church, and the priest's house, 900 yards' distance from the city wall, were taken possession of by the 79th Regiment, as to maintain that post was of the utmost consequence: for now the monsoon had broken, the surf was more dangerous than ever; the whole country was deluged by rain; and at times there were the most dreadful thunder and lightning while the artillery and stores were being landed. But though a lieutenant, named Hardwick, was swept away and drowned, the activity of the seamen surmounted every obstacle. As the blinding sheets of rain that fell without cessation compelled the troops to seek shelter anywhere, they frequently occupied scattered houses that were under the fire of the town bastions, and much nearer them than the rules of war prescribe. The battalion of seamen was cantoned between the 79th Regiment and the marines.

Under the command of the Chevalier Fayette, 400 Spaniards with two field-pieces issued forth and began to cannonade the invaders on the 26th; but were roughly driven in by the pickets of the 79th, with the loss of one of their guns.

Colonel Draper now discovered that the fortifications of Manilla, though regular, were not complete. In many important places the ditch had never been finished, the covered way was out of repair, the glacis was too low, some of the outworks were without cannon, and the now half-ruined suburbs afforded shelter to the besiegers.

The garrison consisted of 800 purely Spanish troops; but there were many half-castes; and to their assistance the country had poured in 10,000 Indians, of a race who were remarkable for their ferocity, hardihood, and sublime contempt of death.

The governor, who was also the Archbishop of the Philippine Isles, united in his own person, by a policy that was not without precedent in the colonies of Spain, the command of the forces, together with the civil power and the ecclesiastical dignity; but, says Cormick:

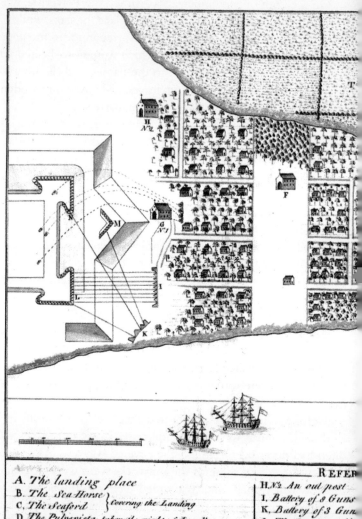

A. The landing place
B. The Sea-Horse } covering the Landing
C. The Seaford
D. The Pulverista, taken the night of Landing
E. The Magazine
F. The Generals head quarters
G. { Where the Mortars were fired from and the
N.I. { repository for stores.

REFER

H, N.2 An out post
I, Battery of 8 Guns
K, Battery of 3 Gun
L, The Bastion whic
M { The Ravelin wh
  { by the 3 Gun Ba
N, { The Flank of th
  { the 3 Gun Bat

THE ATTACK OF

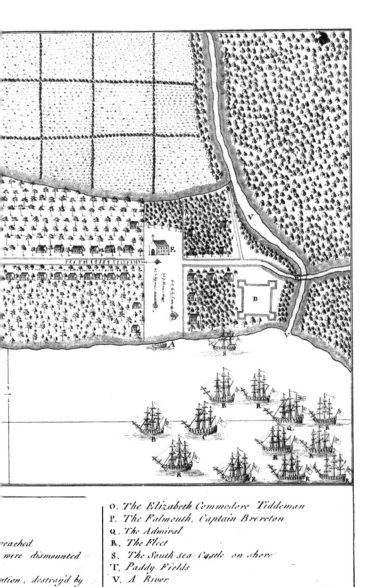

O. *The Elizabeth Commodore Tiddeman*
P. *The Falmouth, Captain Brereton*
Q. *The Admiral*
R. *The Fleet*
S. *The South-sea-Castle on shore*
T. *Paddy Fields*
V. *A River*
W. *A Bridge*

eached
were dismounted
tion, destroy'd by

NILLA, October 1762.

However unqualified by his priestly character for the defence of a city attacked, he seemed not unfit for it by his intrepidity and resolution.

As it was evident that the archbishop would defend himself to the last, the operations against the town were pushed forward with unremitting vigour; and after batteries for cannon and mortars were raised, the bombardment continued day and night. Colonel Draper wrote:

> The front we were obliged to attack, was defended by the bastions of St Diego and St. Andrew, with orillons and retired flanks; a ravelin, which covered the Royal Gate; a wet ditch, covered way, and glacis. The bastions were in excellent order, and lined with a great number of fine brass cannon.

As the colonel's force was too small to invest completely a city of the magnitude of Manilla, two sides of it were constantly open to those who poured in provisions, and to the hordes of armed Pampangos, of whose services the Marquis de Villa Medina, commandant of the place, fully availed himself. The attacks of these people from time to time molested rather than obstructed the progress of the besiegers; and, by frequent acts of savage cruelty, provoked the most dreadful retaliation. Several English seamen, when straggling along the coast, were murdered by them. They even perpetrated the same cruelty upon an officer, Lieutenant Fryar, whom Colonel Draper had sent to the city with a flag of truce, accompanied by the nephew of the archbishop, who had been taken prisoner. Fryar's body, we are told, was mangled:

> In a manner too shocking too mention; and in their fury, they mortally wounded the other gentleman, who endeavoured to save him.

On the 1st of October there was a dreadful storm of wind, accompanied by a deluge of rain; the fleet was in great peril, and all communication with it was cut off. And now, to raise the spirit of the people, the archbishop announced that:

> An angel from the Lord had gone forth to destroy the British, like the host of Sennacherib.

But this illusion was of brief continuance; for, notwithstanding the fury of the tempest, the soldiers and seamen completed a new battery for twenty-four-pounders and for thirteen-inch mortars, the roaring of the waves on the beach preventing the Spaniards from hearing the workmen, who toiled at their task all night.

About three hours before daylight on the morning of the 4th, more than a thousand Pampangos attacked the cantonment of the seamen. They were encouraged by a conviction that the incessant rain would render the firearms useless; and their stealthy approach was favoured by a quantity of thick bushes that bordered a rivulet, by the bed of which they stole unseen in the dark.

Our brave seamen, though taken completely by surprise, and unable, in consequence of the darkness, to learn who or where their assailants were, maintained their ground till daybreak, when a strong picket of the 79th Regiment attacked them in flank, and totally routed them, with the loss of 300 killed. Although armed with only bows, arrows, and lances, they rushed up to the very muzzles of our muskets, and died like wild beasts, gnawing with their teeth the bayonets that pierced them. In this affair Captain Porter, of the *Norfolk*, 74 guns, and many seamen were killed.

At the same time when the Pampangos made this sortie, another was made by them at a different point; the *sepoys* who occupied a church gave way before them, and the building was instantly occupied by Spanish musketeers of the Royal Regiment. The field-pieces were brought up to dislodge them, and they were driven in with the loss of seventy men; but not before Captain Strachan, of the 79th Regiment, and forty more were *hors de combat*. After this the Pampangos lost heart, and all save 1,800 of them abandoned the city to its fate.

The fire from the garrison now became faint, while that of the besiegers was stronger than ever, and ere long a breach became practicable. In such circumstances it might naturally have been expected that the governor would have offered to capitulate, to save the lives and property of the inhabitants. But no such proposal was made, and, what was still more strange, the Marquis de Villa Medina neither attempted to repair the works nor to make any preparations to defend the breach. Colonel Draper therefore resolved to bring matters to a speedy issue.

At daybreak on the 6th the troops were under arms, and advancing towards the breach in the Bastion of St Andrew, where a large body of Spaniards appeared; but on a few shells exploding among them, these retired. Colonel Draper says:

We took immediate advantage of this, and, by the signal of a general discharge of our artillery and mortars, rushed furiously to the assault, under cover of a thick smoke that blew directly on the town. Sixty volunteers of different corps, under Lieutenant Russell, of the 49th, led the way, supported by the grenadiers of that regiment. The engineers, with the pioneers and other workmen, to clear and enlarge the breach and make lodgements, in case the enemy should have been too strongly intrenched in the gorge of the bastion, followed. Colonel Monson and Major More were at the head of two grand divisions of the 79th; the battalion of seamen advanced next, sustained by other two divisions of the 79th; the Company's troops closing the rear.

In this order, with bayonets fixed, they rushed on with incredible ardour; and as they swarmed up the breach with loud cheers, the Spaniards fired a scattered volley upon them, and retired. But little resistance was offered, save at the Royal Gate, where Major More was shot dead by an arrow, and in the Grand Square, from the galleries and lofty houses of which the Royal Regiment d'Espana fired briskly, and the Pampango archers shot with deadly aim.

In the guard-house above the Royal Gate, 100 Spaniards and Indians, who refused all terms, were put to the sword; and 300 more, who endeavoured to escape over a rapid river, were drowned in the attempt.

The archbishop and principal officers retired into the town-house, where, after a time, they capitulated to Captain Dupont, of the 79th.

The humanity and generosity of the British commanders saved Manilla from a general and justly-merited pillage. A ransom of four millions of dollars only was demanded for this relaxation of the laws of war. The Spanish officers taken were all released upon their parole of honour. They were eighty-eight in number, and among them were some Spanish noblesse of high rank. By that time the King's Regiment was reduced to 261 rank and file. There were taken no less than 556 pieces of brass and iron cannon and mortars, and a vast quantity of all kinds of munition of war.

It was expressly stipulated that all the other fortified places in the island of Luconia, and in all the isles dependent on its government, should also be surrendered to His Britannic Majesty. Thus, the whole archipelago of the Philippines fell with the wealthy city of Manilla.

In concluding his dispatch to Lord Egremont, Colonel Draper speaks thus of his favourite corps, the old 79th:—

May I presume to point out the services of the 79th Regiment, which, from the good conduct of its former and present field-officers, has the peculiar merit of having stayed the progress of the French in India, and not a little contributed to the happy turn and decision of that war, under Colonel Coote; and has since extended the glory of His Majesty's arms to the utmost verge of Asia? Twenty-three officers and upwards of 800 men have fallen in the cause of their country since the regiment left England; numbers of the survivors are wounded. Your lordship's goodness encourages me to mention them as objects of compassion and protection. Captain Fletcher has nine colours to lay at His Majesty's feet.

But the regiment was disbanded, when all corps were reduced to the present 70th Foot, in 1763, when a treaty of peace was signed at Paris; and so ill were the services of the army requited, that in the following year the London papers record that there were no less than "500 reduced and half-pay officers confined for debt in the several gaols of the kingdom."

'MILITARY UNIFORMS, 1762.

Valencia de Alcantara, 1762

In 1762, the British were fighting the French by land and sea in every quarter of the globe, or wherever they possessed ships, troops, or colonies; and the spring of the year saw our colours unfurled in a part of Europe where they had not been seen since the days of Galway and Peterborough—the Peninsula.

During the progress of the war the sovereigns of France and Spain had been endeavouring, by arguments and menaces, to induce the King of Portugal to unite with them against Great Britain. Portugal was extremely weak at this period. Its capital had been destroyed by the great earthquake in 1755, when nearly 30,000 inhabitants perished in its ruins; a conspiracy against the king's life followed this disaster, and the little realm had been shaken by civil dissension.

Its army was weak in numbers, and deficient in arms and in discipline; but notwithstanding his weakness, and the haughty threats of France and Spain, King Joseph adhered to his alliance with Britain. He urged their Most Christian and Catholic Majesties:

> To open their eyes to the crying injustice of turning upon Portugal the hostilities kindled against Great Britain, and to consider that they were giving an example which would lead to the utter destruction of mankind. . . . .that he would rather see the last tile of his palace fall, and his faithful subjects spill the last drop of their blood, than sacrifice the independence of his crown, and afford to ambitious princes, in his submission, a pretext for invading the sacred rights of neutrality.

Before the actual commencement of hostilities. Lord Tyrawley, a peer of great military talent and experience, formerly our ambassador at Lisbon, was sent there, with instructions to examine into the state of the Portuguese forces, and to assist the Ministry with his best advice in the organisation of the army and defence of the frontier. He was also to have command of the British auxiliary forces, consisting of nearly 10,000 men, drawn partly from Belleisle and partly from Ireland, where two regiments entirely composed of Catholics were raised for this service.

But Lord Tyrawley, being hot-tempered and impetuous, took some offence at the lack of vigour which he found in King Joseph and his Ministry, whom he charged with want of sincerity; and as these suspicions were supposed to be the result of pride and caprice, he was recalled very early in the campaign, and the command of the British troops was bestowed on Lieutenant-General the Earl of Loudon, under whom Colonels Crawford and Burgoyne, with Lord George Lennox, acted as brigadiers; while the whole allied British and Portuguese force was led by Marshal Count de la Lippe Buckeburg, who had commanded our artillery in Westphalia during the whole course of the war, and given unequivocal proofs of his valour and capacity.

The names of several Scottish officers appear in the Portuguese lists at this time. Among these were General Maclean, who, in 1773, succeeded the Conde Oriolo as Governor of Estramadura, and had been previously Governor of Lisbon; Captain Forbes, famous in those times as the antagonist of Wilkes (he won the highest rank and honours, and died at Brazil in 1808); Colonel John Macdonell, of the Regiment of Peniche; Brigadier Sharpe, Governor of Olivenza and colonel of the Monca Infantry; Major-General Bethune Lindsay; and Lieutenant-Colonel Anderson, commanding the Battalion of Lagos, of which St. Anthony of Padua—or his name at least—figured as full colonel, until it was replaced by that of the Count de la Lippe!

As the French and Spaniards did not deem it possible to cut off Great Britain from the use of the Portuguese ports by naval operations, they attempted it by military ones, and Lisbon and Oporto were the two points aimed at. With this view three inroads were proposed to be made—one to the north; another to the south; and the third in the middle provinces, to preserve a communication between the two former.

The first army that entered upon the execution of this plan was commanded by the Marquis de Sarria. Penetrating into the north-east angle of Portugal, he marched towards Miranda, which, though indifferently fortified, might have made some resistance but for the explosion of a powder magazine, which utterly ruined its defences, enabling the Spaniards to enter by the breaches before they had formed a single battery. The marquis met with still less opposition at Braganza, the city from which the royal family derive their ducal title, as the garrison fled with precipitation, and the magistrates presented the keys to him. Moncorvo surrendered in the same pitiful fashion, and then all the country lay open to the banks of the Douro.

Under Alexander Count O'Reilly, who had drilled the Spanish infantry according to the best system of tactics and exercise then practised in the British service, a detachment made a forced march of fourteen leagues, as far as the city of Chaves, which was immediately evacuated. These successes made them masters of the whole province; of Tralos Montes, and caused so much alarm that Oporto was deemed lost. Thus, the Lords of the Admiralty prepared transports to carry off the effects of the British factory.

The second column of Spanish troops, which took the central route, entered the province of Beira, and immediately laid siege to Almeida, the strongest and best-provided place on the frontiers of Portugal; while the third column, 80,000 strong, destined for the subjugation of that country, assembled on the borders of Estramadura, with the intention of penetrating into Alentijo. Had these three corps been permitted to make a junction, they must have formed an army which the allied British and Portuguese could never have withstood.

Armed and animated by some British officers with a body of regular troops, the inhabitants seized a strong pass in the mountains, and drove the invaders back to Torre de Moncorvo. In ravaging the country, the Spanish troops perpetrated dreadful outrages upon the peasantry. The latter, naturally revengeful and ferocious, retaliated to the fullest extent; and in every encounter the victors attended to the dictates of rancour and hate.

The column which invested Almeida opened the trenches before that place on the 25th of July, and next day it was joined by 8,000 French auxiliaries. The siege was pushed with vigour, as the fortress was of the greatest importance from its central situation, and its reduction would facilitate the operations on every side, and ultimately lead to the fall of Lisbon.

On the 25th of August the fortress capitulated, before even a practicable breach had been effected; and 1,500 regulars, with 2,000 armed peasants, were permitted to march out with the honours of war, on condition of not serving for six months against the King of Spain or his allies—94 pieces of cannon, 32 mortars, and 700 quintals of powder fell into the hands of the victors. This rapid career of the latter was

VIEW OF OPORTO.

not fated, however, to be of long continuance.

It was imperatively necessary to prevent the entrance into Portugal of that column of the Spanish Army which had halted on the borders of Estramadura, since that movement would have been almost equal to a victory on their side. The Count de la Lippe, therefore, formed the design of attacking an advanced party of them in a strong town upon the frontier, named Valencia de Alcantara, in the province of Caseros, and on the left bank of the Aird, where he heard they had amassed vast munitions of war.

The conduct of this enterprise he committed to Brigadier Burgoyne, who took with him his own regiment, the 16th Light Dragoons (now Lancers), then mustering only 400 rank and file, under Major the Hon. Hugh Somerville, son of Hugh thirteenth Lord Somerville, and a distinguished cavalry officer of those days.

The orders given to Burgoyne by the Count de la Lippe on this occasion were somewhat peculiar.

If he found it impossible to withstand the force of the Spaniards, he was to abandon to them his baggage, provisions, and everything, save what his troops could carry on their backs or on their horses, and to retreat as slowly as he could into the mountains on his left, and thence rejoin the main army.

The count added:

I know to how severe a trial I expose the feelings of a gallant officer when I order him to abandon his camp to the enemy; but the nature of the service requires such a sacrifice. Do you execute the orders; I shall take the measure upon myself, and justify you in the sight of the world.

Burgoyne crossed the Tagus at midnight on the 23rd of August, and proceeded by forced marches to Castel de Vide, the troops dismounting from time to time to permit the detachment of grenadiers who accompanied them to ride.

After a five days' march, and in spite of all disappointments and obstructions to which a secret expedition of this kind is so liable, on the night of the 26th the troops left Castel de Vide, the 16th Dragoons taking the lead, and passing the borders of Portugal, approached Valencia de Alcantara, not as Burgoyne had intended, while the darkness left it, but just as the rising sun was beginning to redden its walls and spires.

All was silent and tranquil, however, in the town when the advanced guard of the dragoons, under Lieutenant James Lewis, finding the avenues clear and unguarded, galloped along the main street, sword in hand, followed by the whole regiment. Springing from bed in their shirts, the Spanish infantry, alarmed by the clatter of the hoofs and the ringing cheers of the light dragoons, seized their muskets, and fired a few shots from the windows of their billets. But the 16th pressed on to the great central *plaza*, where they attacked the main guard, and cut down or captured every man. At the same time other parties of the regiment secured the ends of all the streets, while the main body of it formed by troops in the square, where it was attacked by several unformed parties of Spaniards, all of whom were taken or destroyed.

There the Spanish Regiment of Seville was annihilated by the sword alone; three stand of colours were captured; Major-General Don Michael de Irunibeni, his *aide-de-camp*, and a colonel, with many other officers, were taken prisoners; and on the grenadiers coming in double-quick, with their bayonets fixed, all resistance ceased.

The cavalry were then detached to scour the adjacent country, and intercept fugitives. They captured a number of horses, but the Spanish soldiers concealed themselves successfully. One small detachment of the 16th, consisting only of a sergeant and six troopers, penetrated to a considerable distance, and unexpectedly fell upon twenty-five Spanish dragoons, led by an officer. Undismayed by this great disparity of numbers, the seven gallant Britons dashed upon their adversaries with resolution:

And used their broadswords with such terrible effect that in a few moments six Spaniards lay dead upon the road, and the other twenty demanded quarter, and were marched prisoners, with twenty-six horses, into the town.

A quantity of military stores were afterwards seized, hostages were taken for a year's revenue, and then the dragoons and grenadiers retired leisurely across the frontier.

Save fifty-nine men, the whole battalion of Seville was destroyed; while the British loss was only one lieutenant, one sergeant, and three men killed, with twenty privates and ten horses wounded. The conduct of the 16th Dragoons on this occasion was commended by the Count de la Lippe in his public dispatch.

The field-marshal thinks it his duty to acquaint the army with the glorious conduct of Brigadier Burgoyne, who, after having marched fifteen leagues without halting, took Valencia de Alcantara, sword in hand, made the general who was to have invaded Alentejo prisoner, destroyed the Spanish Regiment of Seville, took three stand of colours, a colonel, many officers of distinction, and a great number of soldiers.

Soon after this the Spaniards poured into Portugal in very great force, and though the steady valour of the British troops did much to keep them in check, some retrograde movements were necessary; and in the beginning of October fifty troopers of the 16th alone served to cover the retreat of the Conde St. Jago's Portuguese battalions from the Pass of Alviato towards Sabrino Formosa, and on many occasions, they evinced the most heroic valour.

To arrest the progress of the Spaniards, for whom nothing now remained but the passage of the Tagus, to enable them to take up their quarters in Alentejo, a body of troops was posted on the southern bank of that river, opposite Villa Velha, under the command of Brigadier Burgoyne. The enemy had captured the ancient Moorish castle, and filled it with infantry, while a considerable body of their cavalry occupied two eminences in a plain near the village of Villa Velha.

As General Burgoyne—ever sharp and observant—detected that:

They kept no very soldierly guard in this post, and were uncovered in their rear and on the flanks, he conceived a design of falling on them by surprise, and confided the execution of this to Colonel Lee.

On the 4th of October, fifty men of the 16th Dragoons, with a few Portuguese horse, advanced to a deep and rocky ravine two miles up the Tagus, where, on the following day, they were joined by a number of Royal Volunteers and grenadiers, under Colonel Lee. Leaving their place of concealment during the night of the 5th, these troops forded the river unseen; and making a long detour through unfrequented tracts and lonely passes amid the mountains, they gained the rear of the Spanish camps on the two eminences about two o'clock the following morning.

The grenadiers and volunteers burst in at a rush, and bayoneted the Spaniards in their tents. The yells and execrations of the wounded, the groans and cries of the dying, with a few straggling shots flashing redly amid the gloom of the October morning, gave the alarm on all sides; and getting into their saddles, some of the Spanish cavalry attempted to make a stand, but were charged by the men of the 16th, under Lieutenant Charles Maitland, who the *Regimental Record* says:

Broke in upon the adverse ranks, and cut them down with a terrible carnage, while the infantry continued the work of destruction with the bayonet, and the surviving soldiers of the army fled without making further resistance. The Spanish magazines were taken and destroyed; six pieces of cannon, sixty artillery mules, some horses, and a considerable quantity of valuable baggage, were captured, (while the allied loss was trivial).

The Count de la Lippe, in his dispatch says:

So brilliant a stroke speaks for itself; and there is no necessity to lengthen this letter with the well-deserved applause due to Brigadier-General Burgoyne, as well as to Colonel Lee and the British troops.

These advantages, gained at most critical moments, disheartened even the vast forces of the Spaniards, who began to fall back towards their own frontier, and thus was Portugal saved by British skill and bravery.

There never was, says Cormick, so heavy a storm of national calamity, ready to fall upon an unprovided people as the Portuguese, so happily averted and so speedily blown over. Everything at the beginning of this campaign in Portugal bore the most lowering and ominous aspect to the affairs of Great Britain. As it advanced, the sky gradually cleared up, and towards the close of it the fortune of no nation was enlivened with a more brilliant and more unclouded prosperity.

But in the wars of a future time. General Burgoyne was less fortunate than when leading his light dragoons on the frontier of Alentejo.

Graebenstein and Bruckermuhl, 1762

After the glorious Battle of Minden, the Seven Years' War still continued to be waged in Germany with varying success, and the British troops had been under fire in the general actions of Warbourg and Kirkdenkern, in 1761, and at the capture of several towns, such as Wesel and Campen; and then followed the successful surprise of the French army at Graebenstein in the following year.

Prior to this, we find in the *London Gazette* of the 17th of November, 1761, a record of one of the most extraordinary requisitions ever made in war:—

The French have demanded from the country of Eischsfeld and Hohenstein 400 cats; and 180 have been delivered to them. The motive for the demand is, that the mice eat up their magazines.

In April, 1762, the enemy assembled in force near Muhlhausen, while the Allies about the same time got into motion at Eimbeck. In conjunction with Marshal d'Estrées, Marshal Soubise arrived at Cassel to command the French army on the Upper Rhine and the Maine; while the Prince of Condé placed himself at the head of that on the Lower Rhine.

Our British troops, who were in cantonments near Bielevelt, formed a junction with the column of General Sporcken near Blomberg, and encamped on the heights of Belle. On the 20th of June the main body of the allied army marched for Burgholtz, and the gallant Marquis of Granby's corps, forming the vanguard, advanced to Warbourg; so next day saw the army in position near Buhne, under Prince Ferdinand of Brunswick.

Under the Marshals d'Estrées and Soubise, the French proceeded to Graebenstein and Meijenbracksen; while a corps under the Marshal de Castries got into position on their right flank, between Carlsdorff and Graebenstein. The latter place, which was fated to be the first scene of hostile operations in the new campaign, was a village on the frontiers of Hesse, and the ground was judiciously chosen, both for command of the country and difficulty of approaching it.

Their infantry consisted of one hundred battalions, while that of the Allies was only sixty.

Their centre occupied an advantageous eminence, and was almost inaccessible, in consequence of several deep ravines; their right flank was covered by the village, a number of deep marshy rivulets, and the column of Marshal de Castries. In such a position they deemed themselves impregnable, especially as a considerable corps of the allied army, under Lieutenant-General Luckner, had ample occupation in watching Prince Xavier of Saxony, between the Werra and Gottingen.

Prince Ferdinand resolved to avail himself of this fancied security, by making a sudden and furious attack. He dispatched an officer to Luckner, with instructions to leave a corps of Hessian hussars in his rear to amuse the prince, and, by forced marches in the night, to bring his force into position after crossing the Weser, turn the right of the French army, and, without being discovered, place himself in their rear.

The allied army then crossed the Dymel in several columns, between Liebenau and Siegen. The left wing, under General Sporcken, consisting of Hanoverians, moved towards Beverae, for the purpose of forming on the enemy's right; and the orders were to attack that point under Marshal de Castries, while General Luckner—whose presence was not suspected—was to fall upon their rear. Prince Ferdinand was to attack the centre, while the honour of assailing the left wing was assigned to the Marquis of Granby. All the necessary preparations were made with so much judgment, celerity, and order, that the French had no intimation of the design till they were greeted by the sound of musketry in front, in rear, and on both flanks.

It was between two and three in the morning of the 24th of June that Lord Granby's column marched from the camp to an eminence opposite Furstenwald, in order to attack the enemy's left; and by four o'clock the whole line was in motion to the front.

Sixteen squadrons of cavalry halted near Giesmar, to menace the front of the French; while the more furious attack was being made on the right.

The prince, at the head of five columns, consisting of twelve British, eleven Brunswick, and eight Hessian regiments, with part of the Germans of the left wing and our cavalry (among whom were the Scots Greys, the 7th, 10th, 11th, and other Dragoons), moved to Langelberg, and formed before Keltz, fairly in the enemy's front.

The pickets of the army formed the left advance; the chasseurs of the British infantry and some Hanoverians the right. The moment the firing began, Marshal de Castries found that his right flank had been turned in the night; and, in order to make head against General Sporcken, commenced a sharp cannonade on one hand, and on the other formed up his cavalry to oppose Luckner.

Sword in hand, the allied cavalry advanced at a gallop, broke his hastily-formed infantry, took two pieces of cannon, and, after some severe fighting, wherein many men fell killed or wounded in the ravines and rivulets, the column of Marshal de Castries was driven in great disorder full upon the enemy's right. Amid a roar of musketry, the allied main body, consisting of thirty-one battalions in line, was pressing upon the front; while the Marquis of Granby pushed on from Furstenwald to turn the left.

Finding their once strong situation had now become most critical, the French suddenly broke into as many columns as the rough and undulating nature of the ground would permit, endeavouring to reach the heights of Wilhelmstal; but in doing this they were compelled to abandon all their wagons and equipages at Graebenstein, and a general rout must have ensued, had not General Stainville, on seeing that by the manoeuvre of Lord Granby the retreat was cut off, and more particularly that of his own corps, gained the wood of Meijenbracksen with the Grenadiers of France, the Royal Grenadiers, and the Regiment of Aquitaine (or French 19th, a corps old as the days of Henri IV.), and other chosen troops, the flower of King Louis' infantry.

He took this step to cover the retreat, but it cost him dear, as he was resolutely attacked by Granby; and, after a deadly contest, the whole of his infantry, with the exception of two battalions, were killed, taken, or dispersed. The loss of the enemy exceeded 5,000 men. There were taken prisoners 200 officers and 3,000 men.

The losses of the Allies were small in comparison, and no officer of rank fell save Lieutenant-Colonel Townshend, who was greatly regretted by the army.

The French retired till under the cannon of Cassel, and a great many of them rapidly flung themselves across the Fulda.

In following up the fugitives, the 7th and 10th Light Dragoons made many prisoners in the woods of Wilhelmstal, and on the road to Cassel, which was afterwards captured by the Allies. In the *London*

Gazette, we are told that "Lord Granby acquitted himself" at Graeben-stein "with remarkable valour, and had a great share in the victory."

The colours taken were presented to George III. at St. James's, on the 26th of July, 1762.

A series of successful operations followed this victory, and the enemy were compelled to abandon several posts, till the 21st of September, when a most obstinate contest ensued on the height of Brucker-muhl, near Amoneburg.

BRUCKERMUHL.

Prince Ferdinand had made his arrangements to drive the enemy from Wetter, where they had a strong force, supported by a column under the Prince of Condé. His troops reached their destined positions at the appointed hour. The cannonade commenced at the back of the green and woody hill above Wartzbach, whence the enemy soon fell back. Shortly after the arrival of General Conway they began to retreat in great disorder, and recrossed the Lahn. During this movement their ranks were ploughed up by cannon-shot, and long lines of killed and wounded bodies, maimed, torn, and disembowelled, marked their route.

The Allies then encamped, their posts extending from Hombourg, on the Ohen, to Wartzbach, on the Lahn.

On the 21st of September the fighting began again. The Allies occupied a redoubt on one side of the road, and the French a mill on the other—the *bruckermuhl,* so named from its walls being built of mud. Near their position was the singular eminence of Amoneburg; and their formation was covered by the river Ohen, with marshy banks, broad, but not deep.

The action which ensued here was remarkable for its extreme obstinacy. It commenced when the morning was very foggy, about the hour of six, between two small bodies with a few guns; but, as the engagement grew warmer, the artillery was gradually augmented to twenty-five pieces of heavy cannon on either side. The Allies had originally but one hundred men at this post, but before the action was decided no less than seventeen of their regiments took a share in this now-forgotten battle, one successively relieving the other, as the ammunition became exhausted.

Thus, a constant fire was maintained by these troops without intermission for fifteen hours, from dawn of day till nightfall. Neither side gave way; and this resolute conflict for a trifling object left the combatants in their former positions—the Allies in possession of their redoubt, and the French of their *bruckermuhl*.

But in the redoubt, says Sir James Campbell, in his *Memoirs*, there fell Major Alexander Maclean, of Keith's Highlanders, and many other gallant officers, he relates:

> The fire was so incessant, and the slaughter so great, that it was necessary to relieve the troops in this part of the field every half hour; and I may say without hyperbole that towards the close of the day that which truly served as a redoubt was the dead bodies of the men heaped up for the purpose.

During the defence of the redoubt, the brigade of Guards was ordered to the left, to support a battery of guns on the bank of the river above and below the mill. They came into action at a moment when the Hanoverians had suffered great loss, and expended the last of their cartridges. The grenadiers of the Guards received orders to enter the battery and relieve them, which was done with the greatest bravery, the grenadiers having to march four hundred paces over open ground swept by a storm of grape and musketry, the former from twelve-pound guns. No attempt was made to cross the bridge of the Lahn by either party, although within three hundred paces of the French batteries. Within the limited space of four hundred paces, fifty pieces of cannon poured an adverse fire around that fatal mill.

At a time when the Coldstream Guards were maintaining a fire over the rampart formed by the bodies of the slain, Thomas Viscount Saye and Sele, an officer of the corps, reprimanded a sergeant for uttering an exclamation of horror, and was answered—

> Oh, sir, you are now supporting yourself on the body of your own brother!

This was his elder brother, Captain John Twiselton, who had just been slain, and added to the fatal breastwork; and the sergeant who spoke was an old and attached servant of the family of Lord Saye.

The loss of the Coldstream Guards on this occasion was only thirty-one of all ranks; that of the Scots Guards amounted to sixty. The total losses of the Allies were 600, and of the. French 1,100 men.

At the close of the Seven Years' War, there passed of the British army through Holland, on the 1st of January, 1763, to embark for England, 637 officers, 16,454 soldiers, 506 servants and grooms, 1,666 women, and 7,391 horses.

At this time the standard uniform of the Line was a three-cornered cocked hat, bound with white lace, and ornamented with a white loop and the black cockade of the House of Hanover; the scarlet coats were lined with the facings of the regiment, and laced with white; the vests and breeches were scarlet, and the long gaiters were white. In 1764 the swords of the grenadiers were abolished, and our cavalry first wore an epaulet in lieu of an aiguilet on the left shoulder; their jack-boots were discontinued, and the horses were ordered to have long in lieu of nag tails. All regimental buttons were of flat metal, and numbers were not put upon them till the year 1767.

In the year 1764 Highland music was first played by the bands of the Guards and English regiments; and, according to the *London Chronicle*:

> It was no uncommon thing to see a file of English red-coats beating time to the tune of "Over the Water to Charlie."

The Havanah, 1763

George III. was now upon the throne of Britain. The monarchs of France and Spain, being both of the race of Bourbon, leagued themselves against him and his realms by what was then known as "The Family Compact."

Pitt, the great Commoner, knew of this secret treaty, and urged immediate war with Spain; but his plans were overruled, and he resigned in disgust. The Earl of Bute then became Premier. As Pitt had foreseen, Spain declared war to aid France. But France was stripped of her most valuable West Indian colonies, whilst Spain lost the Havanah and Manilla; and it is the stories of the conquest of the two last-named places we now propose to narrate.

The expedition destined for the Havanah, the principal seaport in Cuba, the key of the Gulf of Mexico, and the centre of Spanish trade and navigation in the New World, required an armament equal to an object so great It consisted of nineteen ships of the line and eighteen frigates, carrying 2,042 guns, under the command of Admiral Sir George Pocock, K.B., who had served with distinction in the Indian seas; and there were 150 transports, having on board 10,000 land forces. These were to be joined by 4,000 more from America. The troops were under the orders of General the Earl of Albemarle; and the whole armament, which assembled off the north-west point of Hispaniola, was, for the sake of expedition, conducted, with skilful seamanship, through the Old Channel of Bahama, and on the 6th of June arrived in sight of the far-famed Havanah.

The object of their long and perilous voyage, and of so many ardent hopes, was now before them. The appearance of the city at the entrance of the port is one of the most picturesque and beautiful in equinoctial America. The strong fortifications that crown the rocks on the eastern side; the noble internal basin, where more than a thousand

VIEW OF THE CITY OF HAVANAH.

ships might anchor, sheltered from every wind; the majesty of the groves of palms, which there grow to a vast height; the city itself, with its white houses, all of the Saracenic and Gothic style, with quaint galleries and deep red roofs, the pillars and pinnacles, towers and domes, half seen and half hidden amid the forest of masts and sails, seen under a clear and burning sun, all conspire to present a most imposing tout ensemble.

The north side of the entrance to the harbour is formed by a high ridge called the Cabana, the face of which is almost perpendicular, and crowned by bastions which overlook the city and the sea. At the extreme point of the entrance stands the Moro, or Castello de los Santos Reges. This range of fortifications, together with Fort Principe and the castle of Altares to the west, some ridges of low elevation, and rows of palm trees, encompass the plain on which, on the western side of the harbour, stands the city, in the form of a semicircle, with its Barrios estra Muros, or suburbs, in its rear.

The name of the fortress, Moro, was a ward applied to the dungeon-towers of the ancient Moorish castles in Spain, and serves to show us, as Scott mentions in a note to "Marmion," "from what notion the Gothic style of castle-building was originally derived."

The Moro Castle was then, and is still, an edifice of great strength, having two bastions towards the sea, and two more on the land side, with a deep wide ditch cut out of the solid rock. The opposite point of entrance was secured by another fort, frequently called the Puntal, which was girt by ditches, and every way calculated for co-operating with the Moro in defence of the harbour. It had also some batteries that faced the country and enfiladed the city wall.

But the latter, and the fortifications of the city itself, were not in a good condition; the wall and its bastions lacked repair, the ditch was a dry one, and the covered way was almost in ruins. It was therefore thought by some officers that the town should have been attacked by land, especially as it was utterly impracticable to assail it by sea; the entrance to the harbour being subject to a crossfire from the Moro and Puntal, and defended by fourteen Spanish ships of the line, three of which were afterwards sunk in the channel, across which a boom was thrown.

Either from being ignorant of the real state of the defences, or from seeing objects in a different manner, the Earl of Albemarle resolved to begin with the reduction of the great Moro Castle, the fall of which would, he thought, ensure that of the city. He believed that if he attacked the latter first, his force might become too weak to take the fort, defended as it was by a garrison, and the flower of the male populace, zealous alike to save their own and the public treasure.

On the other hand, it was alleged that, if the city had been attacked, its wall could not have been defended for twenty-four hours. If the earl committed errors, the Spaniards were guilty of greater. Though apprised a month before that George III. had declared war against Charles III., they were not roused from their apathy; and when the British armament was off the shore of Cuba, they had taken no means for defence: scarcely a cannon or musket was fit for use—they were almost without shot of proper sizes for the former, and without cartridges for the latter. All was confusion and alarm when the sails of the hostile fleet were first descried covering all the sea between the Old Channel and the Gulf of Florida. Instead of having their fleet at sea and ready for action, it was retained in the harbour. A naval victory, however dearly bought, might have saved the city; but now, the city and harbour once taken, nothing could save the fleet.

When the troops were ready to land, the admiral, with a great portion of the fleet, bore away to the westward, and made a feint of disembarking; while a detachment, protected by Commodore Keppel and Captain Harvey, of the *Dragon*, 74 guns, approached the shore to the eastward and landed without opposition—a small fort, which might have opposed them, having been previously destroyed by a cannonade from the ships. On this side the main body of the troops were meant to act. They were formed in two columns, one being immediately occupied in the attack of the Moro, and the other in covering the siege and protecting the foragers, who procured water, wood, and provisions. The former column was led by Major-General Keppel, and the covering force by Lieutenant-General Elliot; while a detachment, under Colonel Howe, was encamped near the west end of the city, to cut off its communication with the country, and to divide the attention of the enemy.

Incredible were the hardships sustained by the troops during these operations. The earth was everywhere so thin that it was with the greatest difficulty they could make their approaches under cover; and the want of water, together with the heat, proved most distressing. Fatigue parties had to convey it from a vast distance; and so scanty and precarious was the quantity, that the troops had frequently to be supplied from the casks of the shipping. Through the thick dense woods, that grew in all the rank luxuriance peculiar to the torrid zone, roads of communication had to be cut; and the artillery had to be dragged by pathless ways, from a rough and rocky shore.

In these painful efforts, under a burning West Indian sun, many of the soldiers and seamen, worn with toil, drenched with perspiration, and maddened by thirst, dropped down dead in the drag-ropes, in the trenches, and at their posts, slain by sheer heat and fatigue. Every obstacle was at length overcome, by the happy unanimity which existed between the two branches of the service; and batteries were erected along a ridge on a level with the fort, and from these the bombs were first thrown on the 20th of the month. The ships in the harbour were driven farther back, so that their guns could not molest the besiegers, and a sally made by the garrison was repulsed with great slaughter by the trench-guards.

To aid the troops, on the evening of the 30th of June, the *Cambridge*, 80 guns, and the *Dragon* and *Marlborough*, each of 74 guns, were stationed as near the Moro as ships so large could venture, with orders to dismount the guns, and, if possible, to breach the wall. The governor, Don Louis de Velasco, a captain of the Spanish Navy, and his second in command, the Marquis de Gonzales, defended themselves with great bravery. The three ships began their cannonade at eight o'clock in the morning of the 1st of July: and after keeping up a constant fire until two in the afternoon, the *Cambridge*, under Captain Goostrey, was found to be so much damaged in her hull, masts, yards, and rigging, by the shot of the Spaniards, that she had to sheer off out of range; and soon after the *Dragon*, under Captain Augustus Harvey, which had also suffered severely, followed her; and then the *Marlborough*, after a loss of 162 men killed and wounded. Among the former was the captain of the *Cambridge*.

The crews of the sunken ships were added to the garrison of the Moro, and for many days an unremitting cannonade was maintained op both sides, with fierce emulation. In the midst of this, the principal battery of the besiegers, being constructed chiefly of timber and fascines, caught fire. Dried by the intense heat, the material burned fiercely, and the battery was almost consumed; the labour of 600 men for seventeen days was destroyed in an hour, and had to be begun again. This was a severe stroke of fortune, as it occurred at a time when the hardships of the British were well-nigh intolerable. Increased by rigorous duty, the diseases of the climate reduced the army to half its strength.

Cormick records that at one time no less than 5,000 soldiers were

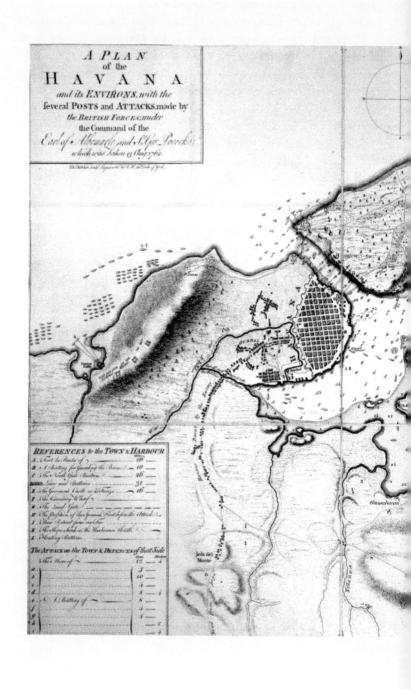

A PLAN
of the
HAVANA
and its ENVIRONS, with the
several POSTS and ATTACKS made by
the BRITISH FORCES; under
the Command of the
Earl of Albemarle and S.r Geo. Pocock:
which was taken 13 Aug.r 1762.

REFERENCES to the TOWN & HARBOUR

The ATTACK on the TOWN & DEFENCES of Left Side

REFERENCES to the MORO.

The ATTACK on the MORO.

quite unfit for service. The provisions were bad, the water more scanty than ever; and as the season advanced, the prospect of success grew fainter. The hearts of the most sanguine began to sink, when they beheld our army wasting away, and remembered that the fleet anchored upon the open shore must be exposed to certain destruction if the West Indian hurricanes came on before the Havanah was reduced.

Daily impatient eyes were turned seaward, looking for the expected reinforcement from America, but none appeared, delays having occurred by the wreck of the transports in the Straits of Bahama. And now another battery took fire, before the first had been replaced; and the toil of the troops was increased exactly in proportion as their strength diminished. Many fell into despair, and died, overcome by fatigue, anguish, and disappointment.

The riches of the Spanish Indies lay almost within the grasp of the survivors, and the shame of returning home baffled made them redouble their efforts. The batteries were renewed; their fire became more equal, and soon proved superior, to that of the fort; they silenced its guns, dismantled and destroyed its upper works; and on the 20th of July the troops made a lodgement in the covered way.

In gaining this advantage, they were greatly assisted by the arrival of some merchant ships bound from Jamaica to England, under the convoy of Sir James Douglas. By these they were supplied with many conveniences for the siege, particularly bales of cotton, which were of the utmost service to the engineers; as they could not otherwise have pushed on their sap, the soil being so scanty on the lower stratum of rock as not to afford sufficient to cover them.

Fresh vigour was now given to the operations of the siege, but an unforeseen difficulty suddenly appeared. An immense ditch, cut in the living rock on which the Moro stands, yawned before them, barring all advance. It was eighty feet deep and forty feet wide.

To fill it up appeared an impossibility; and difficult though the task of mining was, it proved the only expedient. Even mining might have been impracticable, had not a thin ridge of rock been fortunately left, to protect the ditch towards the sea. Over this narrow ridge, though exposed to a fire of cannon and musketry, and showers of hand-grenades, the miners finally passed with little loss, and buried themselves in the wall.

The close approach to the Moro so greatly alarmed the Spanish governor of the city, which takes its name from *La Habana* (or "The Harbour"), that he resolved to attempt something for its relief. Accordingly, on the 22nd of July he had a body of 1,500 men, chiefly composed of the country militia, *mulattoes*, and negroes, ferried across the harbour. Thence they crossed the hills, and made three separate attacks upon the British line. The ordinary trench-guards, though taken by surprise, defended themselves so resolutely that the Spaniards made but little impression. The attacked posts were speedily reinforced by the covering column, from which four companies of the 1st Royal Scots were dispatched; and the Spaniards were driven down the hill at the point of the bayonet, with heavy slaughter, for many were shot down, some gained their boats, and others were drowned. In this well-imagined but ill-executed sally, they lost 400 men.

Among the officers wounded on this occasion was Andrew Lord Rollo, of Duncrub, a colonel of infantry, who acted as brigadier. This was the last attempt made to relieve the Moro, the garrison of which, abandoned as it was by the city, with an enemy undermining its walls, held sullenly and sternly out; but on the 30th of July, at one in the day, the mines were sprung. A dreadful roar and splitting sound were heard; and when the smoke and dust cleared away, there was seen in the massive wall of the Moro a breach which the Earl of Albemarle, in his letter to the Earl of Egremont, describes as being "just practicable for a file of men in front."

With all their bayonets glittering in the sun, the enemy were seen crowding resolutely about the gap, ready to defend it with vigour.

The Royal Scots, the Regiment of Marksmen, and the 90th Regiment were detailed as the storming party, to be supported by the 56th Regiment, then and still popularly known as the "Pompadours," their facings being purple, the chosen colour of the royal favourite.

Lieutenant Charles Forbes, of the Royal Scots, led the assault, and ascending the breach untouched amid the storm of musketry that swept it, with signal gallantry formed the survivors of his party on the summit, and with the charged bayonet scoured the whole line of the rampart. The Earl of Albemarle wrote:

> The attack was so vigorous and impetuous, that the enemy were instantly driven from the breach, and His Majesty's standard was instantly planted upon the bastion.

The garrison was taken by surprise. The Spanish governor, Don Louis de Velasco, formerly captain of the *Reyna*, a seventy-gun ship, exerted himself to save the fortress, but fell mortally wounded when attempting to rally his men, sword in hand, around the flagstaff. His

THE CAPTURE OF HAVANAH

second in command, the Marquis de Gonzales, captain of the *Aquilon*, 70 guns, was killed; and the King of Spain, to commemorate the fate of the former, created his son Viscount de Moro, and directed that for ever after there should be a ship in his navy called the *Velasco*.

The fall of these two officers augmented the confusion in the ranks of the enemy; 150 Spaniards were shot or bayoneted, 400 threw down their arms and were made prisoners, the rest were either killed in the boats, or drowned miserably when attempting to escape to the Havanah. Thus, was the Moro won, with a total loss to the British of only two officers and thirty men of those engaged in the assault, who numbered 39 officers, 29 sergeants, and 421 rank and file.

As Lieutenants Forbes, of the Royals, Nugent, of the 9th, and Holroyd, of the 90th Regiment, were congratulating each other on their sudden and splendid success, the two latter were shot down by a party of desperate Spaniards, who fired from an adjacent lighthouse. Lieutenant Forbes was so exasperated by the death of his friends, that he attacked the lighthouse, at the head of a few of his Scots, and put all who were in it to the sword.

No sooner did the Spaniards in the town and Fort Puntal see the British colours flying over the Moro, than they directed all their fire upon it. Meanwhile the victors, encouraged by their success, were actively employed in remounting the guns of the Moro, and in erecting batteries upon an eminence that commanded the city; and ere long sixty heavy pieces of cannon were ready to open on it.

Lord Albemarle, anxious to spare unnecessary carnage, on the 10th of August sent an *aide-de-camp* with a flag of truce to summon the governor to surrender, and to make him certain of the destruction that must fall upon the place if he resisted.

"I am under no uneasy apprehensions," replied the Spaniard, proudly, "and shall hold out to the last extremity."

But he was soon brought to reason. The batteries opened fire, and says Lord Albemarle, were:

So well served by artillerymen and sailors, and their effect was so great, that in less than six hours all the guns in the Puntal Fort and the north bastion were completely silenced.

White flags of truce were now displayed on every quarter of the city, and a cessation of hostilities took place; and as soon as the terms were adjusted, the magnificent city of Havanah, with a district of 180 miles to the westward included in its government, the Puntal Castle, and the ships in the harbour, were surrendered to His Britannic Majesty.

The Spaniards struggled hard to save their men-of-war, and have the harbour declared neutral; but after two days of vehement altercation, they were compelled to submit. The garrison was allowed to march out with the honours of war, and was conveyed to Old Spain. Private property was secured to the inhabitants, with their former laws and religion. The money and valuable merchandise, with the naval and military stores, including 361 brass and iron guns and mortars, which were found in the city and arsenal, amounted to nearly three millions sterling. Nine sail of the line were taken in the harbour fit for sea; two on the stocks were burnt by our seamen.

Thus, fell the Havanah; but our loss in the capture amounted to 1,790 officers and men killed in action, exclusive of those who perished by fever, fatigue, and sunstroke.

The ensign of the Moro was brought to London by Captain Nugent, *aide-de-camp* to Lord Albemarle, with whose dispatches he was entrusted.

Preceded by a troop of light horse, with kettledrums beating, and French horns and trumpets sounding, in eleven wagons surmounted by Union Jacks, having the Spanish flag beneath, the captured gold and silver was conveyed through the streets of London, and carried to the Tower with great parade. Each wagon was escorted by four marines, with bayonets fixed, and the procession was concluded by a mounted officer carrying the British flag.

As the procession passed through St. James's Street, on the 12th of August, just after Her Majesty had been delivered of a prince—the George IV. of after years—the king, with many of the nobility who were with him, went to the windows above the palace gate to see the trophies, and joined their acclamations to those of the people.

The Havanah Trophies passing St. James's Palace

LEONAUR

ALSO FROM LEONAUR
AVAILABLE IN SOFTCOVER OR HARDCOVER WITH DUST JACKET

OFFICERS & GENTLEMEN *by Peter Hawker & William Graham*—Two Accounts of British Officers During the Peninsula War: Officer of Light Dragoons by Peter Hawker & Campaign in Portugal and Spain by William Graham .

THE WALCHEREN EXPEDITION *by Anonymous*—The Experiences of a British Officer of the 81st Regt. During the Campaign in the Low Countries of 1809.

LADIES OF WATERLOO *by Charlotte A. Eaton, Magdalene de Lancey & Juana Smith*—The Experiences of Three Women During the Campaign of 1815: Waterloo Days by Charlotte A. Eaton, A Week at Waterloo by Magdalene de Lancey & Juana's Story by Juana Smith.

JOURNAL OF AN OFFICER IN THE KING'S GERMAN LEGION *by John Frederick Hering*—Recollections of Campaigning During the Napoleonic Wars.

JOURNAL OF AN ARMY SURGEON IN THE PENINSULAR WAR *by Charles Boutflower*—The Recollections of a British Army Medical Man on Campaign During the Napoleonic Wars.

ON CAMPAIGN WITH MOORE AND WELLINGTON *by Anthony Hamilton*—The Experiences of a Soldier of the 43rd Regiment During the Peninsular War.

THE ROAD TO AUSTERLITZ *by R. G. Burton*—Napoleon's Campaign of 1805.

SOLDIERS OF NAPOLEON *by A. J. Doisy De Villargennes & Arthur Chuquet*—The Experiences of the Men of the French First Empire: Under the Eagles by A. J. Doisy De Villargennes & Voices of 1812 by Arthur Chuquet .

INVASION OF FRANCE, 1814 *by F. W. O. Maycock*—The Final Battles of the Napoleonic First Empire.

LEIPZIG—A CONFLICT OF TITANS *by Frederic Shoberl*—A Personal Experience of the 'Battle of the Nations' During the Napoleonic Wars, October 14th-19th, 1813.

SLASHERS *by Charles Cadell*—The Campaigns of the 28th Regiment of Foot During the Napoleonic Wars by a Serving Officer.

BATTLE IMPERIAL *by Charles William Vane*—The Campaigns in Germany & France for the Defeat of Napoleon 1813-1814.

SWIFT & BOLD *by Gibbes Rigaud*—The 60th Rifles During the Peninsula War.

LEONAUR

ALSO FROM LEONAUR
AVAILABLE IN SOFTCOVER OR HARDCOVER WITH DUST JACKET

THE 9TH—THE KING'S (LIVERPOOL REGIMENT) IN THE GREAT WAR 1914 - 1918 *by Enos H. G. Roberts*—Mersey to mud—war and Liverpool men.

THE GAMBARDIER *by Mark Severn*—The experiences of a battery of Heavy artillery on the Western Front during the First World War.

FROM MESSINES TO THIRD YPRES *by Thomas Floyd*—A personal account of the First World War on the Western front by a 2/5th Lancashire Fusilier.

THE IRISH GUARDS IN THE GREAT WAR - VOLUME 1 *by Rudyard Kipling*—Edited and Compiled from Their Diaries and Papers—The First Battalion.

THE IRISH GUARDS IN THE GREAT WAR - VOLUME 1 *by Rudyard Kipling*—Edited and Compiled from Their Diaries and Papers—The Second Battalion.

ARMOURED CARS IN EDEN *by K. Roosevelt*—An American President's son serving in Rolls Royce armoured cars with the British in Mesopatamia & with the American Artillery in France during the First World War.

CHASSEUR OF 1914 *by Marcel Dupont*—Experiences of the twilight of the French Light Cavalry by a young officer during the early battles of the great war in Europe.

TROOP HORSE & TRENCH *by R.A. Lloyd*—The experiences of a British Lifeguardsman of the household cavalry fighting on the western front during the First World War 1914-18.

THE EAST AFRICAN MOUNTED RIFLES *by C.J. Wilson*—Experiences of the campaign in the East African bush during the First World War.

THE LONG PATROL *by George Berrie*—A Novel of Light Horsemen from Gallipoli to the Palestine campaign of the First World War.

THE FIGHTING CAMELIERS *by Frank Reid*—The exploits of the Imperial Camel Corps in the desert and Palestine campaigns of the First World War.

STEEL CHARIOTS IN THE DESERT *by S. C. Rolls*—The first world war experiences of a Rolls Royce armoured car driver with the Duke of Westminster in Libya and in Arabia with T.E. Lawrence.

WITH THE IMPERIAL CAMEL CORPS IN THE GREAT WAR *by Geoffrey Inchbald*—The story of a serving officer with the British 2nd battalion against the Senussi and during the Palestine campaign.

LEONAUR

ALSO FROM LEONAUR

AN APACHE CAMPAIGN IN THE SIERRA MADRE *by John G. Bourke*—An Account of the Expedition in Pursuit of the Chiricahua Apaches in Arizona, 1883.

BILLY DIXON & ADOBE WALLS *by Billy Dixon and Edward Campbell Little*—Scout, Plainsman & Buffalo Hunter, *Life and Adventures of "Billy" Dixon* by Billy Dixon and *The Battle of Adobe Walls* by Edward Campbell Little (*Pearson's Magazine*).

WITH THE CALIFORNIA COLUMN *by George H. Petis*—Against Confederates and Hostile Indians During the American Civil War on the South Western Frontier, *The California Column, Frontier Service During the Rebellion* and *Kit Carson's Fight With the Comanche and Kiowa Indians*.

THRILLING DAYS IN ARMY LIFE *by George Alexander Forsyth*—Experiences of the Beecher's Island Battle 1868, the Apache Campaign of 1882, and the American Civil War.

INDIAN FIGHTS AND FIGHTERS *by Cyrus Townsend Brady*—Indian Fights and Fighters of the American Western Frontier of the 19th Century.

THE NEZ PERCÉ CAMPAIGN, 1877 *by G. O. Shields & Edmond Stephen Meany*—Two Accounts of Chief Joseph and the Defeat of the Nez Percé, *The Battle of Big Hole* by G. O. Shields and *Chief Joseph, the Nez Percé* by Edmond Stephen Meany.

CAPTAIN JEFF OF THE TEXAS RANGERS *by W. J. Maltby*—Fighting Comanche & Kiowa Indians on the South Western Frontier 1863-1874.

SHERIDAN'S TROOPERS ON THE BORDERS *by De Benneville Randolph Keim*—The Winter Campaign of the U. S. Army Against the Indian Tribes of the Southern Plains, 1868-9.

GERONIMO *by Geronimo*—The Life of the Famous Apache Warrior in His Own Words.

WILD LIFE IN THE FAR WEST *by James Hobbs*—The Adventures of a Hunter, Trapper, Guide, Prospector and Soldier.

THE OLD SANTA FE TRAIL *by Henry Inman*—The Story of a Great Highway.

LIFE IN THE FAR WEST *by George F. Ruxton*—The Experiences of a British Officer in America and Mexico During the 1840's.

ADVENTURES IN MEXICO AND THE ROCKY MOUNTAINS *by George F. Ruxton*—Experiences of Mexico and the South West During the 1840's.

Lightning Source UK Ltd.
Milton Keynes UK
UKHW010629080920
369553UK00002B/208